MAKING GLOBAL SENSE

Had the spirit of prophesy
decreed the birth of this production,
it could not have brought it forth
at a more seasonable juncture,
or a more necessary time.

THOMAS PAINE

About *Making Global Sense*

"Thomas Paine rallied Americans to a new sense of themselves and their possibilities. Judah Freed does likewise for citizens of the planet."

– **Bill McKibben**, *The Flag, the Cross, and the Station Wagon; Falter; The End of Nature*; 350.org; ThirdAct,org, People's Climate March

"Judah Freed has taken the gauntlet from Thomas Paine and other great innovators of democracy to guide us toward the evolution of democracy itself. *Making Global Sense* is a vital and wonderful book, well written and inspired by the very same passion that founded this country, and can carry the world into the next era of evolution."

– **Barbara Marx Hubbard**, *Conscious Evolution*; Foundation for Conscious Evolution (re. first edition of *Making Global Sense*)

"*Making Global Sense* is at once vast and tangible, disturbing and inspiring. The book provides a sweeping overview of the critical challenges of our times. It conveys both a penetrating diagnosis and a galvanizing vision of possibility."

– **Ocean Robbins**, *Transform Your World*; cofounder and CEO, Food Revolution Network.

"*Making Global Sense* by Judah Freed is truly a masterpiece. He is the first to sense the whole, to track the future of our planet in terms of the bio-psycho-socio-spiritual dynamics that are now waking up. Freed provides humanity with the insights and tools to survive and prosper."

   – Don E. Beck, PhD, *8*

"*Making Global Sense* is compelling in its ideas and wonderful in its personal elements!"

   – Herb Goldberg, PhD, *The Hazards of Being Male; The New Male; What Men Still Don't Know*

"Judah Freed has written the only book I know that recognizes the need to face issues like alpha male rule, authority addiction, and the absurdity of sacrificing liberty for a false sense of security. Judah tells the truth with clarity, passion and humor."

   – Jed Diamond, *MenAlive; Warrior's Journey Home; The Irritable Male Syndrome; 12 Rules for Good Men*

"*Making Global Sense* is a breakthrough book for people who care about their social and environmental impact in the world. Judah Freed shows how global awareness is already changing life on earth, such as conscious consumers. The book offers us real hope when we need it most."

   – John Mackey, *Conscious Capitalism,* co-author Rajendra Sisodia; co-founder, Whole Foods Market

"In a thought-provoking book, Judah Freed holds an unflinching mirror up to human nature and offers a blueprint for the spirit and substance we will need to survive and thrive on Planet Earth long into the future."

   – Terry Tamminen, *Cracking the Carbon Code; Lives Per Gallon;* former Secretary of the California EPA

"The book is clear-eyed and novel. Judah Freed charts a path towards greener and more responsible economies that would be good for people and the planet."

    – **Jules Pretty**, **OBE**, *The Edge of Extinction*; Professor of
        Environment and Society, University of Essex

"Judah Freed guides us toward an urgent paradigm shift for creating a sustainable future. Beautifully written, engaging and inspirational, this transformational book is a must-read for enlightened thinkers and instruments of change."

    – **Jill Heinerth**, *Into The Planet*; filmmaker, *We Are Water:*
        award-winning underwater explorer

"Judah Freed has managed something quite remarkable: A sweeping, ambitious, holistic approach to replacing what's wrong in the world with what's right. This is the first book I can remember reading that synthesizes so much into a coherent whole."

    – **Shel Horowitz**, *Grassroots Marketing*; co-author with Jay
        Conrad Levinson, *Guerrilla Marketing Goes Green*; *Guerrilla*
        Marketing to Heal the World

"*Making Global Sense* is an inspirational, empowering call to action and a comprehensive look at the ways in which a global revolution would affect our species and our world. It is a very timely book."

    – **Marian McCain**, *Elderwoman*; editor, *GreenSpirit*

"In *Making Global Sense*, we each may find a firmer reckoning of the part we play in the blaze of liberation illuminating the world."

    – **Paul Goldman**, *Journey to Oneness*; visionary poet

"In my fifty years as a practitioner in the field of interpersonal relationships, and as a passionately concerned planetary citizen, I have never come across a book that so brilliantly marries the two. *Making Global Sense* is breathtakingly scholarly without being pedantic. The easily readable book is idealistic yet down-to-earth, filled with practical ideas about what each of us can do to transform our lives and our world into the dream we long to make real."

— **Jordan Paul, PhD,** *Becoming Your Own Hero*; co-author with Margaret Paul, *Do I Have to Give Up Me to Be Loved by You?*

"*Making Global Sense* is many things: Original, captivating, wise, provocative, inspiring, and hopeful. Moreover, it is an omnibus journey documenting the arising global consciousness through an argument sustained by a sophisticated presentation and analysis of the facts. Enjoy and be transformed toward an enlightened world."

— **Leslie E. Sponsel PhD,** *Spiritual Ecology*; Emeritus Professor of Anthropology, University of Hawaii

"An amazingly astute analysis of the current disarray that is the human race, our inability to govern ourselves wisely. I particularly enjoyed the crash course on Thomas Paine's writing and insights; an amazing mind. Freed picks up where Thomas Paine left off."

— **Gregory SETH Harris,** *The Perfect Stranger;* performance poet

"*Making Global Sense* speaks to my heart."

— **Martin Adams,** *Land: A New Paradigm*

Common sense is not so common.

VOLTAIRE

MAKING GLOBAL SENSE

Grounded HOPE
for democracy and the earth

Inspired by Thomas Paine's
COMMON SENSE

Judah Freed

My journey in these times that try our souls

Hoku House

2025 Edition

MAKING GLOBAL SENSE
Grounded hope for democracy and the earth,
inspired by Thomas Paine's *Common Sense*

Author: Judah Freed
    Published by Hoku House
    Denver, Colorado, USA, Earth
    HokuHouse.com | GlobalSense.com

Published in the United States of America, available worldwide (if not banned).
    Cloth Hardcover: ISBN: 979-8-9900288-7-6
    Trade Softcover   ISBN: 978-1-7373985-7-8
    eBook: ISBN: 978-1-7373985-4-7
    Audiobook   ISBN: 979-8-9900288-0-7

10 Percent of book royalties donated to literacy projects.

Readers, Booksellers, Libraries and Schools, go to globalsense.com/read-book
    Publisher at Hoku House handles special orders.

International rights & translation rights represented by DropCap.com

Library of Congress Control Number: 2024935556

Cataloging-in-Publication Data:

Freed, Judah Ken 1950 —
    MAKING GLOBAL SENSE

278 pages with Preface, 17 Chapters, Appendices, Bibliography, Index.
    Illustrations: 4 photographs, 2 diagrams, 2 cartoons.

    1. Current Affairs. 2. Democracy. 3. Climate Change. 4. Mindfulness.
    5. Philosophy. 6. Ethics. 7. Gender. 8. Memoir

Dedications

For Thomas Paine, a student of nature and natural laws,
who showed up, paid attention, told the truth, shifted society,
suffered blows, and carried on. May his old soul smile in peace.

For Mohandas K. Gandhi,
who embodied the change
he wished to see in the world.
May we all do likewise,
each in our own way.

For all awakened global thinkers on earth
willing to claim the natural power and responsibility
flowing from our connectivity, our oneness, our unity.
May you find here insights, inspiration and hope.

New opinions are always suspected,
and usually opposed, without any other reason
but because they are not already common.

JOHN LOCKE

Table of Contents

Detailed Table of Contents

APPENDICES

THIRD EDITION NOTE: Preamble and Epilogue from prior editions are now spun off together as *A Fable of Liberty Lost and Found.*

List of Illustrations

A long habit of not thinking
a thing wrong gives it a superficial
appearance of being right.

THOMAS PAINE

Making Sense of Global Life

THE CAUSE of global awakening is the cause of all humankind.

Making Global Sense revives ideas and ideals from Thomas Paine and the Enlightenment to champion 21st century enlightenment.

Weaving essay and memoir, I update and extend *Common Sense*. Where Paine in 1776 challenged monarchy and hereditary succession, I challenge alpha male rule and authority addiction, our craving for kings. Where Paine proposed independence and the very first modern republic, I propose interdependence with mindful self rule and personal democracy in direct republics. Where he urged revolution, I urge evolution.

A global sense of all life as One helps us govern our free will, or helps me. Mindfulness grounds my hope we can make democracy work.

Autocracies outnumber democracies. Our world is overrun with oppression. As Paine wrote, "Freedom hath been hunted round the globe." Akin to the crisis moving Paine to write, these times try our souls. Global climate change frightens many into trusting leaders promising to save us from the mess we humans created on earth. During upheavals, societies historically seek safety under kings or other masters. Despots prey on valid fears and grievances to rule our minds and lives. An absurdity.

By design and default, humanity as a whole is poisoning our planet. We let business and government put wealth and power above our natural human rights. We let ruinous corrupt policies persist despite our protests. We let lying leaders lure us into appeasement and consent.

To survive the global crises humanity has generated over centuries, do we look to a king, or do we look to ourselves and one another?

As a young yet dominant species on the planet, are we now ready for adulthood? Are we willing to mature as global citizens? Am I?

Echoing Paine in *Common Sense,* to end our suffering and victimhood, we have a natural right and moral duty to name the abusers in our world and in our minds. We have a right and duty to end our reliance on despots by actually taking personal responsibility for liberty. We have a right and duty to be conscious in ourselves and in the world.

In our emergency, we also have a right and duty to consider scientific evidence of our universal connectivity or coherence. All existence is light, energy slowing to matter. Atoms sing we are stardust. Our global oneness gives us each global reach. We all are naturally powerful.

At least one billion of us on earth today accept our oneness as a fact. We're generating a cultural wave to awaken humanity and avert calamity. As part of this wave, I write to encourage practical enlightenment. We can create a future that *does* works for all. And we can do it without kings.

Why Thomas Paine

Making Global Sense is inspired by Thomas Paine's *Common Sense.* Colonial Americans' rebellion against their king, historians say, would have failed without Paine's 1776 pamphlet. It swung public opinion in favor of the revolution. We again need such motivational works galvanizing us for evolution. Toward that end, I'm revitalizing his worldview.

Paine voiced in plain language for his day the basic "big ideas" of the Enlightenment. That 18th century democracy movement was ignited by the 17th century Age of Reason, kindled by the 16th century Protestant Reformation, sparked by the 15th century Renaissance, fueled by classical Greek and Roman writings, preserved by Islam until looted by Crusaders. Paine made sense of the big ideas from Enlightenment writers like Locke, Rousseau, Voltaire, Burke, Hume, and Kant. He distilled their insights to help common people see democracy *is* possible.

Paine's writings changed the course of human events as few have. His freethinking, egalitarian, democratic vision and values can assist us today. Ideas from the Enlightenment, I believe, can help stimulate enlightenment in our own times. I say this from testing these ideas in my life.

Common Sense animates *Global Sense.* I sought to write what Paine would write today, ofttimes in his voice. His thinking on hereditary kings and aristocracy spurs my thinking on male dominance and addiction to authority. His natural deism imbues my global sense of oneness. His views on freedom inform my thoughts on individuality, personal responsibility, self-government, and free republics. Paine's clarion call for a declaration of independence stirs my call for a declaration of interdependence.

For us to heal our planet and mature into democracy, we need hope, grounded in reason. Paine' offers guidance and hope for us today.

Why My Story

To balance head and heart here, I tell the life story behind my ideas. Stories tell truths beyond ideas alone. Stories help make sense of life.

I narrate childhood abuse, school bullying; joining a cult at age 20, fleeing at 23; facing my authority addiction and committing to self rule. I recall ego follies in decades of local to international journalism. I relate world travel adventures, like landing in Fiji amid a coup. I share my soul choice at 65 to survive cancer, so I can finish this book. I stand on Paine's shoulders, I admit, with insecurity in standing on my own feet.

My literary model for weaving essay and memoir is *Zen and the Art of Motorcycle Maintenance* by Robert M. Persig. His union of theory and story helped me find myself. As a writer, I like what he did there.

Style and Readability

My literary styles are journalistic, narrative and discourse. I write American English at high school reading levels. Where I get technical for precision, I resay simply. My tone runs from playful to somber.

My talent is synthesis, distilling years of thought in a sentence. I write tight, a fast brush painting a global canvas. See the big picture. Read for ideas. Finish the book for the payoff. Let it sit a bit. Allow gestalt.

For brevity, I skip explaining common knowledge (lookup if new). For rereading, I layer in meanings, themes, symbols, and allusions.

Punctuation note: I write the compound-term "self rule" without the usual hyphen (self-rule) to spotlight the autonomy of the Self.

Book Structure and Preview

Global Sense follows the structure and logic in *Common Sense.*

Part I. Where Paine explained the nature of government under law, I explain our lives are governed by how we make sense of life. A billion of us see our oneness, I report. We form a global sense movement.

Part II. Where Paine blamed monarchy and hereditary succession for tyranny, I name ancient alpha male rule and authority addiction for the wealth and power abuses now menacing life and liberty on earth.

Part III. Where Paine surveyed the upset state of American affairs, I survey the state of world affairs, the threats to democracy and the planet, the real dangers of tyranny in our lands and in our minds.

Part IV. Where Paine told how to win a revolution and proposed a republic, I propose our evolution through gender quality and new men, through mindful self rule, personal democracy, and direct republics.

Clarion Calls are Overdue

Paine speaks for me in his introduction to *Common Sense:*

> Perhaps the sentiments contained in the following pages, are not yet sufficiently fashionable to procure them general favor; a long habit of not thinking a thing wrong, gives it a superficial appearance of being right, and raises at first a formidable outcry in defense of custom. But tumult soon subsides. Time makes more converts than reason.

Global thinking uplifts how we make sense of life together on earth. I see global thinkers joining hands to voice global sensibilities peacefully. Those not yet awake to our oneness may now safely open their eyes.

Regardless of our age, gender, race, origin, health, ability, class, party, religion, ideology, or nation, rousing clarion calls of alarm are overdue for ensuring the future of freedom and life on earth. Among all those inviting humanity to unite for democratic global change, gratefully writes...

Judah Freed,
Denver, 2024

MAKING GLOBAL SENSE

We have it in our power
to begin the world over again.

THOMAS PAINE

PART I

Our Global Awakening

The mind once enlightened
cannot again become dark.

THOMAS PAINE

CHAPTER 1

World Enlightenment

1971: WASHINGTON, DC — *One day after the big May Day antiwar demonstration, I am blessed at age 20 by my first real taste of global sense. I feel a peaceful loving connection to universal oneness beyond all words for what's real in life. The awakening transforms me to this day.*

I'm in DC at the end of an idealistic "odyssey for truth," as I call it in my journal. There I write, "I want to understand the world and myself in it." I write often in my journal because I'm so confused. When I left home in Denver three months ago, journals and pens went first into my backpack. I write because I have to write. I write to make sense of life.

Risking a college draft deferment, I've gone "on the road" to find myself as a writer and as a man. After hitchhiking from Denver to New York, living in Greenwich Village, I'm now in DC to oppose the war in Viet Nam.

Protest organizers, the Mayday Tribe, have a camping permit from the U.S. Park Service for West Potomac Park, the peninsula on the tidal basin across from the Jefferson Memorial.

I arrive on Saturday to join the 35,000 protestors gathering for Monday morning's civil disobedience action. Since the U.S. government will not shut down the corrupt war in Southeast Asia, we will shut down the government for one day by playfully blocking traffic.

I wander around in the park through a party atmosphere of communal cooking, blue smoke and shared determination. At a teach-in under a tree, I learn Gandhi's methods of passive resistance. I learn how to get arrested without getting hurt. Standing up for democracy is risky business.

That night is a live Beach Boys concert at the Washington Monument. I run into Billy Mitchell, a New York singer-songwriter in a buckskin jacket. We'd hung out at the Fat Black Pussycat, the show room of the Feenjon Café on MacDougal, where I briefly worked back end. Billy asks me to join him backstage. I'm delighted to watch from behind the scenes.

An insecure guy, I need to justify my privilege. When a roadie falls and cuts his knee, I offer to take him to the medic tent. While he gets treated (likely to make myself look good), I mention to the lead doctor that I have Boy Scouts' Advanced Red Cross First Aid training. He glances up, remarks he's understaffed, and hands me a white medic armband with a red cross. Gesturing around him, he says, "Start anywhere."

Toward the end of the concert, a hippie in his thirties staggers into the tent. He's the sixth one that night on a bummer trip. The man blurts he's a federal agent assigned to send protesters to hospitals on drug overdoses. He babbles that he took a hit of his own bad acid by mistake. Not the good stuff. Save that for getting to protest leaders. Dose them with bad stuff. Put them out of action. I do not ask for proof. It's only a trip. Just keep him calm. An ambulance carries him away. I think wildness is groovy.

At dawn on Sunday, I leave my campsite to go across the bridge to the Thomas Jefferson Memorial, where I watch the sunrise. Jefferson's inscribed words enter my soul: "I have sworn upon the altar of God eternal hostility against every form of tyranny over the mind of man." Seems he means both God eternal and eternal hostility against tyranny over our minds.

I return to find a line of troops in riot gear surrounds the encampment. Helicopter loudspeakers blare orders to leave the area. A uniformed trooper with an assault rifle stops me. I want to retrieve my backpack and my sister's sleeping bag. I offer to be escorted. I beg him. Can I at least get my journals? He retorts, "Do you want to get arrested?" I walk away.

Protesters regroup that morning at local churches. I hear that hospital admissions for overdoses justified revoking the camping permit. We get word from Mayday Tribe organizers that on Monday morning, we will go ahead with shutting down traffic to symbolically shut down the war machine. This afternoon, as planned, we will peacefully march to end the war.

Duality and Unity

The freethinking idealistic countercultures of my youth and today demonstrate how awakened and aroused people change the course of history. Universal ideals transcend generations. Ideals offer purpose and hope for folks anywhere who choose to improve their lives and our world. Ideals grounded in reason can transform life on earth.

What builds civilizations is our abiding belief we can change life for the better. This faith cuts across all politics and religions, even atheism, lending hope and courage when darkness seems bottomless.

Most of us recognize our global challenges. I'll name climate change, overpopulation, pandemics, biological and nuclear weapons, cyber wars, food and water scarcity, rampant racism, sexism, rankism, social injustice, corruption, losses of civil liberties, erosions of human rights, the ascent of despots. Despite all of it, maybe because of it, awareness of our global oneness makes common sense to more of us than ever.

Some of us on the planet inherit or obtain concentrated wealth and power. Those vested in the *status quo*, enjoying privileged lives, tend to resist universal rights for everybody. "They" tend to repress movements calling for equality and social justice. Instead of letting us enjoy freedom in peace, they offer the peace of appeasement and compliance.

The "elites" among us tend to mute rational voices declaring liberty without responsibility is insanity. They hire fossil-fuel shills to call climate change a hoax. They suppress, harass, detain, and kill vocal defenders of civil rights and endangered species. They assassinate journalists and ban books to stifle a free press. They invade democratic lands to build empires. Our silence gives them permission to reign supreme.

The "1 percent" ruling without our explicit consent distracts us with mindless media mayhem. Sensationalism numbs us to suffering in the world, trauma in ourselves. They undermine education, erode curiosity and degrade critical thinking, all to assure malleable ignorance.

They make "democracy" a hollow shell game. They claim voter fraud if they lose, and then rig elections to win. They legalize their villainy. They make politics so disgusting that we take pride in never voting.

They fund dictators who gain control by making us feel terrified of "the other." They sow the chaos inducing us into trusting heroes pledging "law and order" to end the chaos. They normalize big lies.

Worst of all, they get us to think of them as "them," *the other.* We make sense of life as "us or them." Alienating binary tropes seduce us into the delusions of *dualism* and dueling worldviews — be right or die.

Instead, some of us make sense of life in a whole way. We form social contracts based on a global sense of our innate unity and equality, so we live sensibly, kindly, guided by the fact of our planetary oneness.

Ancient abuses of natural rights and natural law today imperil our lives and our world. Today's global crises concern all who honor life and the power of love. We are at a global "tipping point," an inflection point. Civilizations worldwide are being disrupted by globalization.

Global Consciousness

In the long march of humanity on this pale blue dot in space we call home, civilization is going global. The form it will take is uncertain. I see the risk of collapse, and it scares me. Yet I see real causes for hope we will avoid the worst, turn around before we drive off a cliff.

The effect of globalization is like the effect of shifting from agrarian to industrial societies. Future shock stuns us. Life changes faster than we can cope. We feel afraid and unsafe. Hate mongers exploit our fears. Our grievances get turned against us. We feel victimized, so we give away our power to leaders, let them do our thinking for us.

We regain personal power by seeing our objective global oneness, connectivity, interactivity. When the mind knows what the heart and gut knows (we alter all in all we do), we make better choices, or I do.

Our 21st century choices will chart the course of humanity on Earth, or the Moon or Mars or Jupiter's moons, or out among the stars. To help freedom and democracy survive and thrive, I am distilling here what I've learned about *why* and *how* global thinkers are building a movement for shifting to a global sensibility. Old ways are fighting back, fighting hard. I write to help build critical mass for a shift into enlightenment.

At least one billion of us worldwide, my research shows, live in ways that make global sense (in any lingo). To help understand why and how, my guide here is Thomas Paine, the influential 18th century writer and liberty advocate. He's best known for his 1776 pamphlet, *Common Sense*, which galvanized support for the American Revolution.

Paine persuaded frightened and confused American colonists to declare independence from monarchy and establish the first modern republic. If Britain's king held sway in that pivotal moment, he warned, they would get too absorbed in survival ever to stand up for their natural rights and win their freedom. *Common Sense* tipped the balance.

In our global crises now, I want to help galvanize support for human evolution. Most of us feel afraid and confused by global upheavals. I argue for declaring our interdependence. We can free ourselves from needing kings, learn to practice personal democracy. We can renew republics with the rule of law, not rule by men. If our old authoritarian habits hold sway in this pivotal moment, we may soon get too absorbed in survival ever to stand up for our natural rights and make freedom safe for us all.

"Youth is the seed time of good habits," wrote Thomas Paine. His metaphor fits today for individuals, families, communities, organizations, governments, and the whole earth. Now is the seedtime of globalization, a megatrend that transcends tribalism, nationalism and isolationism. The worldwide shift into interdependent global systems will impact us all, for good or ill, and in between. What happens is up to us.

Today and into the next century, the "new world order" that we are co-creating together, whatever we name it, mirrors how we individually and collectively make sense of "globalization" in the years ahead.

If we define globalization as establishing global autocratic corporate superstates above all governments, then we are not ready, and we never will be ready for such a dystopian world order. In our hearts, we can never consent to such "globalist" rule. Discontent from injustice breeds trouble. Social unrest invites despots to quell uprisings with force. We risk going down the dark tunnel of tyranny, where leaders dictate what we think and feel and do. If we go along to get along now. we might never gain the clarity and courage to stand up for ourselves and our world.

Instead, if we define "globalization" as awakening into a sense of our globality, the power latent in connectivity, then humanity is more ready now than ever. We can use globalization to give us each global reach — energetically, socially, culturally, economically, politically. If we consent to healing ourselves, our societies and our planet by making global sense of life (in any words), we can learn to live free responsibly and creatively together in peace without any kings or other masters.

We are creating in the 21st century a new world order of some form or another. A global shift into an interdependent world is now inevitable. As with climate change, it's too late to stop it. Reality bites. We may steer this megatrend most effectively by transforming our own consciousness. We can evolve a global sense of our natural unity on earth. We can co-operate with nature and each other. We can govern liberty better.

From our families and cultures through countless generations, we have inherited a horde of "false beliefs" that hinder our global awakening. These accepted yet mistaken "social truths" include:

- We each exist apart from the rest of life. We are alone, powerless.

- The world is a hostile place. We must be violent to survive.

- Humans are selfish and cannot be trusted with freedom.

- We need a king or a savior to save us from evil in the world and in our own selves.

- The forces of tyranny within the world are too entrenched to be defeated, so resistance is futile.

- There are not enough enlightened people on earth to save the world from ruin, so personal action is pointless.

Such notions are "Big Lies" that we tell ourselves, that I tell myself, to avoid responsibility for using natural global power mindfully.

The evidence I've gathered convinces me that more than one billion "global thinkers" already are changing our world for the better. Yet were we a mere fraction of our current numbers, we'd still be more than a match for any despot leaving us no other recourse but nonviolent civil disobedience with peaceful and playful mass demonstrations.

Granted, a tyrant can crush any one of us like a gnat, but the swarm of us altogether is enough to drive any despot out of office — *if* we persist in our buzz for democracy. For example, our buying power alone places corporations at our mercy. Markets respond to our demand. If conscious consumers learn about a toxic food ingredient, as the news spreads, our marketplace clout is deployed all at once, so the product fails. No central leader needs to call a boycott. Our activism is spontaneous. In this way, trusting conscience and reason, acting alone and in concert, we have an advantage over all the masters of society.

We can let the "1 percent" impose corporate globalization on us, and we can anoint a populist messiah as our savior king. Alternatively, we can unite to help humanity shift into "higher consciousness," a mindset any skeptic can test. We can create democracies that balance equality and uniqueness. We can use our global power to change the world.

A sense of universal oneness, in any lingo, inspires us to live more responsibly. We outgrow monarchies, dictatorships or corrupt republics. We end tyranny in our minds and in the world.

A global sense of life guides us to support civil society and ecological sustainability. We uphold human rights, curiosity, creativity, liberty, and lasting peace. A sense of life's harmony diffuses ego battles and opens us for living free safely together. Uniting personal growth and social change uplifts our quality of life now and for generations yet unborn.

Preparing Us for Global Sense

I have rarely met anyone, when asked, who has not voiced belief that humanity will become enlightened someday — in a far, far distant future. However, our survival depends on shifting into global consciousness now, before climate change and tyranny can overwhelm us.

The good news is that more us than ever feel our connection to the whole of life on earth, and we live accordingly. Chapter 4 proves there's at least one billion globally awake people on earth. At this pivotal cultural "tipping point," *if* we act before it's too late in this decade and this century, *if* we do our inner personal growth work and our outer social change work, both at once, reason tells me we can create a truly livable future.

Humanity has been preparing for generations to make the shift into global consciousness. Below are some of the cultural influences:

Earth images saturate our societies. The iconic Apollo XVII color photograph of our whole globe in space has permeated our cultural consciousness. We can see no lines between nations. We cannot pretend to live apart from one another and all life on our world. Earth images instill a global sense of our planetary connectivity, our oneness — often subtly below our conscious awareness.

From a religious faith in our unity within creation, the earth photos offer visible proof. We go from the Age of Faith into the Age of Knowledge. We enter a new age of global thinking. A global worldview shifts how we see all life. A popularized Lakota term for awareness of the interwoven family of life is *mitákuye oyás'iŋ* — "all my relations."

Environmentalism has progressed from fringe activists io a mainstream movement, shifting public and private policies, shown by the international climate deals. Climate changes render undeniable the natural law of global interdependence, connectivity. Climate change deniers spit in the wind of reality. As eco-disasters magnify in severity, like the recent drought and later floods in Europe, so will a global sense of life.

Economics are globally intertwined. Natural resources production and distribution are global. World monetary and financial conditions affect us locally. Local commerce supports communities, yet selling local to global is now possible online. The macro impacts of micro economics reinforce public awareness of our global interdependence.

Workplace Equality is gaining traction in organizations, at least in developed nations. Ethical and sustainable governance (ESG) gets paired with diversity, equity and inclusion (DEI). Job discrimination lawsuits exhibit the cost of race and gender bias. Declaring pronouns honors a right to self-identify, lest bias disadvantages one. Behind all this is awareness of our natural equality in oneness, a growing global sensibility.

News Media awaken us to globality in daily headlines about global warming, global climate change, global financial crises, global trade wars, global internet, global cybercrime, global terrorism, global pandemics, global supply chain shortages, global food or water shortages, global mass migrations, and global overpopulation. The constant litany boils down to saturation messaging about our global interconnectivity.

Advertising often indoctrinates us as good globalization consumers. Ironically, in conditioning us to believe global "free trade" is good, mass media invite a global sensibility that favors "fair trade" first.

The Movies for decades have saturated cultural consciousness with a sense of our globality. Classic films like *Star Wars, Star Trek, Avatar,* or *Cocoon* frame a galactic view of life on any planet. Films like *Blade Runner, Terminator* or *The Matrix* warn us against dystopian despotism.

Global Internet usage increases global awareness. We had 5.3 billion internet users by 2024, comprising 68 percent of the world population, reports Statista, Ninety percent use mobile devices. Counting usage by regions, Asia leads the world (mostly China). Next is Europe (Northern Europe has highest per-capita usage), followed by Africa, Latin America/ Caribbean, North America (mostly USA), Middle East, and Oceania- Australia. Even where internet content is censored (like Russia and China) the act of interacting, by itself, subtly conveys a sense of our connectivity. The very existence of a global internet induces a global sensibility.

Bestsellers popularize the cultural meme of a global shift. An early influence is the trilogy *Future Shock* and *The Third Wave* by Alvin Toffler beside *Megatrends* by John Naisbitt. Next came *The Aquarian Conspiracy* by Marilyn Ferguson, *Earth in the Balance* by Al Gore, *A New Earth* by Eckhart Tolle, and other global bestsellers. Responding to world reality , all such "Big Ideas" books plant cultural seedthoughts blossoming into a global sense movement. (I am a steadfast believer in the dynamic power of books to change the world, so I write, and so you read.)

Philosophy infuses cultures with a sense of global oneness. Ludwig von Bertalanffy developed *General Systems Theory.* Pierre Teilhard de Chardin conceived a *nooosphere.* Buckminster Fuller discussed *Spaceship Earth.* Marshall McLuhan predicted a *global village.* Ross Ashby gave us *cybernetics.* Peter Russell portrays our living planet as a *global brain.* Howard Bloom says our mass mind is the *global brain.* Pierre Lévy talks about g*lobal collective intelligence.* Matthew Fox offers *creation spirituality.* Ken Wilber describes *integral theory.* Tu Weiming invites *global harmony.* Roland Robertson coined *globality.* Barbara Marx Hubbard envisioned the birth of *global consciousness.* A full list of all global philosophers and thought leaders would fill a book, which rather makes my point.

Biology confirms a global sense of our interdependence. Scientists are finding that cooperative *symbiosis* and *coexistence,* from microbes up, are more crucial for survival than competition. Mutations from habitat changes reinforce global awareness. Edward O. Wilson calls it *biodiversity* and *sociobiology.* James Lovelock and Lynn Margulis offer the *Gaia Hypothesis* for how intelligence pervades the biosphere.

Pandemics boost awareness of world interdependence. An airborne coronavirus disease arose in 2019, for example, and spread globally. New vaccines have not yielded global herd immunity, partly from politicizing public health. The World Health Organization by 2024 reported seven million deaths among 800 million Covid cases. That's one percent of the eight billion global population. For context, the Black Death killed up to 50 percent across Europe, Asia, and North Africa. Global microbiological perils, atop climate change, deepen our global sense of life.

Quantum physics is finding that light interacts at the subtlest levels in our universe, which is composed of light. The material realm is energy slowing to matter, vibrating below the threshold of $E=MC^2$. Light energy exists as waves and particles. Energetically, vibrationally, being condensed light, we interact with everyone and everything on earth, perhaps in other universes, even other dimensions, as Stephen Hawking posits.

Physicists study how electrons in atoms jump orbital shells instantly. Subatomic particles quantum-mirror across space and time, reflecting the presence and intention of researchers. Werner Heisenberg's "Observer Effect" admits mind-over-matter as a fact. Noetic science tests this notion in the Global Consciousness Project. Physics is proving metaphysics. We exist in quantum space where our minds turn waves of infinite possibility into particles of finite experience. A global sensibility.

New Spirituality arises as more of us sense our oneness on the earth, a mindset transcending religion and humanism. If our nature is pure light, we innately have the power to unify with our lightsource, divine or not. As more of us see how dueling duality damages us, more of us will see all life is one, that oneness gives us personal and universal power. Awareness of our natural unity and equality evokes a global sensibility.

Freethinking is growing among those choosing to define reality for themselves through reason. Thinking outside conventional belief boxes is vital for any viable creative society. Thomas Paine, a key Enlightenment Age freethinker, embraced humanism and deism. He trusted reason and science to discover nature and natural law, thereby the nature of "God." Paine was spiritual but overtly *not* religious. Distrusting "revealed" truths, freethinking deists today ally with skeptics, agnostics and atheists, who see religions as control schemes. For me, freethinking defends democracy. More free thinking means more global thinking.

All the factors I've named here, and *many* more, cumulatively, are preparing humanity to evolve a global sense of life. With global minds, we can unite as equals, outgrow bullies, stand up for democracy, and agree to cooperate for solving world crises. Our survival is at stake.

∿

A sea of chanting demonstrators floods the streets of Washington on Sunday afternoon. We march past marble office buildings. We sing to give peace a chance. This is what democracy looks like. I feel in my joyful heart that together we really can change our world. We can end the war. We can end all war. Let there be peace on earth, and let it begin with me.

We turn corners as we march to avoid government troops in riot gear. They finally outflank us and charge. We scatter. I barely outrun a screaming soldier swinging his billy club at my head. I feel terrified and yet jubilant! I am young, invulnerable and immortal.

Sunday night, I sleep on a church basement floor under a donated wool blanket that scratches my chin. More irritating are angry murmurs of plans for the morning, like setting tires on fire, dropping them from bridges.

The more I hear, the less I can be part of it. I am unwilling to be a thug. I've suffered enough from bullies in my life. I can't become one now in good conscience. I love peaceful ends and shun violent means. I'm here to protest an unjust war as wrong, so where can I make my stand?

Monday morning, I slip on the red cross armband and volunteer in a medic unit off DuPont Circle. This becomes the scene of the heaviest fighting between protesters and troops. We stay busy treating bruises and lacerations. I treat eyes and skin burned by tear gas, pepper spray, and what a vet medic says is illegal mustard gas "or worse."

In late afternoon, I call my sister in Silver Spring, Maryland, to say that I plan to stay in DC another day before I come back to her house. She puts her foot down, says no brother of hers is going to get arrested. She sends her husband into the city to retrieve me. She had met him in Colorado when he was an Air Force Academy cadet. They both support the war.

Once in the car, I tune out a requisite lecture. Soon we drive in silence. My sister greets me with love and anger.

Thanks to her, I miss being swept up in the largest mass arrests in U.S. history — almost 13,000 in three days, including bystanders — by 10,000 police and federal troops, such as the 82nd Airborne. The jails fill. Detainees get fenced in at Robert F. Kennedy Stadium. Nixon's use of the military as police is unconstitutional, I later learn. I do not know it then.

I only know my guts feel twisted. I feel disgusted. Witnessing senseless violence on both sides sickens and disillusions me.

That Monday night, I sleep in my sister's apartment in Silver Spring. On Tuesday morning over breakfast, my sister and I argue about the war, masking childhood wounds. In righteous arrogance, I stomp out, slamming the door between us. Takes years to heal.

I go for a walk in the nearby woods. To calm down, I try a meditation taught to me by a Buddhist friend at the Feenjon. In a grove of trees, I kneel, close my eyes and do circular breathing from my belly. Electric tingling in my toes rises up my legs, up my spine and encircles my head. A hum drones in my ears. My noisy mind goes silent. In stillness, I'm aware of myself being aware of myself being aware of myself. Boundaries melt away. I float serene in the eternal now, savoring sweetness in the back of my throat.

At last, I open my eyes. Flowers and leaves radiate shimmering auras beyond any rainbow. The air is granular, filled with dancing specks of light, living prana. A wave of love washes through me. I feel connected invisibly to the grass below, the trees above, the ant crawling across my knee, a barn swallow gliding in slow motion, the distant white clouds. I feel one with all life in the forest, one with all life on earth and our living planet. I feel part of creation. I sense infinity alive in every moment, awake and loving. I see myself as a tiny luminous lightpoint in endless universes of light. I am being here now. I am the one minding the store.

Wordless knowing sinks in for a lifetime. I am forever changed by my first taste of enlightened global sense. The feeling of peace fades when I stand and stroll out of the forest, returning to the "real" world.

Tipping the Pivot Point

In this book, I offer simple facts and common sense about the urgent emergence of global awareness on earth, about our power to generate a worldwide quantum leap into enlightenment in our century. My heartfelt request is that you seek the truth of this for yourself.

My model in writing is *Common Sense* by Thomas Paine. He refuted monarchy and hereditary succession. Kings should not pass power to their sons, he said, for it violates natural law and harms humanity. He looked at the state of American affairs in 1776, and he made clear to the colonists their peril if they failed to renounce regal rule and declare national independence as a democratic republic. Paine wrote:

> In America the law is king. For as in absolute governments the king is law, Independence means no more than this, whether we shall make our own laws or whether the king; the greatest enemy this continent hath or can have [the king], shall tell us 'there shall be no laws but such as I like.

Updating Paine, I'm refuting the principles of male dominance and dependence on despots. I label it *alpha male rule* and *authority addiction*. Like Paine, I'm saying abuses of inherited wealth and power violate natural law and harm humanity. I'm making clear our peril if we fail to renounce autocracy now, if we fail to declare our interdependence.

Paine next looked realistically at the ability of Americans to wage a revolutionary war. He estimated the number of men ready to fight (many women joined in). He calculated the costs to construct a fleet of warships and proposed how to fund the war effort. He offered practical reasons to believe a revolutionary war could actually be won.

Paine said the colonists first needed the strength of will to act. All of their hardships would be justified if they established for humanity a new democratic republic, conceived in liberty and equality.

We face a kindred situation now. So, I look realistically at our ability to conduct a peaceful campaign for world enlightenment. For practicality, I offer ways that global thinkers are taking actions within themselves and in society. I show we do have the ability to change the world.

We first need the strength of will to act, the political will. We need the willingness to do our inner work and outer work at the same time. All of our hardships will be justified if we establish for humanity a world of stronger democracies, conceived in liberty and equality.

To clarify the parallel between Paine's times and ours, I reference Malcolm Gladwell's book, *The Tipping Point*. He extends a term that Alvin Toffler used in *Future Shock* to describe pivotal shifts in society, such as from the Industrial Age to the Information Age.

Gladwell explores how new ideas are adopted culturally and socially. He tells how ideas spread like viruses to become epidemic or "viral." Once a threshold number of people adopt some new idea or behavior, a critical mass is reached for a quantum social shift. People suddenly act and think as if they'd always known the flat earth is round.

Have you heard of the *hundredth monkey phenomenon*? Supposedly, a primatologist started teaching island monkeys to wash their food at the beach before eating. The practice spread. When the "hundredth monkey" adopted the habit, all monkeys on the island suddenly began washing their food. Next, all monkeys on neighboring islands (separated by impassable shark-filled waters, of course) started washing their food, too!

Beyond a fabulous fable of a quantum leap in monkey mindfulness, we have actual historic proof of one worldview replacing another, such as Christianity displacing older nature religions in Europe. Pivotal writings have sparked huge cultural shifts, like the *Diamond Sutra*, Martin Luther's 95 Theses, Paine's *Common Sense*, or Adam Smith's *The Wealth of Nations*. We're at such a tipping point now. Our world wavers between democracy and autocracy. I write to help tip the balance toward liberty.

Paine refuted the principle of monarchy, no matter where found. He urged the colonies to declare independence and form a republic without a king. Today, our myriad cultures around the globe, with few exceptions, display generational dependence on alpha male rule. I propose we choose to rule ourselves without kings, so we practice democracy. The choice can help humanity evolve and ascend into enlightened societies.

※

2011: BRITAIN — *I marry for the first time at age 60 to a New Yorker living on Kauai. When I first met Melissa online in 2009, I lived in Colorado. She said to me, "Distance is solvable, but chemistry is not." One year later, I sell or give away 90 percent of my stuff and move to Kauai.*

We marry in Denver. A honeymoon in Hawaii is silly, so we fly across the pond to Britain. We rent a standard sedan with GPS, buy Ordnance maps, and drive on the left through motorway roundabouts. Mellissa routes us to bed-and-breakfast country houses with wonderful food.

Each day, we visit ancient sacred sites. In Wales, we drive up a narrow mountain road between hedgerows a thousand years old. On top of the pass is an old Roman road lined by ancient standing stones 15 feet tall. We stand on the desolate road among grazing sheep and the row of stones.

In Cornwall, we walk down a lane between farm fields to reach a Bronze Age circle with 19 waist-high stones around a taller tilted stone. We "unlock" the stone circle by walking deosil around it three times. I enter and lay headfirst under the gnomon. My eyes close. Time stops.

Melissa brings me back. We leave the circle and return to the lane. A swarm of odd black flies assails us, darting into our ears, noses and mouths. Realizing we forgot to "relock" the circle, we return and walk widdershins outside the stones once. Moments later, back in the lane, all the black flies are gone. We gain new respect for old powers.

On Salisbury Plain, we visit Avebury, built across 28 acres more than 4,000 years ago. Three giant stone circles are approached by two avenues of standing stones, all managed today by the National Trust.

We miss a tour by Peter Knight, the noted Dorset dowser and author on ancient sites. We walk to the nearest tall stone, pull out copper dowsing rods, start walking around the stone. A small tour group approaches. The guide asks what we're doing. We're detecting the edges of the stone's magnetic field. He nods and invites us to join his tour. It's Peter Knight.

At Stonehenge, having advance reservations, we enter the monument in late afternoon. After the rote talk by a National Trust guide, we're on our own to connect with the monoliths. No touching. I stand in the center of Stonehenge with the setting sun on my face. I ask the earth for guidance in our marriage. How do I become her full and equal partner?

In Glastonbury, Melissa and I visit the Chalice Well near the Tor. Using a map given to us by Peter Knight, we follow the Michael and Mary ley lines in a pilgrimage from the entrance to the ancient well.

We pause to pray and meditate at each sacred spot — the vesica pools, the yew trees, the healing pool, the waterfall, the lion's head (we drink the red spring water), the angel seat, and the sanctuary.

Finally, we sit on the stone ledge around the open wellhead. The vesica piscis symbol on the wellhead cover displays two interlocking circles with a vertical lance passing through them, symbolizing the equal union of male and female, heaven and earth, light and shadow. I welcome divine light for guidance in any shadowlands ahead.

Peace descends on me and arises in me, more sweetly than ever before. Quiet mind. Serene joy. Melissa's eyes glow bright with love and wellbeing. And I love her in my life. We sit silent in gentle tranquility.

Later I wonder, how can I be at peace in the world if I'm not at peace in myself? How can I trust the universe if I don't trust myself?

CHAPTER 2

Shadow Forces

2016: KAUAI — *I nearly die three times this year from cancer and its treatment. Melissa, bless her, anchors me while I find inside the will to live. She has survived cancer and knows what to do. If not for her love, care and logistics, I'd be dead by now. In truth, it's a miracle I'm alive.*

The tale is harrowing and inspiring.

In late January 2016, in response to persistent pain in my left side, I'm diagnosed with Stage IV clear cell renal cancer. A tumor has devoured my left kidney and begun creeping up the inferior vena cava, the central vein to my heart. Lesions grow in a lung. Abdominal lymph nodes are malignant. Cancer is spreading rapidly. I could be dead in a month.

The doctor says this form of cancer does not respond to chemotherapy or radiation, so both treatments are out (sigh of relief). Structural reality says I need surgery, very soon. I'm scheduled for February.

Within days of the dooming diagnosis, I post in my YouTube channel a video in which I call myself a cancer survivor. "I may have cancer," I say, "but cancer does not have me." (Later videos share my adventure.)

As word spreads, dozens of friends and then strangers bless me with prayers and healings for survival and recovery. I'm placed on prayer lists in Hawaii, Colorado, California, and elsewhere. Island healers work on me, as do remote lightworkers on the mainland. It's humbling.

For self-healing, I do vivid visualizations. I bathe my body in the center of the sun as my cells renew. I stand barefoot in zoysia grass in our front yard and feel Mother Kauai rising up my torso and healing me.

To heal my inner child, I visualize young me and adult me climbing up a Colorado mesa. At the plateau, the boy becomes an eagle that lifts to fly in a wide circle, level out and soar straight into my heart. I shift.

Medically, the journey is more treacherous, more amazing.

In mid-February, I fly with Melissa to Honolulu and check into Queen's Medical Center. Surgeons remove the left kidney (the size of a cantaloupe), slide the tumor from the central vein, slip out lymph nodes and a web of cancer tendrils across my belly, touching all organs, entering none. The lead surgeon later says, "We removed all the cancer we could see."

Back on Kauai, I recover slowly. An incision scar arches across my belly like a frown or a rainbow. I'm weak and thin, around 100 lbs. In the mirror, I look like a Dachau survivor. Melissa asks what I want to eat.

An April CT scan shows my abdominal cavity is clear of cancer, but little lesions in my lung have grown. In May, back in Honolulu with Melissa, I undergo Interleukin-2 immunotherapy at Queens.

I'm placed in the dedicated IL-2 room close to the nursing station for constant monitoring. Each infusion triggers severe rigors. Chills make my body shiver and shake violently. My vitals drop dangerously. I tolerate nine doses over five days before the doctors call it quits.

We return home to Kauai. I'm expected back at Queen's in a week for a second course, more of the same. My third night at home, I have a lucid dream of dying in that hospital bed. After a long conversation with Melissa, I call my oncologist to decline any further IL-2 treatments.

We will wait and see and monitor.

Microcosm and Macrocosm

Nearly dying is not the only path to conscious awakening. Any path will do if we sense our oneness. The light being our selves is unbound by space and time, for all is one. If this is so, anything is possible — healing cancer, healing humanity, healing our societies, healing the earth.

Thoughts, fantasies, feelings, words, deeds, and energy fields interact. Thoughts are things. Things affect other things. Physics/metaphysics 101. My individual microcosm reflects our global macrocosm, as does yours and everybody's. I am the world, and the world is me.

To survive cancer, I've gone beyond medical and holistic treatments to face suppressed and denied emotional, mental and ancestral shadow forces that surface in my body as deadly disease. I have to consider a scary possibility. Am I secretly trying to kill myself?

Through introspection, counseling and growth circles, I discovered ways I've made myself ill from unhealed traumas, buried rage, festering bitterness, and chronic victimhood. I played the victim so convincingly that part of me wished to die to escape my duty to live free.

I did not face self-destructive habits of heart and mind that bred illness in my body until a ravenous tumor ate a kidney, filled my gut with cancer, and climbed up the vein to my heart. When it got life-threatening and could not be ignored, I had to take action before it was too late

Humanity likewise now faces suppressed and denied emotional, mental and energetic shadow forces surfacing in our world. Ecological, economic, cultural, social, and political cancers threaten us all. To avoid living free, we may play the victim so convincingly that we worship savior dictators who finally, terribly, make death our only escape.

We tend to play both victims and perpetrators, and rescuers, too, or I do. Will we ever stop hating ourselves and self-destructing? Paine wrote, "Our greatest enemies, the ones we must fight most often, are within." Malignant global conditions feature fossil-fuels pollution causing climate changes, ruining habitats with icecaps melting, coastal and river flooding, storms, freezes, heat waves, wildfires, droughts, famines, and worse. In the "sixth mass extinction" on earth, is human extinction possible?

Societal cancers include business and political corruption, economic and social injustice, the *isms* of sexism, racism, ageism, rankism, ableism. Add child abuse, sexual abuse, slavery. Add fiscal instability and crashes, revolutions and wars. Add the malignant authority addiction of dictators, fed by primal survival fears, devouring our hearts and minds.

Self-destructive habits are woven into our social and cultural fabric. We've grown accustomed to these shadow forces in our world. We never notice nor confront them until some crisis — like a wildfire or a coup to end democracy — grows too urgent to dismiss, no longer can be ignored. Will we now awake and take action before it's too late?

A caveat: When we do act, we tend to triage symptoms and ignore causes. In an offshore oil spill, for instance, we rush in cleanup crews and praise volunteers washing seabirds in kitchen detergent. We don't address the core cause — insanely thinking we can pollute the earth without cost. Similarly, to cure societal cancers like poverty and injustice, let us address the core cause — insanely ignoring the reality we all are one.

Same as I see an acute need to raise my consciousness to heal cancer threatening my life, I also see an acute need for humanity to raise our consciousness to heal the global cancers threatening all life.

We're like the proverbial frog placed in a pot of cool water over a low flame. The frog fable is a trite trope because it's so true. We float placidly as slowly rising heat boils us alive. If we do not act, we will die. Shall we see our peril in time and jump free?

For humanity to survive on the earth, will we awaken to our oneness in time to save ourselves? Will we mature into harmony with life, outgrow fights for ego? It must be done at one time or another. The longer we delay, the harder it will be to accomplish, and the greater the cost.

Before we self-destruct on earth, are we willing to take responsibility for governing our behavior in a globally sensibly way? In binary terms, the same as I will evolve or perish, humanity will evolve or perish — or endure in squalid misery. Shall we change our thinking in time to naysay the doomsayers? Our future hinges on the choice between autocratic shadow forces and democratic self rule. What makes global sense?

In any words we choose to talk about it, for us to survive our epoch, individually and collectively, the conscious evolution of humanity into an enlightened global sensibility, as Paine would say, "is a necessity."

Global sense makes common sense.

〰

More medical news. Fresh PET and MRI scans in August find a tumor thrombus, a blood clot of "neoplastic" cancer cells, is climbing up the inferior vena cava (IVC), the central vein to my heart. Surgery is urgent. My Hawaii doctors all demure. They say I need a "tertiary specialist."

Melissa finds a Los Angeles surgeon who's perfected minimally invasive robotic surgery to remove an IVC tumor thrombus. Seven tiny incisions. Home in ten days. The doctor accepts my case. "Spirit at work."

In September, Melissa and I fly to LA. She's reserved a short-term rental in Silver Lake. Thursday morning, we go for a pre-op exam at the University of Southern California, Keck School of Medicine, Norris Comprehensive Cancer Center. We enter the busy waiting rooms of Big Medicine.

A long day of testing capped by a 3D MRI finds my condition is worse. The clot fully occludes the IVC. No blood flows in the vein. A tumor tendril is on the verge of entering the heart valve.

I could die in a heartbeat.

My condition is beyond what robotics can handle, the doctor reports. Instead, a top surgeon from the urology team will perform "open surgery" (cut me open). I'll go home in about a month.

I email the news to my family and healing network.

Melissa and I meet the surgeon. He says I must be growing collateral veins to bypass the blocked IVC, or else I'd be dead already. He'll do a "cavectomy," removal of the inferior vena cava vein, tumor and all. My recovery will be slow, he cautions, but if I do nothing, I'll be gone in a week.

He explains the procedure. I cringe and feel astounded.

First, he'll break and spread two ribs to enter my thoracic cavity. He'll clamp the IVC vein at both ends. If I don't start to die, he'll snip out the vein. If necessary, he'll replace it with a bovine vein (on hand). If cancer margins imperil the vein to my only kidney, he'll move that organ to a pelvic vein, which means temporary or permanent dialysis. If the clot enters my atrium, he'll crack open my chest and put me on a heart-lung bypass machine, but only if necessary. And he will remove all the cancer he can see.

To me, it's overwhelming. To him, it's routine, his tenth in a week.

Melissa and I exchange looks. Spirit sent the perfect tertiary specialist. He gets my informed consent. Surgery will be Tuesday.

On Monday evening, with the doctor's assurance, Melissa and I go out for dinner at an LA restaurant. We're joined by her older brother, who flew in from Cape Cod, and the co-minister from the Center for Spiritual Living Kauai, who flew in from Hawaii. Their support is magnificent.

At dinner we joke about ridiculous medical outcomes. I wind up with two heads, dragging a colostomy bag behind me down Sunset Boulevard, my hospital gown flapping open in the breeze. My face hurts from laughing so hard. Fun calms fear. I feel loved and safe.

Next morning, I check into Keck. Surgery lasts five hours.

I awake with Melissa at my side in the recovery room. The doctor visits us and calls my surgery "as big as it gets."

I passed the clamp test, so he cut out about five inches of IVC vein. He coaxed the tendril from my heart. My sole surviving kidney stayed in place. The doctor smiles and proclaims, "You're cured!"

Back on Kauai, I feel all my 65 years, and I feel a strong will to live. My resolve springs from the moment I awoke after surgery. Like that awakening at age 20 in a forest glade, I am transformed.

Woozy from anesthesia, not fully back in my body, I am consciously aware of having a choice on whether to take the next breath. I can be done here. The veil between worlds is thin. I can cross so easily. A question arises, is my life complete? Is there anything I must stay alive to do?

In that moment, as much as I love Melissa, I see and know one thing I must do before I die. I need to finish and publish this book on global sense. I must stay alive to get the job done. The writing comes through me more often than from me. The book is my soul work.

And in that moment, I choose to live. I breathe.

Darkness and Shadow

"The greater part of our happiness or misery," Martha Washington advised, "depends on our dispositions and not our circumstances."

Long before my ego was humbled by illness, I started catching myself playing small by acting big. I regret the pretense.

I tell myself the story that any popularity I've enjoyed was due to my talent more than my personality. I've been called "difficult" and "resistant to authority." When I react to injustice, if I am not centered and grounded, if my scared and scarred ego rules me, I'm at my worst with people. Dark and light forces contend in me. I have "unresolved issues."

In my 75th turn around our sun, I'm better at being real and present. I'm better at empathy and love. I must work at mindfulness and kindness. Takes intention and attention to feel whole. If my higher self shows up, by grace, I'm delighted. Behind all my survival-mechanism masks, you see, unforgiven pain still feeds my victimhood habits of self-sabotage.

My denial of self-defeating behavior falls in the realm of *shadow*, the aspects of myself that I "hide, suppress and deny," as I hear in men's circles. Shadow shades the realms of behavior hidden from our conscious minds. Took cancer for me to see self-loathing was trying to kill me. Shadow work sheds light on the wounds and lies I denied rule me. Wanting approval as a writer, for instance, compensates for neglect when young.

Shadow habits are not innately bad or evil, for all is light being all that is. Yet the consequences from unconscious, incongruent shadowy behavior can and does cause harm. The shadow knows my pain.

For all the times I've hidden shame and insecurity with anger, bluster and arrogance, acted superior, like my father; for all the times I tried to control outcomes for safety, been rude, blunt, sharp, or hyper-critical, like my mother; for the times I've excused, deflected, or rationalized, or made others wrong, or lied to look blameless; for all the times I've lost patience, interrupted, overspoke, failed to listen; for the times I've selfishly, unfairly or heedlessly harmed anyone, alive or gone, I am sorry. Take my inventory. My amend is this book, and living from love as best I can.

I'm growing as I go along. Much of my personal growth springs from "shadow work" with counselors and support groups. I also grow by reading classic books. Carl Jung's work on gestalt helps me see my whole myself. Alan Watts' books help me see my life is sacred, how I get in my own way. Robert A. Johnson helps me discover the cost of hiding from my true self. Such illuminating books help me evolve and be more me.

Light dispels shadow, so let's consider the nature of darkness. A room without light is dark. Dark places may scare us. We fear the monster under the bed. We fear chaos and the unknown. We dread the dark night of the soul. Yet traditional cultures do primal initiations in darkness, like a cave or lodge. Dare we behold our darkest visions and bring them into the light? Darkness, darkness, be our teacher; do it all so we may see.

Our central problem is *dualism*. Instead of seeing light and dark as aspects of oneness, monism, we decide light is better than dark.

We adopt light-vs-dark dualism as an *a priori* certainty, but it lacks a valid premise. Astrophysics says invisible "dark matter" fills expanding space between planets, stars and galaxies — so, "nothing" has mass. Our universe naturally exists with light and dark matter. Both are necessary. Despite fact, most of us silently believe light is better than dark.

In writing a book to advance global "enlightenment," I'm challenged by the linguistics of loaded terms like *light, shadow* and *darkness*. I'm alert to connotations for "light" and "dark" in society, extending into all aspects of life, from morality to race to technology, like the "dark web."

In discussing personal and world enlightenment, for rhetorical ease, I frame rulership of our minds as a dualistic battle between autocracy and democracy, a fight between the light and shadow aspects of our full selves. I do so warily. I'm alert to mindtraps. If we fight for the light of liberty, but if we alone are free once we win, our victory begets dark tyranny.

Personal Responsibility

The rise and fall of civilizations tells the story of humanity learning to accept personal responsibility for free will. If we live with awareness of our oneness, naturally empathetic, we need no lofty kings to rule our lowest impulses. If raised since childhood to be mindful of our oneness, trusting conscience and reason to discern light and shadow, we naturally behave ourselves. We barely need any government at all.

I advocate *personal sovereignty*, governed by a sense of natural unity. The term enfolds individuality, self-reliance, self-sufficiency, autonomy, conscience, reason, consent, agency, and personal responsibility.

Modern thinking about personal responsibility, at least in the West, traces to thoughts from the Age of Reason and the Enlightenment. Thomas Paine, voicing Enlightenment ideals, said good society is the responsibility of both individuals and the community, a social contract. He reasoned that Natural Law, the Law of Nature, should govern society. Civil and criminal laws exist because we lack self rule over free will.

I agree with Paine that democracy works best when people accept responsibility for freedom. If government applies the law equally to all, none above or below the law, liberty endures. The natural law of oneness, if enacted into civil and criminal law, guards our natural rights.

The ideal is not current reality.

Sad to say, from us misreading the laws of nature as a fight for the survival of the brutish, our laws codify fear, hate, jealousy, greed, and other shadow forces. Our laws reflect the web of mass consciousness we weave with our thoughts, feelings, words, deeds, and energies. We project our bad habits into the world, and the world reinforces these bad habits within us. A vicious circle eats itself.

Together we co-create our shared global realities of climate change, generational poverty and wealth, toxic habitats, injustice from bias based on gender, race, caste, age, or ability. We co-create societies that fail people with low incomes, chiefly people of color. Scapegoats abound, like Jews, but blaming others does not refute our collective irresponsibility.

In our global crises, the shadow force of fear is the greatest threat to liberty. Survival fears and insecurities drive us to seek safety in such social habits as always needing a boss, or always needing to be the boss, always rebelling against any boss, or hiding from notice to avoid responsibility. Our compulsions deny us the freedom to govern our own lives.

Some of us blame our modern woes on excessive individualism and capitalist selfishness. We notice destructive antics by libertine libertarians who pursue their visions despite harm to others. Selfish crimes give liberty a bad name, costing freedom for all. In contrast are self-reliance libertarians who rule their lives responsibly and treat others as sovereign equals.

Some of us cite "personal responsibility" as an excuse to avoid social responsibility. We do what we want, take what we can, ignore boundaries, ignore other's right to life, liberty and property. We commit outrages and feel justified by our right to live free or die. Personal responsibility slogans are no excuse for reckless disregard and negligent narcissism.

I define "liberty" as the freedom to do as I will, so long as I do no harm. Within that boundary, I claim the natural right to say and do and live as I please, be spontaneous, stretch my limits, be more me.

Inner child me revels in liberty, oblivious to others. If I'm careless, I may ignore caution. If told what I "should" do, the young rebel me reacts, *Oh yeah? Why the funk should I?* What restrains defiantly selfish impulses? What stops me? Elder me wants to live mindfully in peace.

At our best, self rule governs free will.

If I feel inept at self-control, afraid of failure if I try, or too ashamed, I may play the victim, blame another, lie to myself, feel despair, abdicate responsibility for self rule. If I fail to govern shadow impulses, injuries go unforgiven. If restorative justice is denied, old wounds fester.

In a global sense, each of us creates our private personal reality and our public shared reality. By design or default, given our full connectivity, we are individually responsible for the state of our world.

Ultimately, we *consent.* We have *agency.* What happens happens with our permission, even if tacit. Each tiny decision, like selecting sliding doors on trains, decides our future. We may dissent in private, yet unless we act to stop injustice, we somehow must *want* it to happen. One can argue then, that if we consent, if implicitly, to the lives we all create together on earth, there are no victims, which begs questions of karma and fate.

Personal responsibility, for me, means accountability for being true to my soul, that lifeforce being me and all life. Creating a centered, non-verbal connection to our lifesource is on me. The inner and outer work of enlightenment is my personal responsibility.

Social responsibility, for me, means owning how my thoughts, words, feelings, and deeds impact others, society and the earth. I am one with the world as the world is one with me. What's good for the world is good for me; what's honestly good for me is good for the world. Freedom without personal and social responsibility is irrational.

Denial of personal responsibility for self rule plants the dragon's teeth of dictatorship. When we evolve a global sense of life, we outgrow needing kings or masters. We reject those shadowy populist leaders who lie to us, those boastful bullies secretly terrified of being vulnerable.

CHAPTER 3

Common Global Sense

2017: KAUAI — *The morning following the January 20 inauguration of Donald John Trump as the 45th President of the United States, Melissa and I sit at home in Kapahi watching the Women's March on live TV.*

A half million people gather in Washington, DC, to "represent" for the equal human rights of all women, all genders, all races, ages, and abilities. Newscasts report many millions more gathering in cities and towns across the USA, Britain, Europe and around the world.

The massive Women's March convenes the resistance to "Trumpism." Banners and signs warn Trump will ignore the Constitution he's just sworn to protect. Some urge investigating Trump for ties to known Russian election interference on social media, aiding his narrow win in the Electoral College. To me, winning with foreign help feels illegitimate, like cheating.

Melissa and I laugh at the hand-drawn posters poking fun at the ways "The Donald" is unfit for office. Women wear pink hats with pussycat ears, taunting Trump's indiscreet recorded remark that he can't stop himself from kissing beautiful women and grabbing their "pussy" (genitalia). He can get away with anything, he boasts, because he's famous.

I've researched Trump's life (as anyone can). I found a long history of racism, sexism and narcissism; lots of business failures, not paying bills, bankruptcies, frauds; bullying, braggadocio, lying, accusing others of his wrong;, disregard for civil rights, scofflaw disdain for government, contempt for majority rule, and arrogant ignorance of the U.S. Constitution.

Melissa calls him a toddler, "a walking id." I see a wannabe king.

Trump lauds all foreign strongmen, especially Russia's authoritarian leader, Vladimir Putin, said to assassinate critics. I learn about Trump's early mentoring by aging mob lawyer Roy Cohn, the legal counsel behind Sen. Joe McCarthy's 1950s "witch hunt" for Communists. Cohn trained Trump in his mobster defense tactics — deny, deflect, distract, and attack.

I worry about Trump's revival of the 1930s' pro-Nazi "America First" slogan and bigotry. I spy fascist propaganda tactics being scarily successful, like treating opinions or judgments as facts. He poses as a champion of those oppressed by the "deep state." He says, "I am your warrior. I am your justice." In the war of good over evil, he proclaims, "This is the final battle!"

As a cult survivor, I spot his personality cult as authority addiction in action. I see in Trump a feudal lord who will have his way come what may. I fret that an egoist is now "The Leader of the Free World."

In my gut is a sinking sensation that humanity is about to embark on Mr. Toad's wild ride. In the beloved children's novel, Wind in the Willows, *Mr. Toad of Toad Hall steals a car, causes mayhem, gets caught, and goes to prison for 20 years. Will Mr. Trump?*

Melissa and I rejoice at today's turnout for gender equality and human rights. She's retired to Hawaii after decades in New York confronting sexism as a senior executive. I've been engaged in the men's movement for decades. I share her passion as she shouts at the TV, "It's about time!"

Melissa leaves for her singing lesson. I prepare for driving to Lihue, the island capitol. A recent scan says I am "cancer clear" after last September's second surgery in LA. I feel grateful to be driving again. Today will be the furthest I've driven since returning home.

I park on Akuhini mauka of Kapule Highway, across from the airport greeting a million visitors a year. With unsteady steps, pausing for breath, I join the Women's March. We are standing, actually, not marching.

About 1,500 of us, mostly women and "haoles," are singing, chanting, carrying signs, and waving at the passing cars. Drivers honk and wave back. I stand feebly, yet I'm standing up for democracy. Today in 2017, as in 1971, I feel in my heart that together we really can change our world.

Personal Growth and Politics

To improve life on our planet, I encourage bridging a chasm in our minds dividing personal and spiritual growth from social and political change. Closing the gap is as hard, as hard as bridging the gap between our heads and hearts, at least for me. Closing the gap is necessary.

Those of us focused on social change and politics often want nothing to do with personal or spiritual growth. We may attend a church, temple or mosque, yet we seldom or never seek psychotherapy or counseling, never enroll in crazy "woo-woo" workshops. Atheistic, agnostic skeptic, or deist, we may equate mysticism with escapism. We may never bother to pray or meditate. We rarely sit silent alone in nature.

If politics and social change matters most in your life, you may resist me inviting you to think about personal growth and spirituality. You may say contemplating the navel only locates lint, or it wastes time, or it's too frustrating, or too irrational. I've felt these feelings and thought these thoughts. Cynicism is faith disappointed.

Those of us focused on personal growth or spirituality often want nothing to do with politics and social change. We might contribute to ecological or humanitarian causes like saving whales or feeding hungry babies. We seldom or never work on any grassroots campaigns. We equate politics with corruption. We may never bother to vote.

If spirituality or personal growth matter most in your life, you might resist me inviting you to think about government and social justice. You might say politics lowers your vibes too much, or it's too frustrating, too dirty, too disgusting. I have felt these feelings and thought these thoughts. Cynicism is idealism dismayed.

Are such binary views irreconcilable? Black-or-white thinking stops us from seeing our whole world in breathtaking colors. Between dueling duality mountains lays the adventurous land of balance where we dwell creatively from our peaceful center. At the extremes, fear and unease push us to seek shelter under kings or other masters.

By closing the gap between personal growth and politics, we unite self-improvement and world improvement, so freedom thrives.

As we make sense of life with global minds, we discover separation and isolation are illusions. Indeed, we are the world, and the world is us. Our natural oneness or unity or connectivity makes us globally mighty. Why not join hearts and hands instead of giving up?

A Caution — Uniting spirituality and politics is NOT the same as uniting religion and government (or ideology and government). Such an unholy union historically breeds theocracy and tyranny. Whenever any heavenly belief becomes the law, all hell breaks loose.

If I believe everyone is sick, and I have the only cure, then it's my moral duty to force my cure upon everybody, for their own good! Such thinking justified persecutions like Europe's Inquisition, witch burnings, indigenous conversions, the Holocaust, China's Cultural Revolution, or Taliban beheadings. "Every political good carried to the extreme," warned Mary Wollstonecraft, "must be productive of evil."

Paine wrote, "Of all the tyrannies that affect mankind, tyranny in religion is the worst." In a letter to Jefferson, he added, "Give power to a bigot of any sectary [sect] and he [*sic*] will use it to the oppression of the rest." No group has a right to impose its religion or ideology upon society. A "separation of church and state" protects our rights and liberties better than any other measure to avoid the abuse of power.

I would not breach that wall. Instead, I am proposing that a global sense of life unifies spirituality and politics in a freedom-loving, *if* we honor conscience and reason. I'm willing to try.

〰

2019: KAUAI — *In June, Melissa and I agree we're done. The love is there, yet differences and inequalities are irreconcilable. Cordial despite tensions, we agree that I'll move out by December First. I decide to go back home to Denver. The sooner the better, seems to me. I immerse myself in culling and boxing up my life. Goodbye stranger. I'm a free bird.*

I'm about 80 percent packed by mid-September when I visit Oahu to staff a men's weekend. During setup, we're clearing a field of Guinea grass to erect a tent. A man uses a weed whacker with a metal disk blade to cut the thick stalks. I help haul away the cuttings. In an moment of inattention by that man and by me, I stand too close as his saw jumps, bites my front left ankle. I'm in shock. A vet there helps me, says it's like a shrapnel hit.

An Oahu ER does a fast patch. Back on Kauai, I'm told the top tendons are cut. My foot flops. Four surgeries later, I've lost dorsiflexion, so I walk "drop-foot." Physical therapy helps. I'll seeks a specialist in Denver.

While I recover and regain mobility, Melissa graciously postpones my departure until January, giving us the holidays together.

We choose to take the journey of "conscious uncoupling" to forgiveness and release. On the tenth anniversary of the day we met online, an energy retrieval ritual heals our hearts and souls. Telling untold truths, we let go of unmet agendas. Our final weeks together are gentle and open.

Meanwhile, I track the news. The top U.S. story is the impeachment of President Trump. He was caught trying to extort the leader of Ukraine to tell lies about Joe Biden, the most likely 2020 Democratic candidate. Trump orders his administration to ignore Congressional subpoenas. In December, the Democrat-run House impeaches Donald Trump for abuse of power and obstruction of Congress. In January, the Republican-run Senate permits no testimony at Trump's trial and acquits him, a forgone conclusion.

Sensing worse ahead, I return to putting books in boxes.

Society and Government

"We must not confuse the peoples with their governments," Paine wrote. "Society in every state is a blessing. Government even in its best state is but a necessary evil, in its worst state an intolerable one." Government is necessary because we fail to practice self rule in society.

I want to explore the relationship between society and government.

Society and government are not only different, Paine observed, but they have different purposes and origins. Society arises from our virtues. Government arises from our vices, from a need to curb what Paine called "our wickedness." Society promotes our happiness by uniting our virtues and talents within a community. In that community, government restrains our vices or wickedness. We empower government to keep us safe from harm by one another, at best, or the harm we do to ourselves.

The nature of government is defensive. All forms of government arise from a failure to govern our own behavior. Government secures our lives and property against our own and others' abuses of liberty. As we practice more self-restraint, we need less government restraint.

If we all had global sense, if we each trusted reason and conscience as a moral voice within us, government would be unnecessary. "For were the impulses of conscience clear, uniform, and irresistibly obeyed," Paine said, "man [sic] would need no other lawgiver." However, anarchy without responsible self rule is impossible and absurd. Seems we humans remain incapable of sensibly governing ourselves in society. We still require an external authority to protect us from our worst impulses.

Since government is "a necessary evil," Paine said, we should choose the least evil form of government possible. Democratic republics appear to be the least evil, so far, and these are now under threat by the upsurge of authoritarian regimes, outnumbering the democracies.

In binary simplicity, two specters haunt our world — the spirits of absolute despotism and genuine democracy. The great mass of humanity occupies the realms between these two opposing forces.

On the dominant side are transnational corporations, ideologies and religions that rule us through puppet regimes. They exploit our authority addiction to gain our consent to govern. They rely on our willingness to surrender our personal sovereignty to them. If anointed leaders (and their masters) command enough devoted followers to conserve the *status quo*, those in charge stay in charge. They fear revolution and evolution.

The binary flip side is a grassroots global sense movement (going by many names) for ecology, equal rights and democracy — all informed by global consciousness. Aware of our connectivity, we invest energy into inventing a creative, free, peaceful, and just civil society.

We support "good government" ruled by the consent of the governed. We change the world from within. Our minds and actions are generating critical mass for a global quantum shift into world enlightenment.

Dualistic forces of tyranny and liberty compete to shape tomorrow. Which way goes the world pivots on which way goes each one of us.

Autocracy or Democracy?

"No man [*sic*] is prejudiced in favour of a thing, knowing it to be wrong," Paine wrote. "He is attached to it on the belief of its being right; and when he sees it is not so, the prejudice will be gone." Shall we release our prejudice for kings and instead favour democracy?

Paine advocated reading to eradicate prejudice and superstition. Autodidactic, he read books from the Age of Reason and Enlightenment. I want to identify key "big ideas" books that made common sense to him. Four authors distill the era's thinking on autocracy and democracy.

Thomas Hobbes — His 1651 *Leviathan* said we're all selfish animals at constant war in the world, where life is "nasty, brutish, and short." To control our animal impulses, society needs absolute kings to decree laws because might makes right. (Hobbes' ideas inform George Orwell's novels, *Animal Farm* and *Nineteen Eighty-Four*.)

Baruch Spinoza — His 1677 *Ethics* touted the benefits of civil and religious liberties. If society gratifies our base cravings, oppression is not needed to keep us in line. (Spinoza's ideas inform Aldous Huxley's novel, *Brave New World*, where the drug Soma mollifies the masses.)

Such Age of Reason writers, Paine decided, only rationalized tyranny. "A body of men holding themselves accountable to nobody," he concluded, "ought not to be trusted by anybody." Enlightenment writers made more sense to him for the principles of government. Two are iconic.

John Locke — His 1690 *Two Treatises on Civil Government* argued people and the state are ruled by "natural law." In nature, each of us is free and equal, while different, so each of us is our own moral judge. We have "natural rights" to life, liberty, property, and "the pursuit of happiness" — leading us to prefer cooperation over competition. Heedless selfishness gives way to a prudent regard for the common good. A humanist, Locke urged moral self-discipline without government making us behave.

If people violate natural law or natural rights, he said, the state may protect us only as far as we say it can. The state is powerless without the *consent* of the people, if implicit. To protect us from a state abusing power, Locke advocated *checks and balances* in government constitutions.

When the state represses or denies our natural rights, a reasonable revolution is our civil right under natural law, and our moral duty.

Jean Jacques Rousseau — His 1762 *Du Contrat Social* (*The Social Contract*) asserted, "Nature never deceives us; it is we who deceive ourselves." Nature lacks morality in itself, so good people exist only if society makes them good through a social contract. People are prone to competition but may agree to cooperate. He urged moral self-mastery. "Never exceed your rights, and they will soon become unlimited."

Rousseau urged a social contract for democracy, but he warned that the majority is not always right. And what is right? Religious and political morals usually conflict, and religions tend to abuse political power. So, he called for the *separation of church and state*. As for tyrants, "Force does not constitute right," he said; "obedience is due only to legitimate powers." If the state becomes illegitimate, revolution is a right and a duty.

These four authors voiced core differences between autocracy and democracy. Age of Enlightenment values are the true original democratic ideas inspiring the U.S. republic. These are *not* the aristocratic prejudices now being foisted by Federalists as constitutional "Originalism."

〰〰

I love Kaua'i āina and my ohana, yet Denver friends and family await. I also need Denver's better medical care. I'd been cancer clear for two years, but a PET scan finds cancer blips in a lung. A Denver oncologist will restart immunotherapy, which in 2018 helped my body heal malignant hilar lymph nodes near my lungs. We will treat and monitor.

Two friends help me finish packing. In mid-January, a dozen friends help truck my boxes to the mover's dock and load the shipping crate, which cuts my costs. Even so, the credit card takes a gigantic hit.

On January 21, 2020, on the cusp of Aquarius, on the morning of my flight to Denver, a courier delivers our Kauai circuit court divorce decree. Now it's official. I'm free as a bird. This white bird must fly.

At the airport curb, we say goodbye with long hugs and tears and hugs. A marriage ends, not a friendship. My gait is ungainly as I walk away.

I count the wound a blessing.

Global Change

Cynicism and split perceptions close our minds and hearts to hope. Realism opens our minds and hearts to fresh possibilities. Therefore, a reasonable person may accept the following six statements as factual:

1. Global climate change (whatever the cause) increasingly destroys ecosystems, devastates economies, disrupts nations, prompts mass migrations, and threatens human survival.

2. The United States, Britain and European Union, justified or not, have foes around the world who will spit hate at "The West" and at "Capitalism" with their dying breaths.

3. Instead of achieving peace and justice, the "war on terrorism" (foreign and domestic) has yielded more deadly "terrorists," who are driven by revenge for real and perceived injuries.

4. In fighting state enemies, foreign and domestic, real or not, we're witnessing a global erosion and loss of civil liberties and human rights. Undemocratic fascist movements exist in most nations.

5. Autocratic governments outnumber democratic governments in the world. Most of the surviving republics are corrupt.

6. Mass protests against authoritarian governments are increasing worldwide. While risking arrest, or worse, protesters generally lack a unifying vision of what they want instead.

In trying times of tribulations, many expect a messianic savior king to redeem us at the end of the world. They see no point in trying to fix social problems. Why repair a home about to be demolished? Some would tear it all down. Nihilists revel in unruly anarchy.

Instead, I side with global seers like Gregg Braden, Deepak Chopra, Joe Dispensa, Wayne Dyer, Duane Elgin, Marilyn Ferguson, Matthew Fox, R. Buckminster Fuller, Paul Hawken, Ernest Holmes, Jean Houston, Barbara Marx Hubbard, David Korten, Francis Moore Lappé, Ervin

László, Bruce Lipton, Dan Millman, Arnold Mindell, James Redfield, Jeremy Rifkin, Armin Risi, John Robbins, Ocean Robbins, Miguel Ruiz, Eckhart Tolle, Neale Donald Walsch, Allan Watts, Stuart Wilde, Marianne Williamson, and all visionaries who foresee a great leap into our highest human potential. Beyond the varied jargons for a nonverbal sense of our global oneness, we share a vision of world enlightenment.

Thomas Paine wrote in *Common Sense:*

> The Sun never shined on a cause of greater worth. 'Tis not the affair of a City, a County, a Province, or a Kingdom; but of a Continent. 'Tis not the concern of a day, a year, or an age; [our] posterity are virtually involved in the contest, and will be more or less affected even to the end of time, by the proceedings now. Now is the seed-time of Continental union, faith and honour. The least fracture now will be like a name engraved with the point of a pin on the tender rind of a young oak; the wound would enlarge with the tree, and posterity read it in full grown characters.

Paine's vision of continental union in the 18th century can apply to planetary union in the 21st century. Now is the seed time of courage, faith and honor. We can manifest miracles in our lifetimes *if* we do our inner work and outer work, individually and cooperatively, to create fair, safe, free, creative, sustainable, and abundant societies on earth. We can do it if we choose. The choice is up to us.

Every government on earth rightfully belongs in the hands of free people in that land. *Consent of the governed* means we exert our right of consent over the laws governing us. Until we accept personal responsibility for responsive democracy, we stay in peril of being ruled by bullies. Until we govern our lives and societies with a global sensibility, we perpetuate overdependence on authority for our emotional and national security. Democracy is a personal growth process.

CHAPTER 4

A Global Sense Movement

2020: **DENVER** — *Like most people in the USA and globally this spring, I'm self-isolating at home to protect myself and others from the Covid-19 pandemic. Safely living alone could not come at a better time for me. I need space and time to rediscover myself.*

The coronavirus disease that surfaced in 2019, I gather, drowns people in a buildup of lung fluid. In "hot spot" cities, death tolls double in two days. Corpses go in refrigerator trucks. To deter contagion, cities and towns shut down all but the essential services, like food stores. (The toilet paper shortage strikes me as anal.) Streets are empty and eerily quiet, like a post-Apocalypse movie. Air quality improves visibly worldwide.

In the USA, Covid kills five times more of us per capita than the most-infected nations. I blame Trump's highly politicized response. He downplays the plague, I decide, because the public health shutdowns hurt the economy. He needs a robust economy to legitimately win reelection in 2020.

Trump deflects by decrying summer protests for racial equality. The demonstrations began last May in Minneapolis after yet another police killing of yet another unarmed Black man. Four officers forced handcuffed George Floyd, 46, face-down on the pavement beside a police car. An officer knelt on his neck for nine and a half minutes. Bystander video recorded him gasping, "I can't breathe!" before he lay motionless.

Peaceful protests spread from the Twin Cities to cities and towns across the nation and around the world. Tens of thousands march daily to demand an end to abuses of police power and the end of racist policies.

Mostly peaceful protests are spoiled by a few bent on violence. If rioters were paid is unproven. Police in body armor react with tear gas, flash-bang grenades, rubber bullets, batons, or worse. I see video of police using the same "excessive force" that provoked public protests in the first place.

On June 2, in a White House press event, Trump declares he's ordered 4,500 U.S. troops to Washington, DC. Unless the governors and mayors "dominate" the streets, he'll send "heavily armed" troops into America's cities. Minutes later, federal troops in camouflage gear without insignia forcibly clear peaceful protesters out of Lafayette Park across from the White House. Trump (amid security) then leads the press through the park to pose before a long-ago burned-out Episcopal church. Grim-faced and without a mask, he silently holds up a Bible as Pentagon brass stand by him.

For what it's worth, I catch the whiff of a white-rule police state. Dark thoughts of combat troops in our streets keep me awake that night. I picture Trump trumping up excuses to declare martial law to stay in power forever. If it seems he might lose the 2020 election, or if he does lose, will desperation drive him to foment violence, even stage a coup?

I awaken Wednesday morning knowing today I will join the ongoing protests in Denver. I realize the health risks of attending any large gathering, but I cannot stay safe at home and stay true to myself.

That afternoon, I park my used electric car at a street meter by the Denver Art Museum. I walk drop-foot through Civic Center Park to Colfax and cross Broadway to the Colorado statehouse.

I've been going to demonstrations at the west steps of the capitol since the Sixties. I'd always get close to hear the speakers. This time, I'm distancing at the outskirts. I wear a mask and gloves. Buzzy loudspeakers reach me with urgent messages of outrage and calls for change.

I participate in a "die in." We lay flat on our bellies and put our hands behind our backs as if handcuffed. We chant, "I can't breathe!" We lay prone for the minutes it took George Floyd to die. Feels like eternity.

We "take a knee," heads bowed, many with a fist upraised. A pro athlete was driven out of sports for taking a knee during the national anthem to protest police killings of unarmed Blacks. Trump conflated it into disrespect for our flag. Today I see the gesture restored to its rightful meaning.

The rally ends. The march begins. At 14th and Broadway, we cross into Civic Center Park, turn at the Greek Amphitheater, go down the esplanade to the fountains before swinging northwest into downtown.

Choosing not to push my limits for foot pain, I stop at the global man sculpture in the park. I watch the marchers go past. Takes about 20 minutes. All sorts people vote with their feet for equality and justice. We chant, "Black Lives Matter!" We chant, "This is what democracy looks like!"

I do not join in as people chant, "No Justice. No Peace!" It's backwards, says my head and heart. The catchy slogan implies violence, which bothers me, and it misses a practical reality. Only nonviolence deprives the president of any excuse to put down protests with troops. In my mind I chant instead, "No Peace. No Justice!" Protest injustice with inner peace to live justly in freedom. I'm still learning the lessons of Gandhi and Dr. King.

I do not regret quarantining for the next ten days after attending the protest. I took the health risk in the belief that together we really can change our world. I'm keeping the faith.

A Billion Global Thinkers

Awareness of our global oneness, growing over many generations, is shifting human cultures and societies worldwide.

Paul Hawken in *Blessed Unrest* says all the grassroots campaigns for environmental and social justice compose "the largest movement on earth." As a useful label, I dub it the *global sense movement.*

Sociologist Paul H. Ray and psychologist Sherry Ruth Anderson studied this movement in *The Cultural Creatives.* Their book reports on surveys finding that Cultural Creatives care deeply about ecology, saving the planet, world peace, and social justice. They care about their personal relationships, emotional authenticity, spirituality, self-actualization, and self-expression. They display the traits I call "global sense."

In updated surveys, Ray and Anderson report that about 35 percent of the people in developed nations are Cultural Creatives, but few identify themselves by this term. The percentage is much lower in developing and undeveloped lands, where survival is more tenuous.

The researchers lament Cultural Creatives too seldom realize they are creating an "Emerging Planetary Wisdom Culture." To speed the shift, they say, we need a "collective positive image of a future that works for all." I'm writing to help such a global vision emerge.

We need practical, hard-headed reality today. So, I'm going beyond maya fantasies of salvation from a Second Coming, Aquarian Age, Great Turning or cosmic Ascension. While I dearly love lofty utopian visions, and I concur with most of them, given urgent world conditions today, we need to mature beyond the comfort of idealism alone.

From lightworkers to poll workers, we need to exercise our natural global power as global citizens for tangibly improving our world. Raising our personal vibrational level is fully necessary, and it's not sufficient now. To survive, we need to turn ideals into practices for improving ourselves *and* improving life on earth for us all — while we can.

Globally mindful people already live and work at all levels of society, such a democratic teams in companies. We model the countless ways one can think globally and act locally. One need not be rich to go green, be the change, like voluntary simplicity. Evidence of global sense in action surrounds us, like a neighborhood cleanup. It's an increasingly influential cultural and societal force, growing with each world crisis.

For a fast glimpse, we are the people, if we can, who buy organic and natural foods. We purchase holistic health care products and services. We read product labels. We buy fair trade goods produced sustainably. We use compact fluorescent or LED lighting. We drive hybrid or electric cars, someday hydrogen, solar or fusion cars. We use public transit, ride a bicycle, walk or run, if able. Our habits reflects global thinking.

If affluent, we may do ecotourism or voluntourism. We may invest in socially responsible ventures with ethical and sustainable governance. We may construct "green buildings" with solar, wind or other renewable energy systems to power homes, business and communities.

Whatever our means, we donate what we can to good causes. We sign petitions. We volunteer. We vote. We read books about personal growth, spirituality, health, relationships, nature, ecology, conscious commerce, politics, world affairs, and related topics — or we write them.

Seeking tangible expressions of world enlightenment, I've identified more than a dozen *social trends* that reflect and foster global sense:

1. **Environmentalism**
2. **Green Lifestyles**
3. **Holistic Health**
4. **New Spirituality**
5. **Self-Improvement**
6. **Healthy Relationships**
7. **Education and Literacy**
8. **Global Internet Access**
9. **Conscious Consumers**
10. **Conscious Commerce**
11. **Social Entrepreneurs**
12. **Organizational Democracy**
13. **Gender and Racial Equality**
14. **Peaceful Mass Demonstrations**

These trends (and more) show that people with a global mindset are shifting their lives and our world. My pre-cancer research on these trends documented more than one billion global thinkers. After cancer, I tried updating that "body of proof" for this book. Such a research redo proved beyond me, so I'm leaving it for a follow-on book. Yet hard facts are vital, so what's useful for you in the pages here?

As evidence of the global sense movement, I've updated and briefly summarized below six of the world social trends.

Environmentalism — Earth Day, founded April 22, 1971, annually engages (pre/post Covid) one billion people in local to global events.

The 2015 People's Climate March, organized by 350.org, drew one billion people in 166 countries to events in cities like Berlin, Bogotá, Delhi, Denver, Istanbul, Johannesburg, Lagos, London, Los Angeles, Melbourne, New York, Paris, Rio de Janeiro, and Vienna.

A billion people voicing concern for global ecology is a fact, not hype. So, at least an eighth of all humanity is globally awake, which lately gets derided as "woke" — a putdown to avoid awakening.

Global internet — Global interactivity induces a global sensibility. Statista reports 5.3 billion internet users in early 2024. Sadly, open internet access is lost in state or corporate "walled gardens" yielding walled minds, not free thinking. Still, if just one-fifth of us online are thinking globally, if unwittingly, that's a billion people right there.

Literacy — The average world adult literacy rate was 87 percent in 2021, reports the World Bank. UNESCO predicts 90 percent by 2030. Given 5.2 billion adults, that's 4.6 billion of us able to read and write, able to vote smarter, if we *can* vote, *if* we can get factual information. Despite censorship, literacy rates give me hope. (Libraries are digitizing collections, fyi, yet the bulk of world knowledge resides on libraries. Visit one.)

Self-Improvement — The global personal development market grew during Covid to $44 billion in 2022, and will pass $67 billion by 2030, predicts Research and Markets, Dublin. About 35 percent of U.S. adults act to improve themselves, mostly women, Blacks and millennials. Extrapolated globally at about 20 percent, that's at least a billion people.

Conscious Commerce — To hint at the scale, the Global Sustainable Investment Alliance biennially reviews total investments in ethically and sustainably governed ventures, like social entrepreneurs and B-Corps. For 2023 tally is US$30.3 trillion invested in sustainable assets globally. Total global investments pass $1 quadrillion, yet $30 trillion *is* influential.

Conscious Consumers — The Natural Marketing Institute (NMI), surveying a million people in 30 countries since 1990, tracks the US $800 billion global market for green and healthy goods and services.

NMI studies people with "Lifestyles Of Health And Sustainability" (LOHAS). We're the spiritual and secular active stewards of the planet. We're the early adopters and heaviest purchasers of holistic and green products and services. Most of us are female. Most of us are young.

The percentage of LOHAS consumers varies in each nation, reports NMI. While TNS Sifo Orvesto found 30 percent LOHAS rates in Sweden, NMI itself found 22 percent in the USA, 18 percent in Brazil, 17 percent in the UK, 17 percent in South Africa, 16 percent in China, 16 percent in Germany, 14 percent in India, 13 percent in Russia, and 11 percent in Japan. These nine representative nations averaged 16 percent of the adults surveyed by NMI. With 5.2 billion adults on earth, 16 percent translates into a core of 830 million people with a global sense of life.

NMI found a secondary market segment they labeled "Naturalites." These consumers tend to think globally, but do not act locally as reliably. NMI found in the same nine nations that Naturalites averaged 24 percent. Given world population, that means 1.25 billion adults.

Adding primary and secondary groups of global thinkers, the sum passes *two billion.* So, when I say one billion people with global mindsets are creating a global sense movement, I'm being conservative.

Does data from these six trends (among more than a dozen) suffice to convince you the global sense movement is real and measurable?

The global enlightenment movement is now becoming conscious of itself as a movement. Common sense tells me our power as global citizens rests not in our numbers but in our unity. By acting alone and together, we actually can create a better future that works for us all.

At least one billion global thinkers are self-evident proof of the world enlightenment movement. We are a social and cultural force for human awakening. Autocracy advocates are well-organized and well-funded. We need to be better organized, better funded and more effective.

Our local community engagement is crucial. Be active on issues that stir your passion and conscience. Trust the process.

〜〜

2021: COLORADO MOUNTAINS— *At the autumnal equinox, grey skies carry smoke from the wildfires in Colorado and the West Coast. A drive-thru Covid test proves that my cough, runny nose and itchy eyes are not from the pandemic. It's global climate change.*

On Yom Kippur day, I drive up into the mountains to perform Tashlich. Traditionally, Jews symbolically cast away sins from the past year by casting bread or grain upon living water, such as a pond. Tashlich normally is done on Rosh Hashanah, the New Year on the old Jewish agrarian lunar calendar. Yom Kippur, the Day of Atonement (At One-ment). The second High Holy Day. Doing the rite today feels right to me this year.

Defining "sin" as dualism denying divinity, I'll use Tashlich to release beliefs and habits blocking me from feeling whole and free. Instead of grain (safe for fish and fowl), I'll instead use autumn leaves. I'm untraditional in observing traditions.

I drive west on I-70 and turn south on the paved road to Mount Evans (now Mount Blue Sky). At Echo Lake Lodge, I ask for directions and double back to a secluded picnic area by West Chicago Creek. I think it's upstream from the Jewish summer camp of my youth. Perfect spot.

Parking near the creek, I pick up fallen yellow aspen leaves. Ones that shimmer catch my eye. Sitting at a picnic table, I write on every leaf a word or phrase for the thought-forms to release, such as unworthiness, scarcity, illness, loneliness, fears about the future of myself, my nation and our world. Releasing energy creates a void to fill. On other leaves I write positive words, such as inner peace, love, health, abundance, community, faith, gratitude, patience, freedom, integrity, and "perseverance furthers."

Moving warily on my game foot, I climb out onto a wide flat rock that overhangs the rushing brook. Standing firm and centered, I invoke sacred space. I read aloud each leaf, ponder it a moment, drop it in the water, and watch the leaf float away. First, I release what I do not want in my life. Next, I release into the future what I do want. I'm shifting my cellular memory, my DNA. Two leaves slip from my hand and tumble unread into the water, darting away around the rocks and gone. I let go to grace.

Driving back to town, on impulse, I take a side road. Cresting a ridge, I see mountainsides ablaze in color. Evergreen forests surround aspen groves of red and orange and gold. I pull onto an overlook, park the car, get out, inhale pine air. I stand with sunshine on my shoulders. I am home.

Conscious Evolution

Responding to the urgent world situation, at least one billion of us on earth with global minds are exerting our leverage to tip world cultures. Will we act in time to avert the worst?

I believe success depends upon *if* we can let go of seeing ourselves as helpless victims needing kings, *if* we stop feeling alone and powerless, *if* we see our oneness and unite (*ad hoc*) as a global network.

As the global sense movement (whatever we call it) expands to reach cultural critical mass in the years and decades ahead, global sensibilities will penetrate societies worldwide. If we're consistent and conscientious, a gestalt of our globality or oneness will embed into our personal and collective unconscious (our *a priori* autopilot). By daily being mindful of our equality in oneness, we may enjoy liberty in peace.

In promoting global sensibilities in the world, be alert to the danger of authority addiction. When I joined to a cult in youth, I learned to say the magic words for acceptance. I eagerly worked at imposing my beliefs on others. I berated myself for failing as a sycophant. Codependent relationships fostered by organized religions, I learned, instill devotion to holy doctrines instead of encouraging direct connection with the divine. How can the global sense movement avoid this mindtrap?

All cultural influence efforts employ rhetoric and propaganda tools. So, let's be ethical in helping humanity to evolve global awareness. Let's do it without forcing anyone to think like we do. Dissent is a natural right. No bullying. Let others disagree. Obnoxious behavior by those pushing "woke" equity and ecology policies, for instance, provide a handy excuse to avoid awakening. Instead, grow within to grow the movement.

As for myself, I'm learning how to govern my free will by sensing my unity with life. I am responsible for how my words, deeds, emotions, thoughts, fantasies, and energy fields affect my life, all those nearby, all of humanity, all life on earth. Everything I imagine, think, feel, say, and do influences all realities. Given our interactivity, I wish to live mindfully. Like Henry David Thoreau, I wish to "live deliberately."

If the universe is really strings of vibrant light refracting into a broad spectrum, if each of our lives are intertwined like Indra's net of jewels, so every jewel reflects every other jewel, why deny our brilliant oneness? Alone and in community, we can let our spirits shine.

Barbara Marx Hubbard was a champion of *conscious evolution*. A scion of the Marx toy fortune (no relation to Karl or Groucho), she told her early life story in *The Hunger of Eve*. The memoir recalls her youthful existentialist view of the universe as indifferent or hostile. Hungering to understand life, she became a spiritual seeker.

While out walking in 1966, she experienced an epiphany. "A flash of extraordinary insight, more radiant than the sun" sparked a vision of the *Evolutionary Spiral*. She visualized and felt in her woman's body the birth of humanity into higher consciousness.

The clear vision of "a universe full of life and light," she writes, "was imprinted forever upon my very cells." That rare visionary moment would inspire and guide the rest of her joyful journey on earth.

Decades later, encouraged by visionaries like R. Buckminster Fuller, Barbara Marx Hubbard in 1984 campaigned to be nominated as U.S. Vice President, pledging to establish a "Peace Room" in the White House.

Your evolution into global consciousness may not be as dramatic as hers. Mine has been gradual, in spurts, emerging over a lifetime, ongoing. Living with a global sensibility is hard yet getting easier.

I imagine global common sense going global. For peace on earth, seek peace in our loving souls and free minds. Why refuse to give peace a chance when peace is the only chance we've got?

〰

The faster we evolve a global consciousness, the sooner we'll use democracy to solve world crises. Why don't we? What drives us to keep giving power to leaders and kings? What blocks us from making global sense of life and living free responsibly? What's in our way?

What, indeed? What stops us, stops me, from living whole and free? For useful answers, I propose we try some excellent time travel.

CHAPTER 5

Sense and Insanity

*1920: **CHICAGO** — My father is born the son of a short Jewish barber in Lincoln Park. Among the barber's regular customers is a gangster. Every day, the barber holds a sharp straight razor at the bare throat of Al Capone. The little barber has stones.*

As near as I can tell from sparse paternal records, my grandfather, Flischel "Tarnoplitsky," was born 1888 in Bialystok, Belarus. He lived in the Russo-Poland town of Tarnow, thus the namesake. Fleeing pogroms, he and kin emigrate around 1900, landing in Philadelphia harbor.

Flischel enters America as "Philip Freed."

Stories vary on the "Freed" surname. First version: He knows enough English to choose the name for its meaning. Second version: Facing an immigration clerk, he says in poor English, "I freed!" The clerk writes the word. Third version: He claims he's related to a Jewish Philadelphian named Freed, and he enters under that name. Which is true?

I Like the first story, but the third is likely When Philip joins the army to earn citizenship, said my dad, a clerk misspells the name as "Fried." He accepts it. Why not fix it there? Does he fear inquiries and deportation?

Philip Fried moves to Chicago. There he weds Fannie Grassanda from Sokola in Russian Poland. Her father, Isaiah, claims descent from Sephardic aristocracy. Fannie kvetches about "marrying down."

In the 1920s, Philip opens his own barbershop at the corner of Halsted and Webster. He buys a family house two blocks east on Webster, near where today stands bronze Dorothy in Wizard of Oz Park.

My father at birth is named Norman Zander Fried (Nacham Zalman in Yiddish). He's the third and last child. His mother is a peevish complainer, I gather, and his father insists on being obeyed.

My dad later spoke about his Chicago boyhood during Prohibition. When school is out in summer, he sweeps hair clippings in the barbershop, earning a quarter a day plus tips, a tidy fortune. One summer, Al Capone claims the barbershop's back room as his office. The barber tells his wife and children to stay away from the shop. Decades later, my dad confides to me that he still resents the mobster for stealing his summer job.

Norman does well in school, I surmise, and he enjoys sports. His true love is art. For most of the 1930s, he pursues his passion at Jane Addams' Hull House on the Near West Side, an Italian and Greek neighborhood that's now safer for Jews, thanks to Hull House.

Jane Addams opened the Hull mansion as a settlement house in 1889, three years after Haymarket. By 1931, when she wins the Nobel Peace Prize, Hull House is a 13-building campus and citywide network for welfare relief, health care and legal aid, all given freely to immigrants and refugees.

A leader in the progressive "culture and personality" movement, Hull House offers classes in citizenship, literacy, writing, music, and art. The art school and gallery draws my dad into this humanist community. He absorbs disdain for hero aviator Charles Lindbergh, an isolationist "America First" Nazi sympathizer. The enlightened Hull House culture in the Thirties will inspire my father for life just like the enlightened Sixties counterculture will inspire me for life. I inherit his social values.

Young Norman dreams of supporting himself as an art teacher while becoming a fine painter. After high school, he attends Northern Illinois State Normal School for teachers, majoring in art education. In a period photo, he's smoking a Billiard pipe, an intellectual. A snapshot of him in swim trunks displays a hard-bodied, barrel-chested, cleft-chinned hunk.

Graduating with a BA in 1942, he joins the U.S. Army. He's posted as a photography instructor at Lowry Army Air Field in Denver. His secret job is making training films for the Norden bombsight, so bombardiers can rain fiery death on cities like Dresden and Hiroshima. So it goes.

Making Sense of Reality

The way we make sense of life shapes the way we act in life, what we do and how we do it. Generally, if our lives make sense to us, we feel safe. When times are hard or we face a crisis, life may not make sense to us. We do what we can to survive and still be true to ourselves. We do what we think we "must" do. If we later regret our choices, we can find peace in knowing we did what made sense to us at the time.

As a child and youth beaten by bullies, I silently chose to make sense of myself as a victim. A "victim" sees life very differently than a "bully." That difference drives threats to human survival and democracy in our world today, even in my own nation.

To help explain how and why our worldview matters, I next explore the methods we use to make sense of the world and our lives within the world. Understanding the sense-making process improves our decision-making, problem-solving and conflict resolution habits (how we live).

Communication Creates Reality

Changing what makes sense to us changes our lives. Sense-making systems or mindmaps filter our perceptions and inform our expectations. Sense-making skills give us power to rule our minds, so we can think for ourselves, not let others think for us. Sense-making, for me, begins with understanding a model of the communication process.

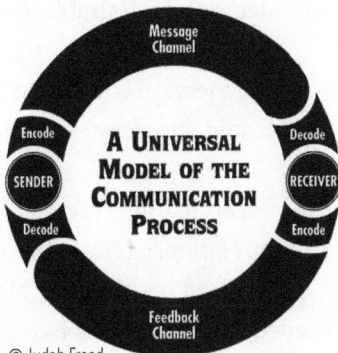

A UNIVERSAL MODEL OF THE COMMUNICATION PROCESS

Message Channel
Encode
SENDER
Decode
Decode
RECEIVER
Encode
Feedback Channel

© Judah Freed

A sender encodes a verbal or nonverbal message, sends it through a message channel to a receiver, who decodes the message and then encodes a response, returning it through a feedback channel to the initial sender, who decodes it, perhaps sends a new message. Without completing the loop or closing the circuit, communication is incomplete. *Yin* and *yang*.

Hampered by noise, communication encoding and decoding are the weakest links. Miscommunication happens when we're mistaken about the meaning of messages, or we misconstrue meanings. It's complicated by limits and failures in our message channels, like a short circuit.

At root, we assign *meaning* to words, sounds, gestures, facial expressions, and all other input through our physical, mental, emotional, and intuitive senses. To communicate with another, we trust the other person assigns similar meanings to the words, gestures, facial expressions and everything else. We assume they define reality like we do. Given the odds against us assigning the same exact meanings to anything, it's amazing we humans can communicate at all, actually.

All of our words are refined grunts to which we assign meaning by mutual consent. A writing implement is a *pen* in English or 筆 in Chinese. If you and I do not speak or write the same language, lacking telepathy, you cannot decode the message I encode. I cannot decode the feedback you encode. If either of us misinterprets or distorts a message, the other may take offense. "We should have a great fewer disputes in the world," said John Locke, "if words were taken for what they are, the signs of our ideas only, and not for the things themselves."

Defining nonverbal reality with words limits our minds. Our words describing the world reflect how we encode and decode our experiences. Words are powerful. Differing interpretations of a word can set the course of societies. If we define "democracy" as corruption, negative denotations and connotations make democracy despicable. If we define "democracy" as ethical self rule, positive associations make democracy desirable. One may chant "freedom" but intend tyranny.

Beware of *bias*. Each incoming and outgoing message is coded to fit inherited and cultural prejudices. Bias gets implanted into our neural nets for pattern recognition in sense-making.

Unconscious and implicit biases form perceptual filters, creating barriers to internal and external communication. (*Intrapersonal* is within the self. *Interpersonal* is with another.) We deny bias at our cost. My bias filter said that I was so healthy that I only needed medical check-ups once a year. I never saw the cancer coming.

Our sense-making processes, our communication habits, form our relationships with all others and our own selves — mentally, emotionally, physically, and spiritually. We create our lives and our world through all the ways we communicate. Clifford Geertz said communication spins the web of culture, the web of life. Biology is communication in action.

See the whole. The ways we interact within ourselves and in families construct the institutions comprising the communities composing the cultures and societies constituting our nations and our world — a daisy chain of causes and effects. Unified string theory.

As earth's overpopulating predominant species, our communication habits imprint on every planetary ecosystem. Witness the impact on the climate and ourselves from how we discuss a dependence on fossils from extinct lifeforms. Witness global warming amid global whining.

Sense-Making

Physiologically, sense-making occurs in the synapses of the brain and neural network. Amid 170 billion brain cells are 100 billion neurons making a quadrillion synaptic connections every second. We electro-chemically encode sensations, emotions, thoughts, and imaginings into the integral neural network of our brain, nervous system, muscles, organs, skeletons, skin, and hair. We each are an "intranet."

Inside the brain itself, simplifying enormously, a stimulus signal first enters the *medulla oblongata*, the oldest instinctive part of the brain stem, the hindbrain, which decides our flight-or-fight-or-freeze reactions. The signal then enters the *cerebral cortex*, the outer skin of the *cerebrum*, that convoluted "grey matter" directly under the skull, the reputed seat of the conscious mind. First I yank my hand away from a hot pot handle, and then I think, "Ow! That pot is hot!"

Our brain's memory-index *hippocampus* and the clearing house *thalamus* connect to the inner-brain *hypothalamus*, a generator of neural peptides that prompt behavior. The midbrain *amygdala* excretions trigger emotional responses. We store our emotions, sensations, memories, and motives in the limbic system, mirror neurons and cellular memories of the brain, muscles, bone marrow, intestines, all the rest of us.

To make sense of burning my hand, a traumatic event, I may encode an aversion to all pot handles. That coding may disperse after a few days, or it may dictate my behavior for years.

My dad told me how his mother would let ripe fruit spoil in the ice box. The rotting smell sickened him, so he refused to eat fruit the rest of his life (watermelon aside), and that made sense to him.

The human body is a scalable, searchable data-processing network for accessing all the information we've stored about "reality." Our sense-making system integrates all of our sensory inputs, genetic traits, lineal memories, past and present life experiences, and working knowledge gained from any "learning mode" we've ever used in life.

We decode and store cultural and social messages from our family, teachers, clergy, friends, coworkers, the media, community culture, and environments. It all shapes how we make sense of our lives and the world. Ideally, it forms a coherent mental model of reality, a functional mindmap and compass we can use to navigate our lives reliably.

Reality Bites

Understanding the sense-making process is necessary yet insufficient. Vital for making sense of reality accurately is accepting we can never be sure what's "real." Philosophers identify three main types of reality.

Objective reality is whatever we can prove exists by observation and testing. Objective reality withstands rigorous inquiry, critical reasoning. Thomas Paine studied nature to make sense of natural law. "Man [*sic*] cannot make principles," Paine said; "he can only discover them."

"The most formidable weapon against errors of every kind is reason," wrote Paine. He knew the *logical syllogism*. If A=B, and if B=C, then A=C. If any premise (A or B) is false, the conclusion (C) is false. Bossy is a cow (first premise). Cows are blue (second premise), Bossy is blue (conclusion). However, cows are not blue, and Bossy is a bull. Assumptions are perilous. Cloudy thinking opens windows for mind thieves to sneak in.

The Scientific Method is a useful tool for discovering objective reality. A process of empirical reasoning, often attributed to ancient Greeks, the Scientific Method has six steps. (1) Develop a question based on careful observation. (2) Collect data from impartial research to form a hypothesis or theory. (3) Test the theory with fair experimentation. (4) Analyze the results and draw conclusions. (5) Share findings, so others can repeat the test and verify. (6) Return to Step 1. Any theory can be disproven.

Subjective reality is whatever we believe is real. The brain's pattern recognition or sense-making system presets what we subjectively perceive is real. A child's subjective reality is not a parent's reality. Subjectivity without objectivity, without verification, leads to absurdity.

Intersubjective (shared) reality is whatever we agree with others is real, like a social contract. Those in love live in their own intersubjective reality. Shared cultural or social beliefs, backed by objective facts or not, are accepted norms, *social truths.* If reality bites and faith is shown invalid, groupthink reactions can become irrational and destructive.

Mediated reality is whatever any external source tells us is real. The message comes through some communication medium or channel. Any perception of reality from secondary sources is not direct evidence from first-hand experience. Second-hand realities, like newscasts, are unreliable until verified by objective facts. Distrust mediated realities.

From my trade press reporting on television and the internet, I know media content is produced and engineered to hook our attention, trigger emotions, fuel addictions. Media manipulate us below our perceptions. Social media is the drug of the masses; AI boosts its potency to implant prejudices. Bias is obdurate. Alertness to bias helps us detect propaganda and make sense of reality more accurately, so we think freely.

If we immerse in media content sharing one worldview, we reinforce our bias, like with conspiracy theories. Instead, *deep media literacy* helps us avoid bias and cynicism. "Suspicion is the companion of mean souls," Paine observed, "and the bane of all good society."

We each have a natural right to define reality for ourselves. So long as we respect others' right to do the same, varied worldviews are delightful and fruitful. If we impose our definition of reality on others, we violate their rights. Clashing realities can end relationships or incite wars. This is why understanding communication is central in global thinking.

Mindmap Illusions

Our mindmap, worldview, *zeitgeist, weltanschauung,* or paradigm organizes life for us, so new data fits into a pattern. Without a Big Picture of how life works, our lives do not make sense to us. We cherish whatever beliefs about life make the most sense to us, so we feel safe. When life stops making sense, we feel unsafe. If we make sense of life as dangerous, we may wish to be saved by a higher power or authority.

Without a working mindmap of reality, we can get lost. We can get frightened and confused. If our subjective mindmap is objectively in error, if we cling to a false mindmap, in extreme cases, madness ensues.

"Insanity" lately is mistakenly defined as "doing the same thing over and over and expecting different results." Misattributed to Einstein, this Rita Mae Brown quote is an *example* of insanity, not a definition. Insanity is far more disturbed and disturbing. Fruitless repetitious behavior may be social or cultural conditioning, after all, not psychosis.

One clinical example of insanity is Narcissistic Personality Disorder, described by the American Psychiatric Association in *The Diagnostic and Statistical Manual of Mental Disorders.* The diagnosis is earned when a person presents at least five of these summarized symptoms:

- Self-perceptions of being unique, superior and high-status.
- Fantasies of power, success, intelligence, and attractiveness.
- Grandiosity with expectations of superior treatment by others.
- A sense of entitlement to special privileges and to being obeyed.
- A pompous and arrogant demeanor.
- Needing constant admiration from others.
- Intense jealousy of others with a belief others are jealous of them.
- Unwillingness to empathize in pursuit of one's own self-interest.
- Exploiting others without conscience to obtain personal gain.

We each may exhibit a few of these behaviors, as I did while a minor local celebrity in youth. But when elected officials present *all* these traits, are they crazy? The legal definition of insanity is a mental illness so severe a person cannot tell fantasy from reality, or right from wrong.

I diagnose our modern view of life as insane. We believe we can spoil the earth without cost. Thinking deeds lack consequences is lunacy. Only an insane person leaps from an airplane without a parachute and gladly sings aloud while plummeting to earth, "So far so good!"

A pebble plopped into a pond radiates ripples lapping every shore. Every thought, feeling, word, and deed reverberates outward. My anger at a store clerk infects the next customers with my grumpy mood. Actions radiate inward, too. My wrath lingers in me, affecting how I feel about myself, which affects how I relate to others and to life, which affects how I relate to the world and how the world responds to me.

We make sense of life through all the ways we communicate. Each communication loop links to all the loops in our families, jobs and social networks, linking our communities, our nations, our planet, and beyond. Understanding *interactivity* helps us see our power. Knowing what we do to others we do to ourselves, we tend to cooperate. We improve the way we interact. We create or co-create together a better world to share.

Our mental model of life sets or presets how we communicate. Communication weaves the warp and weft of our lives. The way we make sense of reality filters our perceptions and choices. False beliefs distort our objective, subjective and shared realities. Mary Wollstonecraft asked, "Who but a fool would part with a reality for a fleeting shadow?"

We get into trouble if we filter out awareness that our oneness makes us objectively powerful. A false belief we're isolated and powerless is the delusion despots depend upon to repress our liberty.

We get into trouble if we insist any belief is the only absolute truth. We may defend that truth, not from reasoned certainty, but from shadow insecurity, so we feel righteously safe in our beloved community.

We get into trouble when our faith ignores objective facts to hide in the shelter of a glorious true leader doing our thinking for us.

We get into trouble when any group sees life in a way that conflicts with other groups seeing life differently (intersubjectively). They may see your property or life as theirs to take. You see them as thieves and killers. How can we enjoy peace if we make sense of life in opposing ways?

The Still, Small Voice

The conflicting worldviews of autocracy or democracy wage a battle to rule our minds and the future we creates on earth. Blind obedience to *any* external authority (person, party, theology, or ideology) evades our responsibility for heeding the "still, small voice" of conscience.

The crux is whether we believe in the natural goodness of humanity. "Human nature of itself is not vicious," said Paine. If we all are born good, then we naturally can govern ourselves from the goodness within. But if we all are born bad, we will always do bad things, so we need a divine hero to save us from our evil ways.

Why consent to mindtraps that let tyrants rule us with fear and lies? More of us than ever now trust our conscience. We speak truth to power, if at our peril. Gandhi proved that nonviolent acts of conscience, passive resistance, civil disobedience, resilient persistence, can unseat any regime. His work persuades me an enlightened free society is possible.

Paine grew up in Quaker meetings where friends sit quietly until conscience speaks. He wrote, "'Tis the business of little minds to shrink; but he [*sic*] whose heart is firm, and whose conscience approves his conduct, will pursue his principles unto death."

Activists jailed or killed for conscience include Cesar Chavez, Mazen Darwish, Chen Guangcheng, Toyohiko Kagawa, Nathan Law, Wangari Maathai, Nelson Mandela, Chico Mendes, Harvey Milk, Narges Mohammadi, Fadhila Mubarak, Alexei Navalny, Leonard Peltier, Liu Ping, Anna Politkovskaya, Nguyen Dan Que, Binayak Sen, too many others.

I do *not* propose we become prisoners of conscience or martyrs. We need living and free peaceful citizen activists to model global thinking locally. For civil society, I invite what James Redfield describes as "a leap into full spiritual consciousness."

Conscience joins objective and subjective realities, like voting my conscience in a close election that tips the balance of power. If I don't vote, as Voltaire said, I am guilty of all the good I did not do.

Every time we act from conscience and reason, we raise the mass consciousness of humanity. This notion is not new.

"Conscience is the voice of the soul," wrote Rousseau. "Conscience never deceives us; it is the true guide of man [*sic*]."

Therefore, George Washington advised, "Labor to keep alive in your breast that little spark of celestial fire called conscience."

"For were the impulses of conscience clear, uniform, and irresistibly obeyed," Paine said, "man [*sic*] would need no other lawgiver." He added, "Don't grant liberty of conscience as a favor, but confirm it as a right."

By acting on conscience and reason, we have an advantage over all the masters of society. For evidence, I offer *Why Civil Resistance Works* by Erica Chenoweth and Maria Stephan. They document numerous cases that cumulatively show Gandhi and King were right about the practical effectiveness of nonviolence in the real world.

Peaceful mass demonstrations are a visible trend in the global sense movement. As proof, see the growing list of 21st century protests in the Appendices. On this page, consider the second half of the 20th century:

- The U.S. civil rights movement in the 1950s and 1960s ended legal segregation and won voting rights for Blacks and minorities.

- The 1968 Prague Spring relit the flame of freedom behind the Iron Curtain. Warsaw Pact troops could not quench the fire.

- Generally peaceful American and global protests in the 1960s, 1970s and 1980s helped end U.S. wars in Asia and Latin America.

- The peaceful Nuclear Freeze campaign in the 1980s leveraged U.S. and Soviet leaders into signing arms limitation deals.

- During China's peaceful 1989 Tiananmen Square pro-democracy protests, one iconic man halted a People's Army tank in its tracks.

- Mass protests in Eastern Europe led to the fall of the Berlin Wall in 1989, which fed into the fall of the Soviet empire in 1991.

- A global boycott of South Africa ended apartheid there in 1994.

Nonviolent demonstrations of conscience, even if silenced violently, give me hope. We participate with faith our united actions do change the world. Every peaceful protest, by its nature, voices a global sense of life.

By engaging, we treat oneness as a fact, for who acts without hope of an effect? Nonviolent mass demonstrations encourage world enlightenment — global thinking in action. (Fun and humor ease the way.)

People who trust reason and the voice of conscience make sense of their lives and the world in ways that expand the global sense movement (going by many names). When a global sensibility informs our conduct, positive results reinforce the hope we can change our world for the better. Hope gives us the will to act. We need more hope now.

∿

1943: DENVER — *My father meets my mother at a chaperoned "mixer" for Jewish singles held at the Lowry base chapel. The community holds such events for brave soldiers going to war. I imagine them dancing to the records of swing jazz bandleader Glenn Miller from Boulder*

Zelda, with her father's permission, as a mitzvah, invites the soldier for Passover seder. The slim young man sits down at my grandmother's dining room table, goes a family fable, and he never leaves. That's a tribute to her cooking, how she serves love with every meal.

Norman and Zelda start "going steady" and soon discuss marriage. My grandfather takes a dim view of such a union. He looks upon marriage in patriarchal terms. His view is from his father, Juda Lasky (my namesake) and from his forefathers (records lost in the Holocaust).

Juda Eisen Laskowitz was born 1867 in Tarnow, Poland, then part of Austria-Hungary. At age 16, he emigrates to America and finally settles in Colorado. In 1897, Juda marries Ida Grossman, the Denver-born daughter of Israel and Rachel Grossman from Ostrow, Poland, in the Russian empire. Juda and Ida live in the mining town of Kremmling, where Juda establishes the Kremmling Mercantile (still in business, new owners). The family later moves to Denver, where Juda opens a store on Larimer Street.

Juda's first son, my grandfather, Abraham William Lasky, born 1898, has five brothers and a sister. As a young man, "William A. Lasky" lands a job in route sales for the new U.S. Tobacco Company. In 1922, he marries Denver-born Goldie Strasberg, a year younger. Her immigrant father, Harris Strasberg, is an scholar and watchmaker with a shop off 16th Street.

Denver in the 1920s is a fearsome place for Jews. The populist Ku Klux Klan controls middle America from Indiana through the Rockies. Colorado Klan members gather atop Table Mountain for giant cross burnings, seen across the city. White-robed marchers fill West Colfax. Their 1925 summer picnic attracts 100,000 people. Denver Jews live in terror.

William and Goldie have two children, my mother and her younger brother. During the Depression, salesman "Willie" Lasky enters management. In 1935, he buys a new three-bedroom Tudor home on Hilltop.

After Pearl Harbor in 1941, my grandfather fears for his only son, who joins the U.S. Navy as a submarine signalman in the Pacific. (He sees action but never speaks of it.) A father hopes his son returns from war.

He also fears for his only daughter, who wants to marry a soldier from Chicago. He doubts this idealistic young man with bohemian ideas can properly support his precious little girl. He puts his foot down. He declares, "No underpaid schoolteacher will ever marry my daughter!"

The war drags on. Norman and Zelda are in love and want a family. He decides marrying her is worth the terms set by her father. He gives up his plan for an art career. He changes what makes sense to him.

My father lines up a graphics job at a big Denver printer, commencing once he's discharged from active duty. For extra pay, he agrees to remain in the Air Force Reserves. My grandfather relents.

In 1944, Norman and Zelda marry at the Lasky family home.

Changing What Makes Sense

Changing our worldview, changing how we make sense of life, changes our lives and our world.

We each have a natural right to define reality for ourselves. We have a duty to let others do the same. When we try to impose our definition of reality on others, we violate their rights. "He [*sic*] who denies to another this right," Paine said, "makes a slave of himself to his present opinion, because he precludes himself the right of changing it."

"There are times," wrote Denis Diderot, "when the greatest change needed is a change of my viewpoint."

What if we choose to adopt an awareness of our universal oneness? Conscious reasoning then starts from the premise that everything is part of everything else. Each is unique while one with all, visible and invisible, known and unknown. We can adopt global thinking as a routine mindset in our cultures. As global sensibilities become commonly agreed shared realities, living free more mindfully becomes second nature.

We can reset the presets in our minds. We can retrain ourselves to think of our unity before we react or respond. For example, I may think of a sarcastic or cutting comment, as I heard at home in youth, but I catch myself before sharp words leave my tongue. Sense-making moments are pivots for leveraging love and higher consciousness.

A sustained or frequent sense of our innate global unity, over time, recodes our neural networks, enters our memes and genes, alters DNA. Just as divisive dualism has passed from generation to generation, so can a unifying sense of oneness. We see our unity beyond duality.

Generating a local to global shift in cultural consciousness across society is the work of the global sense movement. I imagine a freethinking global sense of our connectivity, someday, becoming so engrained in humanity that it's subconscious, as normal as breathing.

Paine proved that such a shift in mindset is possible. *Common Sense* transformed how American colonists made sense of the world. He shifted the prevailing mental model of how to govern ourselves in a society. He persuaded readers that sacrificing natural rights and liberties in trade for feelings of security or kingly glory is an absurd folly. The balance of power tipped from aristocracy to democracy. We can do it again.

ᗏ

To help us move ideals into reality, in the next chapters I look at how so many of us make sense of giving away our power to despots and other bullies. If we grasp how tyranny can make sense to good people, we may better see how democracy makes global sense.

If we use our free will well, our topsy-turvy world can right itself.

CHAPTER 6

Split Perceptions

1950: DENVER — *My birth certificate shows "Kenneth Jay Fried," spelled like my paternal grandfather's changed surname. I'm the third and last child, the only boy. At birth, I do not know my father gave up his dream of being an artist and teacher to be a husband and father. He makes a sacrifice that all men of his day are expected to make. A "real man" must marry and sire sons to carry on his family name and bloodline.*

My father at age 30 is an American post-war Baby Boom family man with a job, a mortgage, a car payment, and a belly. He's still doing graphics for the same printer as when he married. His art is now a hobby.

Does he regret giving up on his dream to beget a boy? He loves his two daughters, yet I am his only boy. How could he not project his fantasies onto me? At birth I do not know my father needs me to be the man he imagined being before becoming a husband and father. I do not know then my father needs me to be the hero he is not any more in his own eyes.

I now believe my father unconsciously feels disappointment in looking on me in a crib, seeing a frail and sickly infant struggling to breathe. Before I can speak, I sense I am not good enough to meet my father's expectations, not good enough for him to love. I am unaware then that I can never give to the man what he does not give to himself.

At the same time as I'm wordlessly (if mistakenly) making sense of what I feel from my father, I am wordlessly (if mistakenly) making sense of what I feel from my mother. From what she says to me, and what I piece together, my mother both loves and resents me before I am born.

My mother is studying biochemistry at the University of Colorado in Boulder when she meets my father. She realizes young women go to college for an Mrs. degree, like her Jewish sorority sisters. But most young men have gone to war. Young women are imagining careers. Given a talent for science and math, youthful Zelda dreams of an exciting life in laboratory research, discovering the cure for cancer. Her ambitions are lofty.

She graduates, but gives up her dream for marriage and motherhood, as expected of all women in her day. By the time I am conceived six years into the marriage (on purpose to get a boy), she has birthed and nurtured two sisters before me, each two years apart. She's tired. But she's a good wife willing to try again to give her husband his son. As does any good mother, she loves the life growing within her.

Six decades later, when I'm doing my inner healings to survive cancer, a clairvoyant says she sees my mother disconnecting emotionally from me as a fetus in her womb. She feels no ill will toward me, the intuitive says, but she's exhausted by motherhood. She reluctantly agreed to try once more for a boy. But what if it's another girl? Could she suffer it all a fourth time? No. Too much! Not again. She disconnects.

Could this be true? I may never know this side of the veil. My intuition and logic says this may be close. An unconscious emotional withdrawal by my mother may explain why, in early childhood, I make sense of myself as unwanted, unloved, unlovable, easily abandoned as worthless.

If infant me makes sense of life as unsafe, this explain why my earliest hold on life is tenuous, why I am born asthmatic. Somehow, I find the will to survive, as I still do. Reckon I'm a stubborn old soul.

The Divided Self

In the early 21st century, at least one billion people around the planet accept our global connectivity as a self-evident truth, an *a priori* premise for reasoning and acting. We see ourselves as individually unique while naturally equal with anyone.

If you see yourself within the global sense movement (any label), we are in the minority. The majority of us on the planet, six to seven billion, do not make sense of life on earth as one whole system.

How do we avoid seeing our oneness? What are the ways and means we use to avoid seeing our connectivity with all life? We've blocked out objective and subjective perceptions of our universal oneness or wholeness. Splitting our minds, we've embraced dualism as our reality.

In most lands, humanity has co-created economic and social systems where wealth and power seem so far removed from most of us that too few of us ever bother to vote. We have co-created cultural belief systems where "God" feels so far removed from most of us that too few of us ever bother to meditate or pray, or simply slow down and be still.

A mental divide may occur when our lives conflict with conscience. Takeo Doi in *The Anatomy of Self* observes that Japanese culture marks differences between inner truth (*ura*), outer face (*omote*) and the need for acceptance (*amae*). Social standards and cultural mores (*tatemae*) might disagree with our inner sense of what is natural and right (*honne*). Conflict between inner and outer can twist us into knots.

Distortions from splitting the self can sicken any life or any culture. Rifts in our minds can rend asunder societies and civilizations.

Perceptual Filters

I want to unpack the process of splitting apart our perceptions. How do we avoid seeing our unity, see only duality. How do we evade living free in a democracy in favor of serving despots in an autocracy? For clarity, I return to the "sense-making process" in communication.

To begin, humans naturally install perceptual filters to avoid sensory overload. This is healthy. Imagine hearing every sound around you all the time, and at full volume. The cacophony would be overwhelming and disabling. The chaos may drive us mad.

Perceptual splitting is inherent and normal in humanity, yet we may misuse it to install mental filters. We may block what we do not want to admit, what does not fit our worldview. This is unhealthy.

In the communication cycle (that circular model in the last chapter), perceptions can split most easily whenever we're encoding and decoding. Messages can be mistaken or misconstrued. We see what we want to see and hear what we want to hear. Nothing else is real to us.

When subjective bias blocks or filters perceptions of objective reality, for accuracy I label this mental schism as *split perceptions*.

I cite the old trope of an alcoholic staggering out of a bar who denies a drinking problem. When we are "in denial," we shackle our minds with chains of thought and deny our imprisonment. We tell ourselves that what we do not know will not hurt us. We pretend that what we do not see does not exist. We act like children who believe they become invisible by putting their hands over their eyes.

We deny addiction to external authority by splitting our perceptions. By denying our liability for the consequences of our choices, we can do horrible things. We can lie, cheat, steal, hate, kill, or die. We can repress others to feel superior. In shame, we may hide our true selves behind ego masks. We may believe the mask is real. When confronted by the harms of self-deception, our minds may divide further.

History tells the results of splitting perceptions to deny our authority addiction. Notice cult mass suicides like Heaven's Gate, Branch Davidians and People's Temple. Mark the "final solution" in Nazi Europe and "ethnic cleansing" in Bosnia, Rwanda, Xinjiang, elsewhere.

M. Scott Peck in *People of the Lie* defines "evil" as the result of refusing to admit any imperfection or vulnerability. He tells about parents gifting their lone surviving child the same gun a sibling used to commit suicide. The more we deny responsibility for the effect of our choices, he said, the more we detach from grace, so the more evil or harm we do in the world. Denying our evil, Peck warned, can lead to "militant ignorance."

From personal experience in a cult, I know how people cling to faith in a religion or ideology or leader despite all scientifically proven "facts" and reason. We tune out shouting in our faces and whispers in our minds. We know our foes are deluded or insane, part of the conspiracy. We shun being disloyal, never asking if our faith is mistaken.

Why parrot any leader's lies while knowing the truth? Paine wrote, "It is necessary to the happiness of man [*sic*] that he be mentally faithful to himself. Infidelity does not consist in believing, or in disbelieving, it consists in professing to believe what he does not believe."

We hide our inner lies with split perceptions.

〰

I grow up hearing a story of my Bris, the ritual male circumcision at eight days old. In the ceremony, Jews give infants Hebrew names, often the names of recently deceased relatives. I'm named "Israel Judah" (ישראל יהודה) after maternal great-grandfathers Israel Grossman and Juda Lasky.

The mohel challenged my parents' naming choice. He reminded them that the ancient nations of Israel and Judah went to war with one another. Giving both names could condemn their son to constant war with himself. Considering my life story, maybe the rebbe was a prophet, nu?

I retain a memory in the crib at night, grasping the bars to pull up while crying for mommy. She does not come. I cry more loudly. She does not come. I wheeze and cry louder. She never comes. Daddy never comes. My sisters never come. Night after night, nobody comes. Nobody cares.

Relentless in fruitless crying, I get fascinated by the sounds of the wails echoing in my head and in the room. I vary the pitch and tone and rhythm. I get lost in musical variations. At last, too tired to toot, I lay down to sleep. I nightly entrain a shadow identity of being neglected, unwanted, unlovable. All this occurs in me before I have any words for the feelings.

What I do not know then is that my mother is trusting in the popular baby and child care book by Dr. Benjamin Spock. Mommy reads that when an infant boy keeps crying in the crib at night, if he's fed, his bottom clean, let the boy cry himself to sleep. Help him grow up to be a strong, independent man. And so, ignoring my cries made sense to her as an act of love. She did not see how it left me feeling worthless and abandoned.

As an adult in the 1980s, I do growth workshops that teach personal responsibility. By the chance of living in Evergreen, I wind up as Dr. Spock's volunteer driver from his host's mountain home to his Denver events. After a long day, connecting as we go, I share with him the impact his book had on me. The good doctor laments my injury. He says that section was revised in later editions. He graciously apologizes. His kindness is real.

I hear him. I'm also telling myself that healing my wounded inner child ultimately is my own responsibility. Forgiveness is up to me.

Signs of Split Perceptions

To help you spot split perceptions in daily life, I summarize below some of the signals or signs of the habit in humanity and in me.

• *Dualism* — Not seeing the oneness of the universe, we split apart life through *polarity thinking*. Natural dualism (*yin* and *yang*, male and female, in and out, up and down, day and night, east and west) twists into unnatural dualism (either/or, good or evil, black or white, us or them, rule or be ruled, kill or be killed, all or nothing). Life looks binary. *Yes or No.* We cannot conceive of life in wholistic terms, *Yes and....* A dualistic mindmap makes sense of life in ways that separate and oppose.

• *Fragmentation* — We see fragments of reality and miss the big picture. We see trees not forests. We cannot imagine all life as one whole when the very idea of wholeness is foreign to us.

• *Selective Reception* — We screen out whatever we do not want to see or hear or know or admit to ourselves. The meme of three monkeys. If I cover my ears and outshout you, I can't hear your truth. Ever told a corrupt politician it's time to resign and go to jail?

• *Compartmentalizing* — We think inside silos that do not readily communicate. We think and behave one way at work and another way at home or with friends. In separate compartments, we can rib a friend, woo a lover, donate to charity, believe a lie, and vote for a tyrant.

• *Disassociation/Detachment* — We detach from the present. We live in the past or future instead of now. It's safer to detach when washing the dishes than driving a car. Dissociation from stress tied to trauma is common in PTSD. If extreme, we may disable empathy and sympathy. Detaching from objective reality altogether is a psychosis.

• *Intellectualizing* — We live in our heads. Noisy thoughts in the front of our skulls divert us from noticing emotions in our bodies. Mental filters mute subconscious and unconscious messages. We get tangled in fascinating threads of abstract thought and tune out hard reality.

• *Judgements* — Our minds divide when ego confuses discernment and judgement. Saying a thing as good or bad prevents seeing it as a fact. Moral judgements, reflecting preconceptions, help us feel superior.

• **Bias, Prejudice** — When we pre-judge a person, place, thing, or idea as acceptable or not, our bias effectively filters our perceptions, splits our minds, alters our sense-making, which alters our behavior. Whether our prejudices are factual or not, the mechanics of splitting perceptions ensures our beliefs are true for us, so the mindlock endures.

• **Rationalizing** — To avoid reality, we rationalize misbehavior to explain away shadows of shame and blame. Like racists justifying slavery, we minimize consequences, invent excuses. Rationalization is instinctive, without forethought, often without awareness we're doing it.

• **Irrationality** — Split perceptions disrupt critical thinking. Valid reasoning relies upon sound logical syllogisms. If any premise is invalid, the conclusion is invalid. Trusting false premises is irrational.

• **Willful Ignorance** — We could be the smartest kid on the block, but if we filter out facts, we lack enough knowledge for sound reasoning. Critical thinking gets waylaid by silently choosing not to know. Trusting the heart and gut is necessary yet insufficient for honest minds.

• **Conditional Love**— We only love those who meet our conditions, pass our tests. We block agape love of all as our equals in nature.

• **Insecurity** — Filtering out our oneness, we think we are all alone in a hostile world, maybe not good enough to compete and survive. We endure in dread of injury. Unless raised lovingly, we may feel unlovable, low self-esteem or self-hate. We seek security from outside ourselves.

• **Victimhood** — If we believe the world is evil and out to get us, we may buy into victimhood so fully that we embody our wounding, as I did with cancer. Victimhood induces inertia and helpless hopelessness. We may play the victim to deny bad choices and shift blame. Victimhood endows a sense of entitlement to pity and special attention. Victimhood can become predatory and cunning, hidden by rationalizations.

• **Complaining** — Filtering out our wholeness, we complain, a lot. We find fault fast. We criticize. We complain without fixing. We voice grievances and forget we are both the problem and solution.

• **Irritability** — If an irrational worldview meets resistance, we can get irritable. When we let our grievances override reason and empathy. we can get peevish, indignant, righteous, unkind, and aggressive.

- *Reactivity/Revenge* — Ignoring our unity, lacking empathy, we may misread situations and unduly lay blame. We may get upset quickly, regret later. We push others' buttons, let others push ours, carry a grudge, nurse grievances. We get even. We think justice means vengeance.

- *No Boundaries* — We each have a natural right to live free in our own space, providing we do not violate others' rights. Split perceptions disrupt sensing boundaries, as with theft. Like infants unaware of personal space, if we want a thing, we grab it. We are space invaders.

- *Irresponsibility* — Blocking oneness from our minds, we abuse freedom without restraint, such as polluting the earth without remorse, corrupting a government without recourse. To sustain our recklessness, we think liberty means no responsibility or accountability. We blame the scapegoats, the alien others. We deny liability for liberty.

- *Self-Deception* — We refuse to admit facts to ourselves. Witness statements by U.S. presidents. Richard Nixon: "I am not a crook." Ronald Reagan: "I did not trade arms for hostages." Bill Clinton: "I did not have sexual relations with that woman." George W. Bush: "Every measure has been taken to avoid war." Barack Obama: "The American people don't have a Big Brother who is snooping into their business." Donald Trump: "The 2020 election was stolen." Joe Biden: "I can win in 2024." If we lie to ourselves and believed it, we invite chaos and madness.

- *Insanity* — When any belief system (mental map) fails to match reality, this splintering of perceptions produces "cognitive dissonance." Ideally, we resolve the tension creatively by shifting reality one choice at a time. When we cannot resolve extreme splits between facts and beliefs, as reality bites, when the denials of denial are undeniable, we might suffer a neural breakdown. Trauma might disable us and induce mental illness. If we cannot tell fact from fancy, at the extremes, we go insane.

- *Self-Destruction* — Denying our unity in life, feeling isolated and lonely, we may unconsciously harm ourselves, self-sabotage. We may feel overwhelming fear of anguish or despair, so we ideate suicide. We may project self-hate onto a demonized "other," so we join militias urging us to kill and die as martyrs to the cause. Nihilism tells us life stinks, so let's destroy ourselves and start over. Split perceptions can be lethal.

• *Tyranny* — If split perceptions induce us to make sense of the world as hostile or evil (not whole), survival fears may leave us vulnerable to leaders promising security in trade for loyalty. Or, we may become the alpha needing power to feel safe. Splitting perceptions, blocking empathy, lets despots use fear to gain compliance with their corruption. If we rebel, we risk becoming rebellion addicts reacting on shadow impulses.

The above signals of split perceptions are not a complete listing. More research is needed. (I'll spot more signs as I catch myself.)

Propaganda and Perceptions

Split perceptions cause problems in our personal lives, such as when I've hidden destructive habits from my conscious mind. On a wider scale, split perceptions cause problems in our societies. By not seeing our power in oneness, humanity choses kings to shirk the work of democracy.

Kings and other despots win our favor and hold our loyalty by splitting our perceptions, so we do not see how their corruption injures us. The ancient art of mass deception has proven itself compelling.

Rulers anywhere control sense-making with *propaganda*. A form of *misinformation*, propaganda uses a suite of persuasion tools to manipulate us with signs and symbols (semiotics) and language (linguistics).

Propaganda preys on our primal feelings. Propaganda distorts human nature, like turning a normal need for safety into a tribal cult. Prejudices, divisions and fears get amplified. Propaganda pushes duality, "us or them" polarity thinking. Our neurology and emotions are exploited to influence our brains and behavior. Modern propaganda propagates media messages massaging our minds and hearts. The most vulnerable are smart people untrained in emotional literacy, media literacy or critical thinking.

Effective propaganda persuades us that black is white, seducing us to forget we ever thought otherwise. The lie becomes truth. When a herd mentality is celebrated as rebellious liberty, then conformity is "freedom." We confuse thinking for ourselves with thinking like our friends.

Propaganda is readily spotted in advertising and political rhetoric. Autocrats are skilled at such techniques as the dirty dozen below:

Ad Hominem — Attack a speaker with name-calling and pejoratives rather than face the truths being spoken. Kill the messenger.

Appeal to Authority — An expert or celebrity says a thing is good or true, even if it's not. The ruse exploits authority addiction.

Bandwagon — Everybody is doing, buying or thinking a thing, so we should, too. It's good for them; it's good for us. Safety in numbers.

Big Lie — Say a lie is true; say it loud enough and long enough until people believe it, or at least give it credence, and so go along.

False Dilemma — Choose this good thing or else be stuck with that bad thing. Such "either/or" duality mindtraps ignore alternatives.

Glittering Generalities — A great something cures ills like nothing ever before. Sweeping appeals to emotion avoid awkward specifics.

Plain Folk — Common people like us buy, think or do something. This instills a false idea of what's ordinary, confirming conformity.

Political Correctness — Talk about a thing in the right way. Variance is heresy. Deplatforming (cancel culture) induces self-censorship.

Red Herring — Blame a problem on something that ignores the real cause. Misdirection is the trick magicians use to get away with stuff.

Slippery Slope — If a thing occurs, a terrible chain reaction follows. Other options are made to look extreme or unacceptable.

Straw Man — Decry a plainly bad idea or deed from a foe which the foe never actually said or did. The ruse knocks down scarecrows.

Whataboutism — If this is bad, what about that? Or, this isn't wrong since that's worse, as if two wrongs make a right. False equivalence.

Autocracies employ propaganda to dominate the popular mentality. Propaganda interferes with our ability to think reasonably. For instance, the technique of *Appeal to Nostalgia* ("Make our country great again!") is a mindtrap baited with the emotions of longing and grievance.

Propaganda exploits our shadow need for external validation, so we identify with leaders. Fo instance, Donald Trump tells aggrieved people, "I am your voice. I am your warrior." Blaming the "deep state" for woes, he attracts those needing a hero to love and an enemy to hate. He plays to the follower and rebel traits in authority addicts (Chapter 9).

Reason and Faith

Paine cautioned, "To argue with a man [sic] who has renounced the use and authority of reason, and whose philosophy consists in holding humanity in contempt, is like administering medicine to the dead."

Split perceptions enable tyranny over our minds. We tend to adopt baseless beliefs that help us make sense of the world. A shared reality and fellowship may lock us into lies. Conflating fact and faith, we reject solid evidence refuting our beliefs. We use motivated reasoning to sidestep inconvenient truths. We reinforce our beliefs by using circular reasoning. "My leader is great because he's great at leading."

Split perceptions impede critical thinking. We miss the range of facts and opinions available. We refuse to test evidence, so thesis and antithesis never synthesize new theories to test. Split perceptions deter reliable sense-making, rational decision-making and effective problem-solving.

Irrational beliefs are true because we believe them. By confusing subjective opinions with objective evidence, as I did in the Moonies, we can make life decisions based on delusions. Convinced I was thinking for myself, I fell into groupthink lockstep. When split perceptions rend our minds, we cannot tell whether a premise is valid. Reasoning is riven by fallacy. We cannot tolerate anyone defining reality differently than we do. If pressed, we may get downright ornery.

Paine wrote, "Reason and Ignorance, the opposites of each other, influence the great bulk of mankind [sic]. Reason obeys itself; and Ignorance submits to whatever is dictated to it." His solution? "The most formidable weapon against errors of every kind is reason."

Paine was pragmatic. "Before anything can be reasoned upon to a conclusion, certain facts, principles, or data, to reason from, must be established, admitted, or denied." As a deist, he maintained, "It is only by the exercise of reason that man [sic] can discover God."

Give faith its due. Our beliefs, as thought forms, do affect objective, subjective and shared reality. For instance, my cancer journey shows how science and faith unite. My lesson is letting go. As I stop trying to control outcomes, surrender gives me more self-control. Life flows easier.

Polarizing debates over fact-versus-faith are solved by a global frame of mind. New Age seekers believe today is The Great Turning and cosmic Ascension. Christians call today the Last Days. Facts and reason support both. The future is in flux and up to us. I deduce human survival on earth hinges on a global sensibility. Reason and faith guides my choices.

Life works best when faith is grounded in reason. If we refuse logical thinking rooted in evident facts, like hard data on our global connectivity, if we ignore our conscience and guts, we may split our perceptions beyond remedy. In wild times of confusion and crises in this decade and century, unless we see our oneness, we risk our sanity and liberty. Paine reasoned that we cannot afford to let fear cost us our freedom.

A global sensibility dispels destructive self-deceptions.

≈

So far in the book, I'm building a framework for making sense of our new global age. I've reported at least a billion of us on earth have a global sense of life. I've explored how we make sense of reality, how changing the way we make sense of reality changes our lives and world, how split perceptions spoil sense-making and skew choices.

Next, we consider the consequences of denying our oneness.

CHAPTER 7

Absurdities and Atrocities

1955: DENVER — *Childhood for me is mostly about trying to feel safe. I absorb early a sense the world is unsafe. Was I born insecure? What filters into my mind about the world is baffling and scary. Newspaper photos frighten me before I can read. I hear radio news about war in Korea. I hear about atomic bombs. I do duck-and-cover drills in preschool. Red meanie Commie bogeymen are hiding everywhere. And when all the swimming pools close, I hear about polio, iron lungs and wheelchairs.*

My child mind learns a bald man, General Eisenhower, is the President. I'm unaware daddy may live in fear of McCarthy blacklists from his ties to Hull House and support for trade unions. He surely knows the fate of those called "pink." All "unAmericans" are outcasts. As an adult today I wonder, did daddy do his duty as family breadwinner by laying low?

My father goes to work at the printer. Mommy stays home to care for us kids. She's always busy feeding, bathing or watching over us. I compete with my sisters for mommy's time and attention. Before I can walk and talk, I discover that being weak and sickly gets my needs met. I cry and whine until I wheeze, and then mommy comes. She rubs my back and chest with vapor salve. Mommy treats me the most tenderly when I'm the most pitiful. I adopt victimhood early as a survival mechanism.

Once I can talk, I'm a chatterbox. However, the phonic "r" is hard for my tongue to reach. I sound like Elmer Fudd saying Wacky Wabbit. Other kids on the block tease me. They make me say my name. "Kenny Fwied." Laughter and pointing fingers. They call me "fried ham and eggs."

Learning to read is magical. Mommy and daddy point to letters and words in picture books, helping me say them out loud. Words open worlds in my mind. Books are doors. I can read story picture books by the first grade, and then chapter books. I love my books more than my toys.

We watch television at my grandparent's house every weekend. Daddy finally buys a boxy Hoffman black and white TV set. I'm a big fan of cowboy heroes. On my birthday, I get a toy six-gun and holster, cowboy boots, a cowboy hat, and a toy horse on wheels to ride. We gallop across the western plains to fight the bad guys and save the day.

Around 1955, I get seriously ill. I'm too weak to get out of bed or stand up. Mommy feeds me in bed. Daddy carries me to the bathroom. My sisters play board games with me on my bed until they get bored.

I recall the family doctor making house calls twice a day to give painful penicillin shots in my rump. I can still see his clipped mustache. As a child, I was told "spinal meningitis," but adult me learns the symptoms don't fit. My adult eldest sister said I survived polio. Logical, yet no proof.

In my childhood bedroom hangs my daddy's oil painting of circus tents. On the walls, he'd painted a clown and circus animals — a lion, seal and elephant. I talk to these figures sometimes, and they listen to me well. At the end of the sickness, imagining myself walking a circus tightrope, I unsteadily step from my bed to the dresser. My family rejoices.

Looking back at me as a child struggling to make sense of that illness, a telling truth is my avoidance at the synagogue of a boy in a wheelchair. (There but for the grace of God roll I?) I recall standing in a line of children at school for a Sabin sugar cube. Later I learn Albert Sabin and Jonas Salk gave away their (virus-based) polio vaccines as patent-free gifts to the world. They put public health before personal wealth.

As I recover my strength, I stop being the household center of attention. My parents are busy. My sisters and their friends won't bother with a little brother. They draw hopscotch on the sidewalk and won't let me play. I feel unwanted. I think there must be something wrong with me.

I have one friend on our block. On a fine summer day, we play barber. I use mommy's sewing scissors to give him a haircut, spikes and bare spots. We are caught moments before switching places.

He gets spanked at home, his worst ever, he'll tell me years later. My daddy spanks me fiercely that night. Not the first nor last time.

Mommy initially does my spankings. As I get older, she declares, "You just wait until your father comes home!" If he comes home in a bad mood, my spankings are harsh. He uses a belt, once a wooden hanger. Provocations arise at any time. His unpredictable outbursts unnerve me.

Mommy does not help me feel safer. She corrects what I do and how I do it. Her sharp sarcasm cuts me. To escape blame and shame, I get evasive, start making up excuses and lying to her. I convince myself the lies are true, so she'll believe me. Lying to myself gets engrained as a survival trait.

We live in a small three-bedroom frame house my father bought when I was born. I do not know then that he secured the mortgage with his dead-end graphics job, which he hates. Around 1956, he quits and opens his own advertising agency. He works from the garage until he rents an office near downtown and takes on a partner.

The year I start first grade, my parents have a loud fight over money. Mommy is angry at daddy because she can buy school clothes for my sisters but not for me. She shouts, "There's not enough for Kenny!" Her words tear me apart. I twist them to mean I am not enough. I'm not worth as much as my sisters. I'm a burden. Low self-esteem encodes engrams.

One night at dinner, I refuse to eat any more of mommy's soggy boiled canned vegetables. Daddy orders me to eat my vegetables. "You won't eat fruit," I protest, "so I won't eat vegetables." He gets furious.

Daddy force-feeds me until I gag. Next night, he makes mommy serve me those same uneaten reheated mushy vegetables. I refuse. Again, he force feeds me. This time I vomit. After a week of dinnertime horror, he relents. (I won't eat cooked vegetables until my early twenties, when I join a cult and discover the joys of veggie wok cooking.)

I shut my childhood bedroom door to be alone, but my folks and sisters walk in anyway. I begin crawling under my bed to hide. I can sit upright against the wall, facing the back of the headboard. In time, I insert Tinker Toys between the mattress and box spring for the knobs of a spaceship, as seen on TV. On the back of the headboard, I tape up my drawing of the ship control screen. I am Buck Rogers or Flash Gordon saving the galaxy!

If I can't sleep after a bedtime beating, I silently slip under the bed and zoom away to safety among the stars. I'm careful never to make any noise nor utter a sound. I dare not wake the daddy starbeast.

Consenting to Scare Tactics

Split perceptions prevent us from seeing the absurd, self-defeating ways we try to meet our natural need for security.

In the 21st century and beyond, we have legitimate reasons for fear. The corruption of local to national governments appears inescapable. Wars, pandemics, droughts, famines, fires, floods, storms, and worse may kill millions or billions of us. Climate changes could leave entire regions uninhabitable. Experts expect waves of mass migrations to upset cultures and societies, spurring political unrest and economic instability. Some believe total collapse is inevitable, even desirable.

By preying upon our fears and legitimate grievances, bullies can gain control over us. Leaders mislead us to blame the bad guys out there who do not look like us or think like us or vote like us. We are taught to fear and loathe and kill some terrible "Great Satan," who embodies all the shadows we refuse to see lurking inside ourselves.

Political leaders keep us afraid to keep themselves in power. The 20th century's H.L. Mencken explained the strategy plainly. "The whole aim of practical politics is to keep the populace alarmed and hence, clamorous to be led to safety — by menacing it with an endless series of hobgoblins, all of them imaginary."

Communism was the 20th century's bogeyman. The 21st century began with Islamist terrorists menacing the USA on "9/11" with hijacked planes flying into U.S. buildings, killing thousands. Terrified, we did not challenge the morality of government intrusions on privacy. Defenders of the surveillance state declared, "If you have nothing to hide, you have nothing to fear." Isn't that what the Gestapo said?

After the Nazis arrested Pastor Martin Niemöller in 1937, he wrote these words (often misquoted): "First they came for the communists, and I did not speak out, because I was not a communist; then they came for the socialists, and I did not speak out, because I was not a socialist; then they came for the trade unionists, and I did not speak out, because I was not a trade unionist; then they came for the Jews, and I did not speak out, because I was not a Jew; then they came for me, and there was no one left to speak out for me."

My own nation is not immune to tyranny. Dare we ignore the risk? I cite the 1935 political satire by Sinclair Lewis, *It Can't Happen Here*. In the novel and stage play, a nationalist with populist slogans wins the 1936 U.S. presidential election. His corrupt loyalists in Congress go along with making him a dictator, same as in Italy and Germany.

Nazi Hermann Göring told a reporter at the Nürnberg Trials how to trick a nation into war. "It is the leaders of the country who determine policy, and it is always a simple matter to drag the people along, whether it's a democracy, a fascist dictatorship, a parliament, or a communist dictatorship. All you have to do is to tell them they are being attacked, and denounce pacifists for lack of patriotism and exposing the country to danger. It works the same in any country."

Voltaire said, "Those who can make you believe absurdities can make you commit atrocities." Genocide anywhere is proof.

Like Paine cautioned in 1776, beware when the enemies of our masters become our enemies, when we are so divided by hate and fear that all we have in common are suffering and death.

∿

Next door to our house in University Hills live two brothers who take pleasure in tormenting little boy me for years of tears.

One day, the bully brothers run into our front yard where I'm playing western hero on a toy horse. They taunt me. They shout, "Dirty Jews can't be cowboys!" They snatch my cowboy hat off my head and play keep-away with it. I chase them, both hands outstretched. I'm screaming, "Give it back! Give it back! That's my hat!"

My middle sister comes outside and yells at the younger neighbor to return my hat. He stops mid-stride at the curb, looks defiantly at my sister, at his brother, and at me. He throws my hat into the gutter, stomps on it and snarls, "Here's your stupid hat!"

The boys run into their house. Their screen door slams. I pick up my crumpled cowboy hat from the gutter. The crown is crushed. Water drips from the torn brim. Water pours from my eyes. My hat is ruined. My life is ruined. Everything is ruined.

I run inside to my bedroom and flop down sobbing on the bed. What's the use? Why am I even alive? Am I here to suffer like that man on a cross the boys next door say I killed? They call me a Christ killer. They call me a kike, a yid, a Hebe, a lousy stinking rat-faced dirty Jew. My mind cannot grasp why they hate me. Why won't they leave me alone?

As the day wears on, my eldest sister knocks on my door to ask if I am okay. My middle sister says in passing I have to stop being such a baby. My father at dinner says, "Don't let them get your goat." My mother at bedtime tells me not to be so sensitive. She says, "Boys will be boys."

The brothers next door never relent. Sometimes, I hear their father yelling at them. Serves them right, I think. I have no clue these brothers take out on me the inner demons their father takes out on them. I know nothing of transference and projection. I'm years away from realizing how bullies in my childhood seal victimhood into my self-image.

I'm just a scared little boy, afraid of other kids, afraid of my father and mother. Life feels unsafe. I make sense of it by blaming myself and feeling resentful. I'm an angry victim invested in feeling victimized.

No Excuses for Tyranny

When I look at world affairs today, I see our natural need for security and liberty being diverted into irrational love for tyrants making big promises. I'd rather see a world where we freely question authority and challenge blind faith in any leader or doctrine. I want a world where heart, conscience, critical thinking, and global sense guide our ways.

I know first-hand how easily we fool ourselves with split perceptions. We go along with nonsense to feel beloved in a community. We say the secret words to get approval. We become faithful to a religion or ideology. The more stubbornly we deny our doubts, the more stridently we assert our beliefs as facts. We may fight and die to prove our righteousness.

Despite doubts, we may find excuses to go along with authoritarian leaders and their lies. We may do so sincerely in honest trust, or cynically from sycophancy, or meekly from intimidation.

Who among us is most responsible for the despots now ruling and ruining our world? Thomas Paine blamed those who never think about public affairs. He said, "The great mass of unthinking people is the source of more harm in the world than all other causes combined."

Many of us live apart from scenes of sorrow in nations where bullies rule and voters do not. In developed lands, mainstream culture trains us to think only of ourselves and ignore the agony of others. We may suspect the needy are faking their anguish to fleece the gullible.

History, we may tell ourselves, teaches us to prize victorious leaders, from Alexander the Great on down. We pretend our leader's glory is our own glory. It's like feeling a sports team's victory is our personal victory. We'd conquer the world while chanting, "Might makes right!"

Trying to rule the world is irrational. How can one person or nation govern every life on earth? As Paine wrote of America and Britain, "There is something absurd in supposing a continent to be perpetually governed by an island." Likewise, it's absurd for the top one percent of us to rule all humanity. Why wage cruel wars over which master should rule us when it makes global sense to mindfully rule ourselves?

Besides, what do we care about war and conquest? If we are globally aware, we value conscious commerce with free and fair trade as the best guarantor of peace. "Peace is a natural effect of trade," said Montesquieu. Why put our freedom or lives at risk for power addicts? Will humanity advance into open democracy or backslide into closed autocracy"

I've heard people say we need strong leaders to protect us from our enemies. The idea is a fallacy. Kings and dictators do defend our lives and property, at our expense, or at their own expense sometimes; that's true. However, the despots only defend themselves, not us. Our leaders often created those enemies on their own. We are liable only if we go along with their deceptions, openly or tacitly, by making their enemies our enemies. When we hate those we are told to hate, we are puppets.

Seeing our oneness sets our minds free, sets my mind free.

The "enemies of the state" usually have no quarrel with us beyond our choice of leadership. Few in the Middle East truly hate all Americans, for example, yet the majority does feel contempt for U.S. government and corporate policies, which are not above reproach.

Tyrant leaders declare their cause is noble. "The greatest tyrannies," Paine warned, "are always perpetuated in the name of the noblest causes." We know without being told that despots are driven by self-interest, not public service, so why be fooled by their speechwriters? Power junkies can tell any lie that feeds their addiction. Let them wave their lies before the world like flags. Let tyrants praise one another. Let them pretend their abuses are moral. The injuries we suffer warn us against trusting any bully, not in our governments, in our jobs, in our schools, in our homes, and not in our own unconscious minds.

Tyrants may seduce us with talk about fatherland, motherland and homeland. More absurdity. Such emotion-laden terms help the despots control unthinking people. They deploy linguistics to exploit our primal survival needs for home, family and security. We unite in fear of the alien. Defending territory is animal instinct, like a dog marking turf.

Our idea of "homeland" is changing. Colonial Americans in 1776 saw each colony as a separate country. A farmer in Virginia did not live in the same country as one in Pennsylvania. Thomas Paine convinced the Americans to view their colonies as states within one nation, which he evidently was first to call "the united states of America."

Nationalism is irrational. Paine wrote, "The World is my country, and to do good is my religion." Why must "homeland" mean one country only when the entire planet as our home? We are world citizens entering an age of global thinking where unity goes beyond borders.

Why risk our lives for the pride and glory of any one leader or nation when the whole globe is our abode? Across history, our faith in the folly of tribalism (dualism) has led humanity into despotism. To survive our world crises today, let us outgrow nationalism as foolishness.

Charlie Chaplin with his little mustache parodies Hitler in his 1940 film, *The Great Dictator*. In his vaulted office, he plays with a large balloon globe of the world. He balances the globe on his finger and flicks it up to the high ceiling. As it floats down, he bounces the globe off his head. He climbs up on his desk and bounces the world off his butt. He spoofs all tyrants treating the world as a toy until it bursts in their faces!

Bullies leave us alone only when we do not interfere with them. We comply with despots at our cost. Count up all the losses if we bow to the abusive boss at work, if we appease an abusive partner or spouse. We let shadowy self-hate habits destroy our health and finances. We rally behind leaders whipping up hate of bad guys to keep us in line as "team players." The cost of trusting tyranny in our minds and the world may be our souls. All humanity, all life on earth, shares equal natural rights. When this idea makes common global sense, there are no excuses for tyranny.

≈≈

1960: DENVER — *The summer I enter third grade, my family moves from a frame house in University Hills to a brick house in Mayfair Park. Moving from south to east Denver upsets my life.*

Mommy and daddy never ask if I want to move. Parents then do not ask. They tell. They tell me the new house is across the street from my new elementary school, where I can get a fresh start. It's closer to daddy's office downtown. It's close to Lowry Air Force Base, where I'll swim in the officer's club pool. It's close to my grandparents' house on Hilltop, which is within sight of the junior high school I'll go to in a few years.

All these benefits are why we moved, they tell me.

I do not learn until years later that my genuinely loving parents moved, in part, to get me away from the bully brothers next door.

On my first day of school, the teacher asks me to say my name out loud. Snickers of Elmer Fudd. At recess, teasing students encircle me on the playground. The bullies among them see I'm afraid to fight back. From then on, they pick on me almost daily.

I resent and resist school due to fear of bullying. I dawdle in the house every morning until the schoolyard five-minute bell. I dash out the door, run across the street, and land in my seat moments ahead of the final bell. I daily defy the clock to escape being harassed before school.

A Denver Public Schools' visiting speech pathologist helps me train my tongue to pronounce the "r" sound. Within a year I can say my last name without humiliation. I do not know it then, but I now realize speech therapy empowers me to find inside the ability to change how I show up in the world, change how people respond to me, change how I feel about myself.

School still feels dangerous, same as at home. By the end of primary school, I've lost my childlike wonder. I've lost faith in a good future for myself. Feeling I'll never meet expectations, I give up trying.

I fracture within a bit more every year. I split apart my perceptions to expect the worst. I decide anything good will always be taken away. I solidify the self-image of a hopeless victim. I get by on others' pity. My imagination is the only place where I feel safe to be my real self.

≈

Entering seventh grade, I enroll at Hill Junior High School, a quarter-block from my grandparents' house. Several primary schools feed into Hill. Bullies from my primary school tell the bullies from other schools about the skinny red-headed kid who's a kick to kick around.

Now I have a pack of old and new bullies dogging me. They goad me on the playground. They shove me at the bicycle racks. When I'm peddling home up Third or Fourth avenues, boys on bikes may jump me from any side street or alley. Whenever they catch me, I get beat up.

By eighth grade, my shell is thicker. I no longer cry when bullies attack. I get silent and sullen. Given a choice, I'd rather flee than fight. Fighting is stupid, I decide, and only stupid people fight.

I further choose not to fight for moral reasons. Violence is wrong.

I'm seeing TV news reports of Buddhist monks in Vietnam, protesting by lighting themselves on fire rather than killing oppressors. I see reports on the Freedom Riders and segregation, about Selma and Rev. Martin Luther King, Jr. In my social studies class, I learn Dr. King practices "nonviolence." He gets this idea from a dead man in India, Mahatma Gandhi. They both say nonviolence is the moral way to change the world.

I adopt peace and nonviolence as a lifelong moral principle.

Morality and Liberty

How do we navigate the uncertain terrain between freedom and responsibility? What stops us from doing whatever we like, regardless of the costs to others or ourselves or the planet? How do we know when or where to stop? For an alcoholic, one drink is too many, and a thousand is not enough. The freedom to fulfill desire is best governed by a reliable moral compass. Free will needs self rule.

Religions have long played the role of our moral arbiter. Paine found fault with organized religions using morality to control the faithful. For me, the central issue is how organized religions tend to promote external validation, reliance on authority outside the self. Rather, I trust reason and conscience to reveal what is moral for me in the world.

The Enlightenment-era writer Immanuel Kant influenced Paine. Kant critiqued pure reason, and he explored the "metaphysics of morals." He moved morality from the realm of religion into the realm of reason by formulating the "Categorical Imperative."

Kant proposed an act is morally good if it passes three tests:

1. We would want all people everywhere doing that action. What if everybody used biodegradable soap? What if every person was kind to animals? Kant advised, "Act is if the maxim from which you act were to become through your will a universal law."

2. The act treats other people as ends unto themselves, not as the means to our own ends, not if our ends justify unjust means.

3. The act treats other people as "mutual lawmakers" (co-creators) in an ideal "realm of ends," where the means justify the ends (Golden Rule, good karma, reciprocity, natural rights, global sense).

For simplicity, Kant says, ask what would happen if everybody does a specific thing? What if we all ate sand, or killed over trifles? If the result of us all doing a thing is absurd or atrocious, then it's immoral.

Any choice that makes global sense will pass Kant's moral test. If each of us on earth senses our natural equality and unity with all life on earth, I reason, our choices would be moral. If we resolve grievances through grieving and forgiveness, we cannot commit absurd atrocities.

Thomas Paine, like other freeethinkers in the 18th century, believed people are naturally good and inclined to do good. Mary Wollstonecraft wrote, "No man [*sic*] chooses evil because it is evil; he only mistakes it for happiness, the good he seeks."

Paine trusted informed people will unite to create a better world. He had faith in the colonists freeing their minds from the shackles of hereditary monarchy, instead declaring independence and creating a republic. His faith was justified.

In our 21st century, I share faith in the innate goodness of humanity. I see people aware of our oneness uniting to improve our world. I see us liberating our minds from the restraints of authority addiction, so we live mindfully free in open democracies. Will my faith be justified?

In the half-millennia since the European Renaissance and the rise of reason over ignorant faith, humanity worldwide has advanced toward freedom and democracy. Now free nations risk relapsing into despotism, even in the USA. Dark dystopian visions seem less far-fetched.

We've overpopulated our planet and unbalanced the ecosphere. We see the results in deadly terms, and it scares the hell out of us. No surprise so many of us believe the comforting lies of alluring leaders.

Illogic is easier than reason. We easily give away ownership of our minds to dogmatic tyrants promising to save us from our recklessness. Paine warned us, "When men [*sic*] yield up the privilege of thinking, the last shadow of liberty quits the horizon."

〰

Why do we give away our power to bullies?

For vital answers, since our freedom and survival is at stake, the next section delves into the darker side of human nature. As spiritual warriors, we'll journey through darkness into light. We'll explore the shadow forces, hidden by split perceptions, driving us to love our leaders, no matter their sins against us. The habit of worshipping kings is ancient.

PART II

Kings and
Other Masters

Remember, all men would be tyrants
if they could.

ABIGAIL ADAMS

CHAPTER 8

Alpha Male Rule

1963: DENVER — *In the Bar Mitzvah rite-of-passage in Judaism, a boy at his 13th birthday reads the Torah in Hebrew before the congregation and declares "Today I am a man." I feel far from manhood at my Bar Mitzvah. I'm a gawky adolescent with pimples and a voice that cracks.*

I suppress simmering rage at my father. Tensions between us saturate our home. My rebellion began a year ago during the Cuban Missile Crisis. In those 13 days hovering on the brink of nuclear war, I beg him to convert his workshop under the basement stairs into a fallout shelter. He refuses and calls it "a waste of time." I take this to mean that I'm not worth his time. He does not care if I live or die. He must not love me.

I do not consider then that he's a captain in the U.S. Air Force Reserves, assigned as a public information officer to the Air Defense Command. He knows Lowry is a target for Soviet missiles. In the event of a war, our nearby home will be vaporized. A basement shelter is pointless.

I also am unaware that his time is needed elsewhere. His ad agency is struggling. He's losing hope for success in business, the plan he'd adopted to replace his lost dream of being an artist and teacher. I do not realize then that my resistance threatens his primal self. Neither does he.

What I decide in my addled adolescent brain is that he treats me more like a servant than his son, and certainly not like a man.

I've been cleaning up after him for years, and I've had enough. This one evening, he's just replaced a closet hinge in his basement den down the hall from my bedroom. My mom shouts that he has a phone call.

Dad treads upstairs. I'm on my bed reading. I hear his muffled voice slowly rise until he's yelling, "For the last time, I don't have anything to pay you! Now leave me alone!" I hear him bang down the telephone receiver. He blasts out curses at the bill collector and his life.

Moments later, he yells down from the top of the stairs for me to put away his tools. I'm absorbed in a Ray Bradbury novel, and I holler back, "I'm busy. Do it yourself!"

He pounds down the stairs into the den. "Get in here!" he shouts.

I do not budge, but I do close the book.

"I said to get in here! Don't make me come and get you!"

With mounting fury, I slide off the bed, charge down the hallway into the den. He points to the drill and screwdriver on the floor at his feet. "I told you to put these tools away!"

"Put away your own tools," I snap. "I'm not your damn slave!"

Before I can flinch, he hits me with an open hand across my face. My legs crumple. I go down with him above me, slapping and hitting. I pull into a fetal ball, my arms covering my head. I'm shrieking at him to stop. I fear for my life. He's lost control.

Out of nowhere arrive my mother and sisters, pulling him off, pushing him out of the den and up the stairs. My mother screeches after him, calling him a madman! I lift up and lean over my knees, my face inches from the linoleum tile floor, inches above a red pool below my nose.

My dad never hits me again. His remorse and shame are real. He shifts. He honestly does try not to boss me around as much anymore.

Still, I do not trust him for years.

The Fall of Man and Rise of Male Rule

I now say my father did the best he knew how to do at the time. His dad likely beat him, same as his forefathers likely beat their boys.

I've thought about my talented father's life and his influences on me. I've come to doubt beliefs he passed to me, directly and indirectly, about the meaning of masculinity. I no longer think that a "real man" dominates others, that "manhood" means violence and war. Instead, I've developed faith in the power of a peaceful spiritual warrior.

For me, male dominance, *alpha male rule*, hinders awakening into global sense. I discern that men fighting other men for glory and power, historically, keeps humanity locked into the self-destructive mindtraps threatening our survival on earth. We need male liberation.

Paine believed in the 18th century that no man has an inborn right to rule society by virtue of lineage or wealth. He challenged the division of society into Kings and Subjects. Today I'd use gender-neutral terms as I agree with his views about monarchs upon hereditary thrones, which inspires my views about patriarchy and inherited power.

Origins of Alpha Male Rule

For clues on the start of male rule, scan human "his-story." Whatever our species genesis, most paleontologists agree Cro-Magnon *homo sapiens* came out of Africa, eventually displacing Neanderthals. Migrating to the Tigris-Euphrates valley (Iraq), "The Cradle of Western Civilization," they evidently began settled agriculture about 10,000 years ago.

Were early human societies ruled by men or women or both?

Folklorist James Frazer in *The Golden Bough* contended that because only women give birth, matriarchs ruled Neolithic Mesopotamia. Lineage was traced from mothers to daughters. They worshiped the goddess, the Mother, the mysterious sacred fertile lifeforce miraculously causing fruit to grow on a tree. Based on the feminine fertility principle, he proffers, women held cultural and political power across the region.

Elise Boulding in *The Underside of History* tells of African women as chiefs in Niger, Chad and Nubia. China was matrilineal until patriarchal Confucianism arose. Women in India held high status until Vedic culture lifted men and repressed women. Boulding gives ample examples.

The Myth of Matriarchal Prehistory by Cynthia Eller disputes the theory humanity lived in utopia until the rise of male rule. Even if women did rule, she asserts, life was imperfect.

Myths of Male Dominance, edited by Eleanor Burke Leacock, shows women as co-leaders with men in diverse early societies.

Riane Eisler in *The Chalice and the Blade* finds early Mediterranean societies, like the Minoans, were egalitarian with gender equality.

When did men realize their role in procreation? Artifacts found in the underground city of Catalhoyuk, Turkey, indicate men understood fatherhood by 6500 BCE (Before the Common Era, or BC).

How did men gain carnal knowledge? I offer a playful theory:

One primeval day, an impassioned woman felt tempted by her man's rising serpent. This archetypal Eve shared with her archetypal Adam the Fruit of the Tree of Knowledge. She told him the secret of the "Holy Hole," that sex creates babies. He realized women held tribal power by hiding the truth of male potency. That man told other men, who rebelled against women and seized control, sparking the "battle of the sexes."

Was the "fall of man" really the rise of male rule?

In support, I cite the Celtic *Mabinogion* recalling oral traditions of the Old Tribes ruled by women defeated in war by the New Tribes ruled by men. Patriarchy replaced matriarchy. Lineage was traced from fathers to sons. To assure the paternity of every son, men invented wedlock, so a wife and her womb are a man's property under patriarchy.

Men's Right to Rule

Paine would say none are born with a right to rule based on ancestry. He challenged the social system of primogeniture, where the firstborn eldest son has the right of inheritance from the father, excluding females. He saw this as a system to keep the aristocracy in power.

Paine objected to kings on inherited thrones holding absolute power over those they rule. Reasoning like Paine, I see no valid basis for us men to assume we have any right or duty to rule the world.

How about science? Neurobiology measures differences in male and female brains that relate to differences in our reproductive functions. My research has found no reliable proof either gender is born to rule.

How about in nature? Our closest relatives are the chimpanzees. Jane Goodall found an alpha male chimpanzee may murder males competing for his harem, even a brother. In contrast, the gentler matriarchal or egalitarian bonobo chimps make love not war. Both breeds of aggressive and amorous primates are 98 percent genetically identical to us humans. Seems either gender is able to lead, and neither is born to rule.

〰

On Friday afternoon, November 22, as I'm leaving Temple Emanuel, as I near the vestibule of dark wood doors with inset squares of blue glass, a fellow student asks if I've heard the news. What news?

President John F. Kennedy has been assassinated in Dallas.

I still recall TV scenes of the funeral cortege in Washington, DC. Three pairs of white horses pull the black caisson carrying JFK's flag-draped coffin. A riderless horse prances as a steady soldier on foot holds the reins. I hear the echoing clop of hoofbeats and the rolling drumbeat dirge.

I decide hate and violence solve nothing. Nobody wins. Hate breeds more hate. Violence breeds more violence. Violence is futile, so it's stupid. Violence is immoral. Surely, there's a way for us to live in peace!

Male Dominance

Humanity has been guided by a mental map of reality that makes sense of life and evolution as a male war for dominance over women and nature. Some call it, "the survival of the fittest." This belief is based on the premise, *might makes right*. This old fallacy, called "Social Darwinism," has caused much of our suffering on earth.

Let's erase a misconception of Charles Darwin's findings on "natural selection." He never said a willingness to lie, cheat, bully, or kill makes us the most fit to survive. *On the Origin of Species* actually says "adaptation" is what best assures survival. When a food source fails, survivors eat other foods. Their digestive systems adapt to the new diet, and then their genes. "Survival of the fittest" means adapting in the right way.

Therefore, *right makes might*.

Did humanity adapt to the rise of alpha male rule in the right way? I think not. For proof, I cite any despotic society ruled by men.

Tyrants have abused our rights, waged wars, and spoiled the planet to gain land, wealth, fame, and power. "The militancy of men, through all the centuries, has drenched the world with blood," wrote Emmeline Pankhurst, "and for these deeds of horror and destruction men have been rewarded with monuments, with great songs and epics."

Men Pay for Male Rule

Male dominance injures us men. Herb Goldberg in *The Hazards of Being Male* and Warren Farrell in *The Myth of Male Power* report women tend to outlive men because men die early from wars, murder, dangerous jobs, stress, and lonely suicides. Men endure "male bashing" in the media (dumb hubby) and in the courts (father's rights).

We damaged men buy into beliefs about the meaning of "manhood" that leave us ruled by fear and shame, by low or no self-esteem. We learn from society to measure our masculinity by our muscles, intelligence, wealth, power, or the length of our — beards.

Society tells us a "real man" does not need anyone. So, we men dare not ask for support or road directions. We learn it's unmanly to cry and express any emotions but anger, mirth or courage. We learn early that men who display embarrassing feelings are shunned. We avoid heartfelt friendships with men, afraid of being called gay, or being gay. A good man fights and kills bad men. I grew up in Colorado, where the movie cowboy hero saves the town and rides off alone into the sunset.

Men tend to adopt the "masculine mystique," says Frank Pittman in *Man Enough*. We become "Philanderers" driven to avoid commitments, "Contenders" driven to compete, and "Controllers" driven to rule.

On the flip side are men afraid of their power. As Dr. Robert Glover observes, men can fixate on being "Mr. Nice Guy" and stop being true to themselves. Another flip side is a "sensitive New Age guy" with empathy who lives powerfully as a conscious peaceful warrior.

Consider the traditional social contract that men and women inherit. As I distill Warren Farrell in *Why Men Are the Way They Are*, a man must excel at something to prove to a woman that he can reliably provide "home, family and security." She must be convinced of his value and valor through symbolic or real combat. As her provider and protector, the man becomes a walking wallet for the woman. In trade, she duly vows sexual fidelity backed by her implicit promise to be modest in public and wanton in bed. Above all, I will add, she must bear sons. Such binary gender roles keep us men in charge so long as enough women consent.

In suppressing women, we men suppress our own feminine natures. We lose access to the range of emotions, especially sadness and grief. We lose access to intuition. We live from our necks up and our waists down. We live cut off from our hearts, spiritually castrated, which is no life at all. Emotional illiteracy make us unfit as mates for women or anyone.

By hiding behind machismo pretensions to secure male dominance, we men become like Ralph Ellison's invisible man in a superhero mask. We hide our secret identity as vulnerable men full of love.

Taoism says the nature of masculine *yang* energy is not taking but giving. Generosity stimulates the flow of fertile *yin* energy, so love grows abundantly. The path of sacred masculinity for "new men" starts with the forbidding hero's journey from the head to the heart.

Women Pay for Male Rule

Male dominance injures women. Worldwide, one in three women suffers violence, reports the UN. Male partners commit 80 percent of the violence against women. If a woman is raped, it's her fault for being sexy. In some lands, to curb male lust and limit competition, men make women hide their beauty under wigs, scarves, veils, or formless clothing.

As a whole, we men resist women controlling their own bodies. We ban contraception and abortion to stop women from discarding our seed. We think we own all the fruit we fertilize. To get moral women to go along, we claim every fetus has a right to life, but we don't extend that same right to adults. If all life is sacred, how can we execute prisoners or wage wars? The true hidden agenda here, I deduce, is womb control.

〰

1964: DENVER — *In front of every student eating lunch in the cafeteria. I finally stand up to the school bully. Now I'm in real trouble.*

I'm still finding my footing after rebelling against my father a year earlier. Dad no longer hits me, but I feel that I'll never be good enough for him. Mom still cuts me with her sharp tongue. I embed her knack for jibes and snide wisecracks, a habit to hide my wounds from the world.

School bullies still see me as meat for the dog pack. They know I don't fight back. I'm most vulnerable in the lunchroom. Their latest gag is tripping me when walking with a lunch tray, so my food flies to the floor. I look like a clumsy idiot. I feel like the school joke, and I'm sick of it.

On this typical schoolday, the leading school bully is hassling me at my lunchroom table, picking a fight after school. "What's wrong with you? Are you a pansy? Are you just a dumb little chicken?"

"I am not afraid to fight you," I say, Joe Cool, "but I don't care to fight. You can beat me up. So what? You're stronger, but I'm smarter."

His reaction is predictable. He picks up my carton of chocolate milk and pours it over my head. Laughter dies when I stand and step into him. Grabbing him by the shirt collar, I push him up against the tile wall and lift him off his feet. He is taller and heavier, and I lift him off his feet. I yell into his face, "Stop picking on me, all of you! Enough is enough! No more!"

I hear students gasp in the suddenly silent cafeteria. I hear a spattering of applause. The gym teacher breaks us apart, pulls me aside. He's seen me teased and bullied in the locker room. He tells me, "You did nothing wrong here, son. Hell, you just became a man!"

What? I'm not getting detention, getting suspended or even expelled? Seems he and other teachers have been waiting and hoping for me to stand up for myself. I broke the school rules, yet this adult man is praising me for being violent. He says, "Atta boy!"

From that day on, fellow students treat me better, even with grudging respect. I can eat lunch in peace with the other nerds. I can ride my bicycle home without attacks. I visit my grandmother from love not fear.

Despite improvements in my daily life, I am beating up on myself for resorting to physical force. My conscience bothers me.

When push came to shove, I acted no better than a bully. I betrayed the principles of King and Gandhi. I did not honor my moral commitment to nonviolence. I betrayed myself. Gaining even a moment of peace at school may be too high a price if the triumph torments my soul.

In the name of brave manhood, I acted like a "real man," and I hate myself for it. Now I'm in real trouble.

The Failure of Monarchy

The ultimate form of alpha male rule is a government under a king or tyrant. How prevalent is royalty? My research identifies 42 monarchies on earth today, 31 bound by democratic constitutions, like the United Kingdom and Japan, and 41 of the monarchs are enthroned by hereditary succession. "We cannot conceive a more ridiculous figure of government," Paine wrote, "than hereditary succession."

Paine blamed "the pride of kings" for "throwing mankind [sic] into confusion." He cited Scriptures as proof. "The quiet and rural lives of the first patriarchs hath a happy something in them, which vanishes away when we come to the history of Jewish royalty." Huh? Jewish royalty? For Christians, Paine retold the old Bible story to make his point.

After escaping slavery in Egypt, the Hebrew tribes conquered the Promised Land. They established assemblies and judges ruled by the Law of Moses. They gave up their basic republic to became a kingdom, which divided, and then was conquered. Choosing a monarchy caused their fall, said Paine, which shows God dislikes government by kings.

Same as ancient Jews discarded a republic for a king, we risk doing so again in our modern republics, at least in mine. Understanding their choice then may help us make better choices now. "History is philosophy teaching by examples," said Thomas Jefferson.

As a frame for Paine's views, let me distill what scriptures and experts say happened before and after the ancient Israelites chose a king from the line of Abraham, Isaac and Jacob. From history and myth, we may garner insights for our world today and tomorrow.

Abraham's Promise Land

About 2000 BCE or 4,000 years ago, a Chaldean nomad, Abram from Ur (Iraq), freed his Bronze Age mind from polytheism and saw one God in all. *Monotheism* was a radical revelation.

Like ancestor Noah, Abram could hear God, who promised his seed would rule the lands from the Euphrates to the Nile rivers (Genesis 15:18), the "Fertile Crescent." Renamed Abraham, he settled in Hebron (southern

Israel). To satisfy his vision of empire, his loving but barren wife and half-sister, Sarah, gave him her slave, Hagar, who bore Ishmael as Abraham's heir. Sarah raised the boy as her own.

Ten years after, post-menopausal Sarah conceived and bore Isaac. Such a miracle! Another decade later, Sarah ordered Abraham to cast out Hagar and Ishmael, so Isaac alone would be heir to the land promised by God. Abraham agreed, but only after God promised his firstborn would sire a nation, too (Genesis 21:8-21). Did El Shaddai promise the same land to both sons? Has Western civilization been at war ever since in a family feud over which half-brother inherits papa's estate?

To mend the rift, Isaac's first son, Esau, married, Ishmael's daughter, Mahalath. But son Jacob (coaxed by grandma Sarah) tricked elder brother Esau into selling his firstborn's birthright to the land promised by God. Ishmael's heirs felt twice cheated out of Abraham's legacy.

Jacob wrestled with an angel and got renamed "Israel." One of his 12 sons, Joseph, was sold by his brothers into slavery in Egypt. Joseph rose to power. His clan joined him on the Nile. The 12 sons multiplied into 12 tribes. Joseph died. Slavery ensued. God spoke to Moses, who led at least 600,000 Israelites out of bondage in Egypt (Exodus 12:37).

The liberated Israelite tribes had no clue how to handle freedom. At Mount Sinai, they formed a Covenant with God, a sacred social contract. They agreed to obey the Ten Commandments and the Law of Moses (Leviticus) in trade for the empire God promised to Abraham.

The Republic and The Kingdom

After two generations or 40 years of wandering in the wilderness, say scriptures, the Israelites invaded Canaan, displacing the Ishmaelites, Philistines and others. Securing conquest by 1200 BC, the Hebraic tribes elected sanhedrin assemblies and judges to apply Mosaic law. The ancient Israelites created the world's first republic.

Israel was the only land in the region ruled by laws, not a king. Insecure tribal elders asked Gideon and his sons to be kings (Judges 8:22). Gideon rebuked them, for God alone rules Israel through the Law.

Around 1050 BCE, Israel's elders begged judge and prophet Samuel to anoint a king. Samuel said the Law rules. But God said to find a king, "for they have rejected me from being king over them." (1 Samuel 8:7)

Samuel staged a rigged lottery. The lot fell to tall and handsome Saul. King Saul's dark moods and darker deeds caused the prophet to anoint a replacement — David. The boy who'd slain Goliath is now a young man, a psalm singer who soothes the king.

David won the throne in a civil war. Descended from Abraham, Isaac and Jacob, King David's anointed bloodline became revered as holy. David sired King Solomon, who built a great mystical temple.

Solomon died in 931 BCE. His sons' turf war for throne inheritance divided the kingdom into Israel in the north (ten tribes) and Judah in the south (two tribes). Each nation had its own generational kings.

Exile and Salvation

Assyria (Syria) invaded Israel in 722 BCE and exiled its tribes north, where they were "lost." Assyria in 609 BCE was conquered by Nebuchadrezzar. His Babylonian-Chaldean empire (from the Euphrates to the Nile) occupied Judah in 604 BCE. To end all the revolts, the empire destroyed the Temple in 586 BCE and exiled the Judeans to Babylon (Iraq).

In Babylon, the Jews absorbed Zoroastrian prophesies of a savior descended from Zoroaster (Zarathustra) who will defeat evil in a cosmic final battle. This faith got conflated with faith in the Abrahamic bloodline. The Zoroastrian-based messianic beliefs adopted in Babylon are as alien to natural Judaism as having a king.

Persia (Iran) conquered Babylon (Iraq) in 539 BCE. About 40,000 Judeans return to Philistia (Palestine). After 70 years of exile, Jews rebuilt the Temple in Jerusalem. Palestinians were displaced.

Across the Mediterranean, in 509 BCE, Rome established a republic. (Julius Caesar would make it a dictatorship.) In 508, Athens instituted an aristocratic democracy, initiating their Golden Age. Two centuries later, Aristotle's student, Alexander the Great, in 333 BCE defeated Persia. The Greeks and their surrogates occupied Palestine.

After Alexander died in 323 BCE, Hellenic Syrians tried forcing Jews to worship Greek gods. The Maccabean revolt in 167 BCE, aided by Rome, restored the Judean kingdom, but not the old republic.

By 63 BCE, Judea was a subject province of Rome. The Babylonian-influenced books (like Ezekiel, Second Isaiah, Daniel) moved Jews to pray for a warrior king messiah from the line of David.

Jesus had Davidian lineage from Mary and Joseph, says Matthew and Luke, but few Jews accepted as their messiah this peaceful cousin of fiery John the Baptist, who also had doubts (Matthew 11:3, Luke 7:19).

Rome ended unruly Judean nationalism in 70 CE (Common Era, or A.D.) by destroying the Second Temple. Isaac's heirs dispersed. Ishmael's heirs reclaimed the Promised Land they'd always felt was theirs.

Worship of Jesus took root in Asia Minor and spread into Europe. Constantine in 311 made suppressed Christianity the state religion.

Christianity later battled with Islam, founded in the 7th century by Muhammad ibn Abdullah, said to be descended from Ishmael. When The Prophet died in 632, Islam spit over how to fill his throne. Persian Shiites wanted hereditary succession. Arabic Sunnis wanted an election. Their feud still shapes the Middle East and world affairs.

When the Moslem Ottoman empire fell in World War I, the British ruled Palestine by mandate. After the Holocaust, facilitated by the United Nations, Israel was reborn in 1948 as a social democracy, ending the Jews' Diaspora. The UN also partitioned a state for Palestinians, who refused it, denying Israel's right to exist again. Many wars later, despite peace activists on all sides, the ancient family feud has burst into flames again. I hear calls for a "two-state solution." Will both be democratic? Any state religion, warned Paine, is a theocracy, not a democracy

God's Judgment Against Kings

Summing up, the urge for alpha male rule inspired Abraham to sire sons and nations, led Israelites to give up a republic for a king, led to their split into rival kingdoms, led to Israel being lost, led to Judeans' exile in Babylon exile and Jews seeking a messiah, led to Christians exalting Jesus, led to Muslims fighting Christians and Jews and each other.

All three Abrahamic faiths venerate alpha males, kings by any name. Yet Paine wrote, "The will of the Almighty, as declared by Gideon and the prophet Samuel, expressly disapproves of government by kings.... 'Tis a form of government which the word of God bears testimony against, and blood will attend it."

Paine argued that "Jewish royalty" failed and perished (or plotzed) because God's way is democracy, not monarchy. Therefore, we ignore God's Will — natural law — by tolerating kings in any guise.

Male Rule Blocks Global Sense

Generations of humans have believed strong men own the right to rule society. Alpha male rule is the primary obstacle, as primal as racism, blocking us from creating a world that makes global sense. Monarchy, like all forms of despotism, Paine reasoned, is a form of government that history bears testimony against. The blood of the slain attests it.

To further invalidate the idea of monarchy, Paine in *Common Sense* sought the origins of all royal bloodlines.

> It could have been no difficult thing in the early and solitary ages of the world, while the chief employment of men was that of attending flocks and herds, for a banditti of ruffians to overrun a country and lay it under contributions [extorting plunder]. Their power being thus established, the chief of the band contrived to lose the name of Robber in that of Monarch; and hence the origin of Monarchy and Kings.
>
> ...What at first was plunder assumed the softer name of revenue.

Does being the roughest of ruffians give any man a right to rule over us? Not under natural law. In reality, the kings and masters of our world seize what they want and wield power over us only because we openly or tacitly consent to them governing us.

We give away our personal sovereignty, our agency, by letting men rule us and put their sons on the seats of power. We let them claim their thrones and reign supreme over us. We let lineal inbred monarchs believe their dynasties are fit to rule. Why enable such silliness? Why let absurdity govern in every generation and in nearly every land?

"All hereditary government is in its nature tyranny," Paine wrote. "To inherit a government is to inherit the people, as if they were flocks and herds." Are we sheep, property, herded anywhere our masters desire? Besides, how can one of any ancestry claim a divine right to rule over all? More absurdity. We each are pure light, so we all are equals.

Cautioned Abigail Adams, "All men would be tyrants if they could." I contend that men battle to be tyrants because men have been taught by society to do so. We let bullies govern us because we have been taught by society to do so. We let alpha-male competition produce abuses of power like poverty, wars, military coups, and ecological catastrophes because we have been taught by society to do so.

Devotion to male dominance filters out full appreciation of feminine energy. We deny our oneness with sacred Mother Earth. We deny our soul responsibility for individual self rule and earth stewardship. We replace inner knowing of what is right and true with unthinking loyalty to alpha leaders who feign those heroic kingly traits we adore.

An ancient myth across cultures teaches us that regal men on golden thrones should always rule us. Notice all the popular novels and movies that glorify kings and royalty. The only question has been whether alpha males (or anyone with alpha male traits) shall take power by force of arms or force of personality. Both choices presume we need a king.

I contend that patriarchy by any name has failed us.

〰〰

If I am correct that alpha male rule is a societal cancer endangering humanity and our planet, why do we keep desiring alpha rulers? Why do we keep trusting despots and bullies despite all the muted alarms in the back of our minds screaming at us to run for our lives?

For answers, we next explore the shadow self to look closer at our habit of wanting kings to rule us. We address a central question:

Why do we idolize our leaders?

CHAPTER 9

Authority Addiction

1971: **DENVER** — *I sit alone in Cheesman Park on a July evening. Hundreds of people surround me on the lawn in front of the Greek Pavilion. We're here to watch a production of the musical,* Guys and Dolls.

A young woman and young man approach me. Turtle-tucking her head with a sweet, wincing smile, she asks, "May we, may we talk with you for a moment?" Jesus Freaks, I guess. My college philosophy classes had whet my appetite for chatting with all sorts of devotees. A real spiritual experience has changed their lives. I want what they're having.

I gesture for this pair to sit. What they say surprises and entices me. They live in a commune called the Unified Family. They follow the teachings of a Korean master who's unified eastern and western thought into a new philosophy that can usher humanity into a new age of world peace.

I'm still unsettled and disillusioned by the senseless violence at the May Day protest months before. I'm seeking a way to combine peaceful spirituality and social change. Could this be that way?

I enjoy the energy of these two. I like their friends, who show up before the show starts to sit nearby. They carry a loving glow inviting confidence. My heart and mind tells me these are good people on an unusual path that may be worth exploring. I'm open-minded.

The musical ends. The woman invites me to "The Center" for dinner sometime. I give her the phone number of my parents' house. I'm living in my old basement bedroom again after returning from my odyssey. Already the old family pressures are driving me crazy.

A few days later, my mother tells me that a young woman called, "and she sounded really excited about something."

I call her back and go to the center for dinner and a free introductory lecture. I can agree with their ideas about "give and take," the yin and yang aspects of God uniting to create new life, like a diamond with God on top. I return to the center for the next lecture in the series. I enjoy good food and deep conversations about the nature and purpose of life.

Over the next months, I receive instructions in "The Divine Principles." Starting with Eastern ideas I already accept, lessons shift to focus on the Fall of Man and reinterpreting God's purpose through Jewish and Christian history, culminating in our present tribulations.

They say that God created Adam and Eve to be the perfect parents of humanity under Him. But jealous archangel Lucifer fell by seducing Eve, who seduced Adam in the Original Sin, putting Satan on top instead of God. To reverse the Fall, God sent Jesus (a perfect human) as the Second Adam to marry a Second Eve, become King of Israel, and ride the Roman Empire as a horse to save the world. When John the Baptist did not accept Jesus as the messiah, neither did the Jews, so Jesus took the path of the cross to marry the feminine Holy Spirit. Christians are reborn spiritually, they explain, but not yet physically. God promises to send a Third Adam, the Second Coming of Christ, a perfect man who marries a perfect wife. They become the True Parents who redeem humanity from Satan through rebirth into one unified world family of harmony and peace.

In the last lesson, they proclaim Christ is here on earth, born in Asia, and he will use the United States to save the world. Obviously, they mean their Korean master, but I must say this truth for myself. I quip, "Is it Mickey Mouse?" They frown. So, I say the name, "Sun Myung Moon." They rejoice. Later, I'm warned my flippancy may be from Satan.

I lack training in critical thinking, which I gain years later. I miss how their logic builds on false premises, so their conclusion must be false. Their ideas sound strangely plausible, even reasonable. Their idealism, spirituality and loving ways strongly appeal to me. I feel called by Spirit. Unconsciously, I choose heart over head and suspend disbelief.

External Validation

A quest for external validation drove my childhood and youth. I told myself a glory story about being my own man, following my star, destined to be a great writer someday. Behind the bravado, I was exploiting natural gifts to obtain approval from others.

When we compulsively deny our true selves to seek validation from some external authority, especially anyone who abuses power, that cluster of behaviors is what I call *authority addiction.*

An extreme form of codependency, authority addiction tends to be unconscious, masked by split perceptions. Compelled by unmet needs for love and security, authority addicts (in various social roles) habitually form self-denying relationships with external power. Loyalty to leaders is common, so is devotion to ideas, like a religion or ideology.

Granted, we all act from habit every day, like how we walk and talk. Here I'm focusing on *authoritarian habits* that govern our choices in life, the habits behind the worst tyrannies in human history.

I'm discussing the personal, cultural, societal, and political shadow forces in our minds, hearts, bodies, and souls. A compulsive addiction to "alpha male rule, or alpha dominance in all genders, is a habit we pass along to every new generation.

Thomas Paine in *Common Sense* said we tend to "promiscuously worship" kings and other masters. We do not care if a king is good or bad, so long as he's a king (or kingly). We need a king to feel safe, like an addict needs drugs, so any king is better than no king at all.

By relying on kings and other masters, we exhibit what psychologists and sociologists call an "external locus of control."

We split our perceptions to avoid seeing how much dependance on external authority injures ourselves, our loved ones and our communities, indeed our whole planet. Split perceptions enable addictions.

Physiologically, authority addiction taps into survival mechanisms encoded in our neurobiology. Genetic traits and intense life experiences stimulate the hypothalamus, for instance, releasing peptides forming emotional links in our neural nets, like adrenal cortisol responses to stress and fear. When life evokes a neurochemical signature similar to a known signal, the brain connects them, merging inputs into a coherent pattern (mindmap), so we feel safer. Survival is the goal of the game.

As I understand the encoding process, repetition and reinforcement of protective stimuli embeds neural survival mechanism deeply into our hindbrains and amygdala. There reside our inborn and learned survival instincts. When an event triggers neurochemical danger signals, we react from habit without conscious thought. Engrained mechanisms take over. We may feel irrational panic, for example, upon whiffing a scent tied to a trauma, like a fragrant person who.... Such neural programming can be disabling, as in PTSD. We may like to say that our heads or our hearts or souls rule our lives, well, so does our biochemistry.

Dr. Fred Von Stief in California identified eight neurotransmitters involved in addiction. These include acetylcholine, dopamine, glutamate, noradrenaline, and serotonin. He found the neurochemistry may become unbalanced by substance abuse or by trauma, which brings on addiction. More research is required, yet such findings are evocative for insights on healthy self-governance, like how we process our feelings.

When neurochemically driven impulsive emotions, often rooted in past pain, compel our behavior now, when we cannot control our habitual reactions, this survival mechanism is an addiction. As with generational alcoholism, our addiction to external validation may be physiologically hard-wired into our neural survival networks.

Cults and despots manipulate our neurochemistry to induce our addiction to their authority. In youth, given my child abuse and religious school indoctrination in Jewish victimhood, my neural receptors were receptive to a cult. Cults prey on us when we deny personal sovereignty, when we depend on external validation to satisfy our insecurity.

As much as I took youthful pride in my mask of independence, rather than honor my own sacred inner light (internal locus of control), I sought someone else to tell me what is right and true. I did not feel loved by my father, who felt unsafe to me, so I found a surrogate father-figure. Feeling unlovable, I joined a cult to feel loved. A sincere spiritual seeker enmeshed in authority addiction, I lost my way.

〽

On Labor Day weekend, I join the center on a camping retreat at Echo Lake. On Mt. Evans (Mt. Blue Sky) at sunrise, clouds fill the valleys below. The world is new. I am born again. I do not know my conversion experience is universal across cultures. I tell myself that if their teachings weren't true, could I feel God's presence so clearly? My illogic eludes me.

In September 1971, I move into the Unified Family center, a three-story red brick Victorian mansion on Capitol Hill in Denver. My dad throws a fit when I pack some of his books to take with me. My mother is glad I've quit smoking everything, cut my hair, enrolled in college, and found a flower delivery job. I'm just happy to get out of their house.

A dozen of us live in the center. We all have outside jobs to pay center bills. We brothers sleep dorm-style on the third floor. Sisters sleep on the second floor. Sex is sin outside marriages arranged by the True Parents in mass weddings. We are one unified family of love, genuinely working hard together on personal growth and spiritual awakening.

Apart from my job and schoolwork, I settle into the house routine of prayer, cooking, cleaning, study, and prayer. Our "unison prayer" of fervent voices resounds like thunder. I vow to help God save the world from Satan. I love God. (I love the group's love for me, actually.)

In earnest faithfulness, I practice the presence of God. I'm passionately praying daily for God to speak to me. After months, I hear a voice outside and within saying, "You have no control." The words baffle me.

Generational Addiction to Authority

Focus on the family going back to mythic Eden. However we define human origins, we may agree our sense-making mindmaps reflect both heredity and environment, both nature and nurture.

Evidence and reason persuade me that the habits of compulsive external validation are the habits that produce kings and dictators. Our habits trace to instinct and our early lives. Habits pass from one generation to the next and the next. Addictive engrams in time become inborn traits. Our families, cultures and societies pass along ancient habits.

As children, we may absorb the social meme that we are unfit to rule ourselves responsibly. (Richard Dawkins coined "memes" as a cultural counterpart of genes.) Generations of parents train children to believe they are too stupid, inept or sinful to be trusted with freedom. This meme says we need a king or messiah to save us from ourselves. We suffer from hero worship. Unsafe in an unfree world, we distrust self rule.

Beyond memes and genes, Caroline Myss says, humans consent to "sacred contracts" based on the "archetypal habits" we learn from parents and peers, who learned from their parents and peers.

The Family Constellations work of Bert Hellinger contends we carry bioenergetic "entanglements" from ancestors. These affect all our bodies, what we magnetically attract into our lives. Rupert Sheldrake suggests core memories from ancestors generate "morphic energy fields" affecting us and our descendants. If a woman suffers a miscarriage, the next seven generations inherit her sense of loss. Is this possible?

Such theories get dismissed as unprovable "pseudoscience." Where's the proof using Scientific Method to earn acceptance? I agree, and I spot a mindtrap. Established scientists distrust devices detecting etheric fields. Until the tech is accepted, spiritual energy stays unverified.

I cannot prove authority addiction moves generation to generation. Nevertheless, as Galileo reputedly said, it does move. He was branded a heretic for saying the earth orbits the sun, contrary to Church doctrine. Likewise, I challenge a generational mindset preset that treats as fact the myth we need a king to be safe. Authoritarian shadow forces in ourselves and in society enable despotism in our world.

Addiction to male rule is scalable from families to nations. Alpha males (or any gender with alpha male traits) may hide their insecurities by forming cults around themselves. "Cult" is the linguistic root of culture. Cults can grow into sects, religions, and ideologies ruling empires.

Cults attract people feeling safest in communities of true believers. We fear or hate those outside our tribes. Tribalism triggers turf wars for security and power. We wage war over which hero will be our holy king. We use shadow mindtricks to avoid ruling ourselves.

〜〜

The Rev. Sun Myung Moon in 1972 returns to the United States from Korea. At the Unified Family headquarters in Washington, DC, he declares the end of separate groups begun by his three U.S. missionaries. All are now one group under a new name: The Unification Church. In Denver, we read the photocopied "Master Speaks" transcripts, sent by mail from HQ.

We learn the family must grow to fulfill our mission of world salvation. We are told our lives will change. Father will send waves of American-born missionaries to pioneer centers in all 50 states. To support the centers, he will dispatch touring buses with members from the USA, Europe, Japan, and Korea. We promise God to help win the war against Satan.

Like my brothers and sisters across the country, I must devote myself to witnessing and fundraising. I must quit my job and drop out of school. I'm in far too deep by then, mentally and emotionally, to question orders. Doubt opens the mind to Satan. Stay pure for God. (In retrospect, I relate to how veterans describe faithful obedience in military life.)

My devotion in Denver earns a place on the One World Crusade, the bus teams visiting new state centers. I'm flown to New York City and housed in a shared room at the New Yorker Hotel. (The Church later will buy and renovate the art deco edifice as its headquarters.) Hundreds of us gather in the ballroom for our assignments. No more hippie communes.

I'm assigned to the central U.S. bus team, touring 16 cities in 16 weeks, Detroit to New Orleans. In every city, we hold a noontime public rally in a downtown plaza. Our trumpet player blows the opening solo of Copeland's "Fanfare for The Common Man." I hear Gabriel rattling Jericho.

We go witnessing in pairs, seeking young people sitting alone in parks and campuses. We invite them to the local center for a free dinner and short lecture. When guests arrive, we practice "love bombing." After guests leave, sisters and brothers crawl into sleeping bags in separate rooms.

Our touring bus breaks down in New Orleans at Christmas time. A replacement bus arrives for the team to continue the tour. I'm told to stay behind and oversee bus repairs, and then I'll rejoin the team. Meanwhile, I'll live in the New Orleans center.

Bus repairs take two months since parts must be shipped. When not calling the garage for reports, I go witnessing and fundraising with center members. We canvass colleges and parks across the city. We go fundraising in the French Quarter at night. I hear Basin Street jazz and blues and want to dance. I can't stop bopping a bit.

To resist temptation, the Church teaches, I must pay indemnity to Satan. I use my stability in the New Orleans center for a ten-day water fast with cold showers. Near the end, miraculously, I feel so much vitality that I jump up on a kitchen counter to get a soup pot atop a cabinet. I happily help cook meals I do not eat. Blessed by peace and grace, I thrive on being in joyful service. I'm so glad God is using me to love everyone!

By the time the bus is repaired, the team has finished its 16-city tour. So, I rejoin them at headquarters in Washington. Maybe it's the high energy I'm radiating, or whatever the reason, I'm chosen to restart the failed center in West Virginia, a Christian stronghold.

I stand in a long row of brothers and sisters facing Father to get our assignments. He hand-selects each missionary. When he stands in front of me, he reaches forward to pinch my suit jacket sleeve at the wrist and tug me toward him. In curt English, Master says, "You go there."

My mission in West Virginia is clear. I must recruit new members, raise funds to support the center, win allies in churches and government, and then "take over the state for God."

I ride a Greyhound bus into Appalachia. I first look at Morgantown, drawn by the personal rapid transit system there. Instead, I choose the larger city of Huntington for starting a new center.

I rent a two-story house with the church seed money and plunge into fundraising. I knock on doors for donations, offering church-made scented candles in snifters. In a tenement, an angry woman opens her door a crack, points a pistol at me and shouts, "You don't belong here!"

When I go out witnessing, I imagine myself a fisher of men, like Jesus' disciples. I get nibbles and bites, but five months pass without landing any new members. My faith is tested, and so is Church patience.

I'm transferred to Kentucky, where another seven months pass without me recruiting anyone. What's in my way? Is it Satan, or is it me?

I'm assigned to the new center in Lexington. When out witnessing, I'm blessed to befriend a young born-again Christian woman who speaks of Christ in her daily life. In the weeks I try to recruit her, I realize she honestly practices unconditional love, just as I want to do. She has no need for what I'm selling. Is my path really the only true path?

I'm transferred to the Louisville center. I feel restless and rebellious. The center director declares Satan is in me, and I'm wounding the suffering heart of God. Take a cold shower. Repent. Stop questioning orders.

One night I get so upset that I stomp out of the center and sleep under a tree in the nearby park. I return in the morning, sheepish and compliant. I'm soon reassigned to a "mobile fundraising team." The new assignment is presented as a special distinction. I interpret it as demotion.

Social Roles of Authority Addicts

From childhood onward, we make sense of our lives and the world in ways that help us survive. We adopt public social roles for safety and love. Among the many useful role-model systems, Transactional Analysis identifies three power roles: *Persecutor, Rescuer and Victim.* They form a "drama triangle." Persecutors and rescuers need victims. Victims need persecutors, so they can be rescued. I attest all three roles are traps.

Since being in a cult, to fathom my behaviors, I've identified four power roles common among authority addicts:

Leader — We feel safe only by being the authority in control. We cannot show any weakness. We depend on being both feared and adored. We dislike being alone with ourselves too long.

Follower — We feel safe only by responsibly obeying authority. We fear thinking deeply for ourselves. We feel unworthy to be our own boss. We feel most secure in communities of fellow followers.

Rebel — We feel safe only by fighting authority. Resentful and often vengeful outrage rules our impulses. We react hot. We seek attention, yet we mistake attention for love. We dread apathy.

Hermit — We feel safe only by being alone. We avoid authority. We shun being a leader, follower or rebel. We isolate ourselves, often in shame. To feel safe, we want to be ignored. We wish to be invisible.

Each social role is natural and vital in any healthy personality and healthy society. A problem arises when we're driven to perform any given role all the time, everywhere, like always having to be a leader or a rebel, no matter the costs to others or ourselves. Roles can conflate, like hermit and follower impulses in online gaming. When we cannot stop ourselves form enacting a habitual power role, we are authority addicts.

Authority addicts occupy other social roles, yet I spotted these four roles by living them. I've been a cult follower, journalist rebel, community leader, and pandemic hermit. I've learned the hard way about how we authority addicts hide from our true selves. We may perform many social roles during the course of our lives. Our social roles evolve as we evolve, yet we tend to stay within our range — at least I do, or I have.

For clarity, imagine a workplace staff meeting of authority addicts. Note the thoughts (l-r) of the Follower, Leader, Rebel and Hermit.

The mobile fundraising team (MFT) travels in two vans pulling two camping trailers for separately sleeping 6 brothers and 6 sisters. Our mission is funding the work of the Second Coming of Christ. We go city to city, selling flowers at street corners and in parking lots. I average $200 a day. In the northern states, we're getting youth off drugs. In the Midwest and South, we're Christian missionaries. Both statements are true, and both are lies. We practice "heavenly deception." God's ends justify any means.

In December 1973, we drive to Washington, DC, and join a thousand members for a "spontaneous" live demonstration at the televised lighting of the National Christmas Tree. We rehearse at an armory. That night, when Nixon throws the switch, on cue we jump up cheering and rush toward him, chanting, "God Loves the President!" We wave red, white and blue pennants reading, "Forgive, Love and Unite." The press calls it unprecedented.

A string of busses carries us to Lafayette Park, across Pennsylvania Avenue from the White House. We sing carols and wait, sing and wait. At last, a phalanx of men in black suits crosses the street, halting all the traffic. In their midst walks President Richard M. Nixon.

Our church president gives Nixon a giant Christmas card and a giant candle that "will burn for the rest of your term in office." The two men talk softly for a moment. Nixon turns, waves a "V" with his best campaign smile. Secret Service men escort him safely back across the street.

All MFTs work extra hard raising money to buy full-page ads in The New York Times, The Washington Post and other major newspapers. The ads proclaim the "National Prayer and Fast for the Watergate Crisis," and they urge Americans to "Forgive, Love and Unite."

In February, Rev. Moon meets President Nixon in the White House. We're told Father advised the president to hold firm, and then they prayed together. Soon afterwards, the media blitz stops. No explanations.

Hoping to upgrade my assignment. I try to recruit uncle Moses Lasky. He asks me, "Do you believe only because you want to believe?" The seed of doubt he plants sprouts weeds of wariness. I start secretly taking time when fundraising to read newspapers on Watergate. I'd marched against Nixon three years earlier. Now I ask, what am I doing here? I feel trapped.

In June 1974, my eyeglasses break just before the MFT leaves Chicago. I'll stay overnight in the center and rejoin the team by bus once my glasses are repaired. Next morning, I go to the Loop to with center members. I'm expected to sell flowers, pick up my glasses, and board a Trailways bus.

Instead, I pick up my glasses, give away the flowers, and board a Red Line train northbound to Rogers Park. I plan to sleep by the lake that night. Steel wheels on steel rails beneath the city carry me to freedom.

The Recovery Paradox

In the traditional Tarot deck is a card called, "The Devil." A horned figure on a throne holds chains looped loosely around the necks of a man and woman. They could easily lift off the chains, but they stand in mute bondage. They cannot conceive of freedom.

"Man [sic] is born free, and everywhere he is in chains." said Jean-Jacques Rousseau, "One man thinks himself the master of others, but remains more of a slave than they are." To paraphrase, we are born free, but everywhere we are enslaved in chains of our own choosing. We are not free unless we know we have a choice, and we can act on it.

Are you bound by authority addiction? Ask yourself: Am I compelled to have power, serve power, fight power, or avoid power? Am I loyal beyond facts and reason? Do grievances drive my reactions? Do I avoid vulnerability? If caught in an error, do I play the victim to get saved from myself? Has my life become unmanageable?

Recovery in Twelve Step work rests in surrendering to "the God of our understanding." Admitting I am powerless to prevent impulses rooted in past pain, I discover inside the strength for responding to my old urges in a new way. I make a decision to turn my life around.

I savor the paradox. Spiritual surrender gives me more self-control. When my behavior or another's action touches a nerve or an unmet need, I'm more resilient, less easily triggered. Intuition, conscience, reason, and heart guide me better than survival instincts. I find serenity in wholeness, and my life makes global sense to me. My behavior is more sensible, more grounded in objective reality, so I'm more genuine in daily life.

〰

1974: CHICAGO — *From The Reader I find odd jobs and a roommate vacancy in a brownstone at Halsted and Newport. I do sales at Downtown Records on Rush Street. I do house cleaning for a Near North maid service. I ghostwrite a book for a Michigan Avenue psychiatrist. I eat egg foo yung at Chester's. I drink beer at The Town Hall Pub and dance at The Road House. I flirt freely in the after-hours clubs and seldom go home alone.*

One autumn day in the Loop public library, I'm reading the Tribune *when I overhear familiar words. Across the table, behind the reading lamp shade, the Chicago center director is witnessing to a young man. Lifting the newspaper in front of my face, I mumble an epithet, stand and turn in one motion, walk away without looking back. Narrow escape.*

That winter, I'm on the train when I get hailed by a Scottish brother I'd known in Kentucky. He greets me warmly, like I'm still in the Family.

Our talk somehow turns to Nixon. He'd resigned last August. Too bad Nixon ignored Father, he laments. What? Roundabout questions elicit that when Moon met Nixon in the White House, unlike what I'd heard, Moon urged Nixon to go on TV, confess all and beg for forgiveness. Moon pledged to wage a media blitz convincing America to forgive the repentant president and unite behind him. Nixon declined. "Too bad," says my friend.

Yeah, too bad. I say farewell to my brogue brother and get off the train. I'm thinking, that plan might have saved Nixon from Watergate resignation. It could have ended the "Koreagate" Congressional investigation into bribing U.S. public officials (akin to Church influence in the Japanese government exposed by the 2022 assassination of their prime minister).

During the year I lived in Chicago, as part of reclaiming myself, I read three books that forever change how I make sense of my life.

The True Believer *by Eric Hoffer helps me realize how I'd been seduced into the cult, and why I chose to believe. The longshoreman philosopher told the truths behind Fascism, Nazism, Stalinism and all cults.*

The Book (On the Taboo Against Knowing Who You Are) *by Alan Watts helps me accept my precious uniqueness in our universe. Validation from Spirit, I recognize, is found within, not in savior gurus.*

Zen and the Art of Motorcycle Maintenance *by Robert Persig clarifies my ethics and reframes my values system. His story of a breakdown and breakthrough helps me heal my soul and restore my wholeness.*

When I finish reading Zen, I'm sitting in the front bay window of the Chicago brownstone. I close the book and sit for hours in silence.

Authority Addiction Blocks Global Sense

Across our cultures, we've let authority addiction and alpha male rule (split perceptions) govern societies for generations. Nepotism runs amok. Devotion to external power blinds us to our inner global power.

Addictions are cunning, baffling and powerful. We may be enslaved by the lack of a plan for managing our addictive urges as easily as we may be enslaved by submitting to urges directly. Follower and rebel authority addicts both, for instance, may join anti-government groups.

Recovery from addiction to alpha rule, chiefly male rule, hastens an end to tyrannies in our governments, communities, workplaces, homes, and our own minds. By declaring personal sovereignty, we choose to live free of loyalty to any lord or master. Aware life is one, we practice mindful self rule in ourselves and personal democracy in the world, or I do. We seek moral self-mastery, as the Enlightenment writers like Paine advised. Our world may never be free of tyrants and kings so long as we depend on leaders for our national, tribal and personal security.

I see my choices always affect myself, my family, our societies, and our planet. I see us evolving a natural global sensibility that helps us heal our authority addictions. The journey of recovery may take the rest of our lives, my life. We may stumble often, as I do. We go on. There are as many paths up lifework mountain as those willing to ascend.

A crucial shift in me was discovering I can feel one with the universe *and* retain my individuality. I can love me as I am, be at peace with myself and the world. I can stop trying to control life for safety. When liberation from my inner tyrant makes sense to me, I feel free.

〰

In the next chapter, I explore how alpha authority addiction shapes our abusive wealth and power habits. Our habits are putting at risk our lives, our cultures, our societies, and the whole earth.

CHAPTER 10

Money and Power

1975: LOS ANGELES — *Out of work in Chicago, I accept an offer from a high school friend for a job and a room in his house near Venice Beach. Packing my typewriter, using savings for airfare, I move to LA.*

I arrive to discover my friend's job never existed. I look for other jobs. Without a car, hard luck. My "friend" kicks me out of his house.

I'm homeless. I sleep on the beach and in crash pads. I get jobs that don't last. I manage a bookstore in Marina Del Rey and a gypsy consignment store in Ocean Park. I cook in a vegetarian diner on the Venice Boardwalk.

I'm reading George Orwell's Down and Out in Paris and London. *I'm down and out in Chicago and Los Angeles. Unlike in the Windy City, here I'm involuntarily celibate. A man without money sleeps alone in LA.*

Living on the street forces me to live in reality. Inspired by Persig's book on motorcycle maintenance, I enroll in the federal "CETA" jobs program at the Venice Skills Center. I earn a stipend for learning automotive mechanics. I buy a used 1964 Valiant and rebuild the slant-six engine.

Mechanic's training anchors me into practicality. When something in a car is broken, it stays broken until I do logical troubleshooting, testing to find what's wrong and fix it. Rational machinery grounds me. In my reality, if something is broken, I need to find what's wrong and fix it.

I live with classmates. After graduation, when I cannot find an honest mechanic's job, then any job, they kick me out. Bang. Homeless again I am. Looks like my life needs a major tune-up.

Inherited Wealth

Consenting to monarchy is bad enough, Paine said, but we make life worse for ourselves by consenting to hereditary succession.

Inherited power in any government or business dynasty exists with our consent. We let some man declare himself a king or tycoon, and pass along entitlement to his sons (lately daughters and bi).

"When we are planning for posterity," Paine wrote, "we ought to remember that virtue is not hereditary." He argued against hereditary succession by saying it cannot ensure only good people govern. Rather, inherited power mostly yields incompetence.

"One of the strongest natural proofs of the folly of hereditary right in kings," Paine wrote, "is that nature disapproves it, otherwise she would not so frequently turn it into ridicule by giving mankind an ass for a lion." He refers to a rampant regal lion.

When children are raised to believe they are born to rule and others are born to obey, he said, once they inherit the seat of power, they're "frequently the most ignorant and unfit" to govern of any in the land.

In lands with hereditary monarchies, Paine stated, royal subjects will say privately they view royalty with contempt. "The Royals" flaunt their wealth, spawn scandals, return nothing of value. Paine saw monarchy as a social evil to be abolished. "The nearer any government approaches to a republic, the less business there is for a king."

The myth of alpha male rule tells us powerful men must pass power to their sons. The practice is harmful in itself. When a man's inherited power is believed to be a divine right, all hell breaks loose. Witness the bloody wars across history to win the game of holy thrones.

Traditional alpha male rule and authority addiction, I submit, cause and enable the abuses of wealth and power that now endanger democracy and our earthly survival. We can create a better tradition.

For evolving global consciousness, I invite us to question the ancient political and economic pillars holding up our modern world order. Such a shift in our shared worldview can transform the real world. Such a shift in our thinking is long overdue.

If male domination of society violates natural law, if government by a hereditary ruler violates natural law, then unearned inheritance of great wealth and power violates natural law. So does abusing wealth and power without regard for others' rights and feelings.

Inherited wealth has long bestowed a right to rule society. Until the rise of corporations, family dynasties held the property and power. A few families in England and America drove the early Industrial Revolution. An aristocracy of 200 families (*les deux cents familles*) has ruled France since *l'Ancien Régime*. Germany has the Junkers. Japan has the Samurai. All nations have hereditary elites and nepotism.

In high society, *le haute monde*, distinctions between "old money" and "new money" persist in the ruling class with private jets. The Cynical Golden Rule prevails — the one with the gold rules. Entitlement breeds arrogance and contempt, spawning corruption and injustice.

A Native American proverb tells us we do not inherit the earth from our ancestors; we borrow it from our children. Such wisdom does not guide our modern world order. We have confused the inheritance of high moral values with inheritance of high property values.

Martin Adams in *Land: A New Paradigm* asserts the "natural wealth" of land belongs to us all, so only human-made property improvements, like buildings, should be privately owned. Ending "fee simple" land titles would reform economic systems from the ground up, literally.

An outlandish idea? It's not new. "You forget that the fruits belong to all and that the land belongs to no one," wrote Rousseau. Paine agreed. In *Agrarian Justice,* he proposed estate taxes for funding pensions and a universal basic income — a surprise to capitalists lauding Paine.

Socialists say inherited wealth results in "oligarchy and plutocracy," the concentration of wealth and power. So each generation starts fresh, they propose high inheritance and estate taxes to redistribute wealth fairly across society. This presumes there's enough abundance for all.

At the other end of the spectrum, some libertarians would ban great hereditary wealth. They reason new generations should learn self-reliance and personal responsibility, not grow up as spoiled rich kids. As a veracity barometer, research the fates of estates left by uber-rich libertarians.

How do you personally feel about inherited wealth?

Does being born with money we did not earn make us any better than those born with less or nothing? Does having less or no money make us any worse than those with more? Does having less make us morally better than those with more? Does our value come from what we own and owe, or from who we are inside? Do we feel worthy of wealth?

"Our incomes are like our shoes," wrote John Locke; "if too small, they gall and pinch us; but if too large, they cause us to stumble and trip." Is his insight keener than a Marxist analysis of "economic determinism"? Mary Wollstonecraft wrote, "The tyranny of wealth is still more galling and debasing than that of rank."

Many of the wealthy among us are mind-locked into the *status quo*. Those born into mansions too often make the term "trust-fund baby" mean "wasted human potential." Conspicuous consumption is the drug-of-choice for external validation among the rich and famous.

Giving me hope, I believe injustices of class and caste will fade and end as global thinking becomes common. When? Up to us.

I see signs of meaningful change. Not all wealthy people are addicted to materialism, possessed by their possessions. Many affluent people consciously refuse to be mere cogs in the mercantile machine.

Growing numbers of us on earth with new or inherited wealth treat money as a form of energy. Green and ethical investments offer evidence people do value the globally sensible idea of using prosperity for posterity. From billionaires to paupers, good people with global minds shine by making positive contributions as best they can.

〰〰

1976: DENVER — *Using up most of my cash, I fly home.*

A happy homecoming. Mom cries at seeing me for the first time in five years. Dad is warm and welcoming. No recriminations.

I settle back into my former basement bedroom. I begin writing a book about my life in the Moonies. I'm writing to make sense of their beliefs and my own choices. I develop the theory of authority addiction.

I propose my book to publishers. Their rejection slips, if not form letters, regret that they already have enough cult books since Jonestown. The market is glutted. I'm too late. The manuscript goes in a drawer.

My parents have been generous while I wrote and pitched the book. That done, they say, it's time for me to get a job and my own place.

The husband of my mother's best friend is a counselor in the Arapahoe County employment office. He slates a job interview at a weekly newspaper, The Aurora Sun. My resume is "thin," to be polite, yet the publisher-editor offers me two audition assignments. Amazing opportunity.

I procrastinate. I say to myself that I want to write novels, not news. Could I earn a living in journalism and still do creative writing on the side? My high school sweetheart, a friend for life, chides me for my fear of failure. "You will never know what you can do unless you try."

So, I mimic the style and story structure in The New York Times and The Denver Post. The editor says my work reads like I've been writing news for years. I'm hired as a cub reporter. Lois Martin's old-school newsroom training ensures I become a skilled professional journalist.

For the next decade, I work freelance or staff as a reporter or editor at most of the newspapers and magazines in metro Denver. By catching government officials in lies, I develop a reputation as a feisty, rebellious reporter. I get the story behind the story. I turn arrogant. I wear the mask of a minor local celebrity. I'm called, "that writer about town." I don't get rich, but I do get laid. I'm using fame and sex for external validation.

Behind my bravado, I'm aspiring to be real.

The Real Adam Smith

In modern capitalist nations, big corporations own the "means of production" more often than dynastic families. Corporations have gained the legal status of persons, but they enjoy more rights than individuals. Corporations may buy or sell companies at will, deciding the fate of employees and their families. Corporations tend to treat employees like medieval feudal lords treated their serfs, like private chattel property. Utilitarian transactional values saturate modern capitalism.

Corporate lobbyists and campaign contributions influence laws and policies. Business corruption of the government is nothing new. Jefferson complained about "the aristocracy of our monied corporations which dare already to challenge our government to a trial by strength, and bid defiance to the laws of our country."

Are all republics so ruled by private capital that these governments no longer can be called "democracies?" Given subversions of our elected officials in our governments, can they still be called "republics?" In fact, can today's economic system still be called "capitalist?" A more apt term is corporate feudalism, approaching fascism in places.

Capitalism today is *not* what Adam Smith had in mind.

Progressives paint the conceiver of capitalism as a villain. His 18th century views are unduly classed with the amoral 16th century views of Machiavelli. Conservatives, in contrast, may worship Smith as a demigod, too often invoking his holy name without clarity on what the man himself envisioned or espoused (much as with Paine). Neither view is true.

Consider what Smith actually wrote:

> Most government is by the rich for the rich. Government comprises a large part of the organized injustice in any society, ancient or modern. Civil government, insofar as it is instituted for the security of property, is in reality instituted for the defence of the rich against the poor, and for the defence of those who have property against those who have none.

Smith also wrote:

> The disposition to admire, and almost to worship, the rich and the powerful, and to despise, or, at least, to neglect persons of poor and mean condition is the great and most universal cause of the corruption of our moral sentiments.

Surprised? May I introduce you to the real Adam Smith?

Moral philosopher and economist Adam Smith was born and raised in Fife, Scotland, near the Firth of Forth. He was a leading influencer and writer in the Scottish Enlightenment movement.

Adam Smith published *The Theory of Moral Sentiments* in 1759. He said morality is an act of imagination. Put yourself in the shoes of another, and then act as they would act. Smith defined morality by the sentiments of empathy or "sympathy," which creates a moral society.

Two decades later in 1776, about three months after Thomas Paine published *Common Sense,* Adam Smith published the first volume in *The Wealth of Nations.* Paine's writing turned politics on its head while Smith's writings turned economics on its head. Their impact was like a one-two punch. Our world is still reeling from the combination.

Since the 1500s, European *mercantilism* had defined national wealth as the gold in state treasuries. Nations earned gold by manufacturing and exporting merchandise, taxing imports, selling off the natural resources of colonies. Mercantilism drove the European plunder of the Americas, Africa and Asia. Christian salvation legitimized conquests.

Adam Smith ended mercantilism by proposing *capitalism.*

He redefined national wealth as the total value of all the goods and services people consume. Simply, capitalism is consumerism. In modern capitalist nations, consumer spending comprises about two-thirds of all the economic activity (GNP) supporting society.

In the utopia that Smith called *laissez faire* (French for "allow to do"), the "invisible hand" of enlightened self-interest in the open marketplace — ruled by moral sentiments — helps all to prosper. He famously wrote, "Every man [*sic*], as long as he does not violate the laws of justice, is left perfectly free to pursue his own interest his own way." Observe that Smith places morality and justice before the freedom to make a profit. His moral values are not valued in capitalism as practiced today.

Smith's vision of sympathy in business and government reflected realism. "No society can surely be flourishing and happy, of which the far greater part of the members are poor and miserable."

He envisioned abundance distributed in society through many small businesses, like local shops selling goods from local farms and factories. He saw monopolies as enemies of free enterprise, trade associations as conspiracies to raise prices. He said, "A criminal is a person with predatory instincts who has not sufficient capital to form a corporation."

Adam Smith favored small government with fair laws and fair taxes. Fraudulent, unfair market practices warrant government regulation. Any person, company or government lacking sympathy in their policies and conduct, Smith argued, violates natural moral laws.

Smith mapped out specific changes he wanted to see in society. For instance, he proposed ending all hereditary occupations, so a son would not be forced to do the same job as his father. If the father is a barber, the son is free to be an artist. (I bet today he'd say it of any gender.)

Smith conceived a functional "division of labor" in early factories that led to mass production on highly efficient assembly lines. Sadly, as a consequence, artisan craft got lost among the spare parts.

Adam Smith underrated the value of human labor. His low valuation of labor was misconstrued to rationalize workers being underpaid and overworked in unhealthy, unsafe working conditions.

A century later, Karl Marx and Friedrich Engels saw capitalist abuses, and they proposed the "labor theory of value" for socialist economies. Marx, unfortunately, underrated the value of profit and private property in producing a higher standard of living.

Both economic visionaries missed the mark on labor, in my opinion. Smith got it right on the freedom to prosper fairly and morally. Marx got it right about social equality. Absent in both is connecting marketplace value with intrinsic self-worth from doing work one loves.

Smith would decry the "techno-capitalism" now being malpracticed in his name, as with unregulated artificial intelligence. AI innovations, while useful, allure humans into letting machines think and decide for us. AI risks mental tyranny, undermining the mindful self rule necessary for democracy to work. At the dawn of the Industrial Age, Smith predicted, "The robot is going to lose. Not by much. But when the final score is tallied, flesh and blood is going to beat the damn monster."

What about libertarianism? Ethical self-reliance libertarians accept moral responsibility for their private and public choices. Amoral libertine libertarians with utilitarian values want liberty without accountability; if caught, lie about lying. Smith would disapprove.

As I said, too few of us know the real Adam Smith.

Adam Smith in the 21st century has become a distorted icon bereft of his actual thinking and ethical morality. How did his pragmatic ideas and humanist ideals go so far astray?

Most utopian writers map out a vision for an ideal world before they offer a compass to navigate life's actual terrain. Smith, however, published his moral compass first. Only decades later did he publish a map for his utopian world of enlightened capitalism.

We have misread Adam Smith's economic map because we have forgotten his moral compass. This is how we lost our way.

Conscious Commerce

What if we go beyond the battle between capitalism and socialism? Why stay stuck in economic dualism? More options exist.

A 2020 Harris/The Hill survey of likely U.S. voters found 60 percent favored capitalism while about 40 percent favored socialism. Bloomberg in 2020 found 43 percent identified as socialists and 38 percent identified as capitalists. How do the remaining people see themselves?

Britain's Institute of Economic Affairs (IEA) in 2021 said about half of Millennials and Zoomers correctly define socialism and capitalism, and a quarter mistake the definitions of one for the other. A fifth identify as capitalists, and another fifth identify as socialists.

Younger people tend to be progressive, thinking beyond the duality of capitalism vs. socialism. Many seek new solutions for income disparity. The nonprofit and for-profit *social entrepreneurs* profiled yearly in Forbes "30 Under 30" offer evidence of young global thinking.

As a fiscal indicator, green and ethical ventures with ESG and DEI principles in 2020 drew US $35 trillion in investments, says the Global Sustainable Investment Alliance dipping to $30 trillion by 2023 from the Covid fiscal crises, but climate change drives renewed growth.

A related trend is more than one billion people identified as globally conscious consumers with lifestyles of health and sustainability. We are the ones who value clean ethics and transparency. We read product labels. We consider how products are produced. Our purchases vote our values. We use our marketplace power for the global good.

"It's no longer a question *if* consumers care about social impact," said Amy Fenton, chief commercial officer at Marketcast. "Consumers do care and show they do through their actions." Gives me hope.

When we know in our minds and hearts and guts that we all are one, any thought of harming others or the earth for raw profit looks too absurd to contemplate. Pillage and plunder does not make global or moral sense to us, not anymore. We seek a better way.

"Civility costs nothing and buys everything," said Mary Whortley Montagu. So, why not foster a sensible economic theory and system that transcends dualistic models of capitalism or socialism?

Conscious commerce helps strengthen the global sense movement. Any business can prosper by mindfully respecting society and the earth. Remember, commerce is older than capitalism or socialism.

Current economic systems and political systems reinforce alpha male rule, historically enabling concentrated wealth and power. The present national debt system mainly benefits big lenders, not the public New models are emerging. Modern Monetary Theory offers debt-free funding of public benefit projects, such as infrastructure.

Society and government are separate things, as Paine pointed out. Likewise, economic and political systems are separate, yet intertwined. Socialism is an economic system promoting equality. Communism is a political system using socialism. Democratic socialism, social democracy, joins liberty and equality, as in Europe. Capitalism and democracy are the American Dream. Capitalism funding autocracy yields fascism. Socialism and capitalism can fund either a democracy or a dictatorship.

For clarity and satire, I update the old "Parable of the Isms."

Socialism — You have two milk cows. The State takes one cow and gives it to your neighbor, so you both have milk.

Democratic Socialism: —You have two cows. The State takes one cow and gives it to your neighbor, but only after a public vote.

Communism — You have two cows. The State takes both cows and gives you spoiled milk.

Fascism— You have two cows. The State takes both cows by force and sells you overpriced milk from a corrupt monopoly.

Nazism — You have two cows. The State takes both cows, slaughters you and gives the milk to the army.

Trumpism — You have two cows. The state buys both cows at a high price, sells the milk at a profit, and then never pays you.

Capitalism — You have two cows. You sell one and buy a bull.

Conscious Commerce: — You have two cows. You sell one and buy a bull, raise a healthy herd, sell organic milk to your member-owned coop dairy, mitigate the methane, and recycle the cow patties.

〰

1982: DENVER — *People are calling me for free advice on writing and publishing. I decide to monetize my know-how and contacts.*

Hippies have become yuppies passing out business cards at networking events in New York. To cash in on a hot trend, I start the Professional Writers Network as "a self-directed referral service" linking writers with each other and those who hire them. I hope to gain national visibility and credibility for the books I'm developing in my sparse spare time.

I host crowded monthly networking parties in Denver and publish a quarterly newsletter. I perform referrals by hand with letters and postcards (pre-internet). Two years in, I'm overwhelmed by administrative paperwork. I can't afford to hire help. Turns out the best writers already have their own networks and don't need me to get work. My venture only attracts newbie writers wanting to be rescued. I'm feeling drained.

I put so much time into the writers' network that I lose freelancing gigs. Dwindling earnings from the network can't cover all of my bills. I'm falling deeper into debt. Mom sometimes gives me money to help make ends meet. In December 1984, on the verge of bankruptcy, I pull the plug.

I feel so humiliated by public failure that I move to the mountain town of Evergreen and hide like a hermit. After a few years of fiscal recovery with local jobs, I gain clarity on my path as a writer.

I had imagined the network would help change my career from writing news to writing books. I saw the venture as a means to an end. I did not go after the end goal directly — writing that great book awaiting inside me, and making the book worth publishing.

I then realize that I do not know enough to write the book in my heart. I move back to Denver and return to school. I enter a self-directed program to earn a double BA in journalism and communication in 1988. In graduate school I research logic, rhetoric, public and organizational communication. To pay the bills, I write resumés for a national company.

Meanwhile, I am involved with John Denver's Windstar Foundation. As the press room aide for five years at his annual summer symposiums in Aspen, I meet leading global thinkers from around the world. They expand how I make sense of life. I adopt futurist views and values.

Graduate school focuses on research for a new book, Self-Rule. *Ideas in the cult book on authority addiction and autonomy inform my writings on "democratic consciousness." A New York literary agent in 1994 pitches the book widely. Too outside the box, sorry. It goes in a drawer.*

In a career reboot, I start writing for media trade magazines. I'm among a handful of journalists who pioneer industry reporting about interactive television and the "Internet." I work for top U.S. and European publishers. I'm known for writings on media social effects and the power of interactivity itself. I call for "deep media literacy" in speeches on four continents.

A big-ego fish in a small pond, I wear English double-breasted suits. My brilliant career ends abruptly in the 2009 financial crash

During that period of world travel, I begin formulating my ideas about "global sense." I foresee a shift in cultural, social and spiritual consciousness that transforms life on earth. I feel it transforming me.

Our Inner Gold

We've let a small ruling class clique control global wealth and power. The middle class shrinks while the rich get richer and the poor get poorer. Our grievances from economic disparity are justified, in my eyes, but we let despots divert our fear into blind faith they will save us.

In a nutshell, the ancient legacies of alpha male rule and authority addiction incite the abuses of wealth and power that today cause injustice, endanger democracy and threaten all life on earth. Authoritarian thinking and predatory economics are blocking global enlightenment.

The pursuit of happiness through external validation has become assault with a deadly thought form. Ruthless selfish competition among combative alpha men is ripping apart our societies and rendering our planet inhospitable. Our misguided male war for the survival of the fittest is making our world unfit for living.

Powerful men with sons believe they have a divine right to rule the world. Men fixate on inherited worldly power, but we men rarely inherit from our fathers an awareness of how to feel all our feelings. If we adopt a global mindset, boys instead can inherit sacred masculinity.

By natural law and natural rights, we each deserve to inherit a rich emotional life, a spiritual life or secular life, so we live true to ourselves in open societies. We can inherit self-worth, not the fool's gold of external validation. The ManKind Project calls this our "inner gold."

Eric Butterworth in *Spiritual Economics* says there is not a spot where God is not. He suggests we can release scarcity and create abundance by opening our inner faucet to Spirit's flow. A freethinker may call it Nature, yet a sense of unity can flow in rich and poor alike. Social entrepreneurs, for instance, model creating abundance to benefit society.

I believe we can evolve beyond selfish utilitarian or transactional values. We can adopt norms, laws and traditions recognizing all unique life has equal rights on earth. We can honor the law of reciprocity, karma, the fact we reap what we sow. We can value empathy and outgrow the "law of the jungle." We can do it. Do no harm and be free.

Ascension, for me, means remaining in a body and living mindfully, being sensitive to light energies and the ripples from my choices. I'm slow, yet as more of us ascend, higher consciousness may someday embed into the genes and memes of humanity, says Bruce Lipton. As humans evolve natural mindfulness, enlightenment will enter our DNA.

If global sense guides us to become humane beings, humanity may ascend into a new species. Alberto Villoldo and Leslie Temple-Thurston independently call it *homo luminus*. David Hawkins calls it *homo spiritus*. Barbara Marx Hubbard coined *homo universalis*. If enlightened evolution is our goal, how do we get there from here?

〜

This midpoint of the book is a good place for an overview of where we've been and where we're going. Recall that I'm emulating the four-part structure of *Common Sense.*

Part I explained sense-making, told how we split our minds to avoid seeing our oneness, and described the global sense movement.

Part II exposed ancient alpha male rule and authority addition as the human habits endangering our freedom and survival.

Part III, next, will assess the state of world affairs, so we realistically understand current conditions and the perils we all face.

Part IV will explore our innate ability to create global enlightenment, both in ourselves and in society, so we build our world anew.

Now you have a useful roadmap for the second half of the book.

PART III

The State of
World Affairs

Reason obeys itself; and
Ignorance submits to whatever is dictated to it.

THOMAS PAINE

CHAPTER 11

The Hazards of Autocracy

2001: ISTANBUL, TURKEY — *The city shimmers under springtime sun. I'm on a packed ferry crossing the Bosporus strait from the Asian continent to the European continent. I'd arrived by train after presenting a paper on media literacy at the International Communication Symposium in Ishkashir. Once on the pier, for a few American dollars, I board a tour bus visiting the remnants of Byzantium and Constantinople.*

What calls to me most is Hagia Sophia. The "Church of Holy Wisdom" was built in the 6th century by Emperor Justinian. The square basilica with soaring dome was the largest cathedral in the world for a thousand years. It survived the European Crusaders sacking and razing Eastern Orthodox Constantinople in 1204. It survived when Islamic Ottoman Turks conquered Constantinople in 1453, renaming it Istanbul. Mehmed II converted the church to a mosque, building tall minarets at each corner. In 1935, Ataturk's secular Republic of Turkey converted it into a museum.

Inside the main entrance is the marble outer narthex, a long corridor once reserved for unbaptized Christians. The inner narthex boasts tall doors for the imperial entrance. I'm drawn to the north porch.

I find a ramp up to the nave. The narrow tunnel with a low ceiling has endless blind switchbacks. Window slits offer poor light. Ascending amid a procession of visitors, I feel boxed in. I sense trudging ghosts from centuries of Christians and Muslims in this confining rampway. Their energies linger in the walls. I bless all who came before me and come after me. After ages in the tunnel, turning a corner, I step out under the dome.

An engineering wonder, the massive scale makes me feel insignificant. That's the intent. Justinian wanted worshipers here to feel powerless before almighty God and His mighty Eastern Roman Empire. Inheriting the throne of Constantine, Justinian enshrined a monument to himself and his empire. I marvel at the majestic building. I'm surprised to detect its ghosts, a rarity for me. I'd hoped to sense ineffable numinous spirit. Instead, I mainly sense the vanity of an emperor, a phantom echo under the dome.

Perils of Addiction to Male Rule

Anyplace a leader rules and the people do not, the result is autocracy. Our ancient addiction to alpha male rulers let bullies govern. The habit degrades the spirit of men and all of us. Few things may solve global crises as fast as gender equality undoing male dominance.

I have heard people say, likely without thinking, that they dread men liberating themselves from patriarchy. They fear it would produce chaos. Rarely are reactive and fearful thoughts correct. There are more reasons to dread the security of dependence on alpha rulers than the insecurity of independence or interdependence in a democracy

No matter how strange this truth may seem, many striking reasons exist to end our devotion to "kings" of all genders or titles.

Authority addiction and alpha male rule pose a peril today greater than most dare admit. For a sobering view of our danger, I advise reading *On Tyranny* by Timothy Snyder, plus *Tyranny of the Minority* and *How Democracies Die* by Steven Levitsky and Daniel Ziblatt. The habits of despots are ancient. Study history books. Read Thomas Paine.

In *Common Sense*, Paine argued for "independency" from King George III. Despite "Redcoats" killing colonials, ardent loyalists loved the monarchy. Paine told the perils of reconciling with the crown and forever remaining subject colonies. He proposed the first modern republic.

In most lands today, ardent loyalists love despotic leaders despite abuses. I decry the perils of reconciling to alpha rule itself and forever remaining as children. Later, I will propose direct republics.

Below are seven of the perils of reliance on alpha male rule, adapted from Paine's writings on monarchy. You may hear his voice here.

1. Appeasing Despots Will Destroy Democracy

Compliance with power addicts is an absurd fantasy and fatal fallacy. Appeasement or reconciliation with alpha abusers is a dangerous doctrine. Consider how Paine refuted the idea of reconciling with the crown:

> I make the sufferers case my own. I protest, that were I driven from house and home, my property destroyed, and my circumstances ruined, that as a man [*sic*] sensible of injuries, I could never relish the doctrine of reconciliation, or consider myself bound thereby."

For those dismissing the dangers of appeasement, he wrote:

> Hath your house been burnt? Hath your property been destroyed before your face? Are your wife and children destitute of a bed to lie on, or bread to live on? Have you lost a parent or a child by their hands, and yourself [made] the ruined and wretched survivor? If you have not, then are you not a judge of those who have. But if you have, and can still shake hands with the murderers, then you are unworthy the name of husband, father [*sic*], friend, or lover; and whatever may be your rank or title in life, you have the heart of a coward, and the spirit of a sycophant.

And if we do reconcile to any autocratic government, even if benign:

> Instead of going forward we shall go backward, or be perpetually quarreling or ridiculously petitioning. We are already greater than the king wishes us to be, and will he not hereafter endeavor to make us less? ...Reconciliation and ruin are nearly related.

I dread the event of public consent to authoritarian rule in any land. If only to ease unrest, consenting to life under a bully might keep a roof overhead and food on the table, but at what grave cost? Compliance with repression is unstable. It inevitably spawns resentment, dissent, protests, uprisings, civil wars. The consequences of rioting among us can be more destructive and deadly than the merged malice of every tyrant.

If injustice ignites unrest, a charismatic rogue may gather aggrieved, alienated people into an army and become a despot. It's happened before.

Mussolini did it. Hitler did it. Mao did it. Pol Pot did it. Trump almost did it and may try again. Our acceptance of bullying lets bullies dominate. As Paine realized, reconciliation with tyranny ends in ruin.

2. Abusive Alpha Males Will Rule Society

Unmet emotional needs compel us to elect or select abusive men as rulers. Our depend-dance with alpha leaders shapes our governments, the laws governing our lives. If we skip trauma healing, if we don't reprogram our survival mechanisms (hard work for me), the habit endures. Our faith in male authority may dominate our future, as it has our past.

If we split perceptions to deny a natural need for external validation, we reject our whole selves. We deny what Gary Zukav calls our "authentic power." Our repressed selves may act out destructively.

Spiritual warriors welcome the inner jihad for mindful self rule. Authority addiction distorts honest spiritual aspirations, as Thomas Paine noted in *Age of Reason*. In modern times, the Islamic State enlists youth with visions of a new caliphate, channeling passion and purpose into serving an underdog movement. Dictators and wannabe despots entice followers into looking outside themselves for demons to slay. Authority addiction lures us into serving atrocious bullies. It lures us into becoming the bullies committing atrocities, blaming others for our outrages.

The devil dwells in our habits. Shifting what we do on autopilot is a challenge. It is for me. Generations of male rule planted in our memes and genes the habit of kings keeping us safe. Until we choose to rule our minds and societies with global sense, tyrants will govern us.

3. Despots Will be Lousy Leaders

If a mania to "rule the world" is proof of insanity, every would-be king or savior is innately unfit for leadership.

Unlike visionary servant leaders, authority addicts crave validation as kings. They create crises to pose as heroes. It's Munchausen Syndrome by Proxy. Caretakers secretly hurt those in their care and gain esteem by rushing to the rescue. If they bungle, they blame others and foment chaos to distract us from their ineptness.

Once in office, a despot is hindered from being an effective leader. Paine said, "There is something exceedingly ridiculous in the composition of monarchy." A wise leader needs a range of information to make sound decisions, but a king is so obsessed with security that his fears isolate him. He surrounds himself with sycophants, who filter what reaches him.

Despite lacking information, the king has the power to act and alter society in situations that require the best judgment possible. Paine wrote,

> The state of a king shuts him from the world, yet the business of a king requires him to know it thoroughly; wherefore the different parts, by unnaturally opposing and destroying each other, prove the whole character [of monarchy] to be absurd and useless.

4. Laws Will be Authoritarian

In modern republics, a presidential signature enacts the laws passed by legislatures. Seldom is a veto overridden. Good measures often die in committees if a president wishes. In the USA, the legislative and executive branches are co-equals on paper. In reality, the president is a king.

Kings have always negated independence, you may reply. Common people have never made laws without royal consent. It's a telling point of right and good order, as Paine noted. Yet Kings and tyrants in all the ages reveal themselves to be hardened enemies of democracy. Paine called it "ridiculous" that King George III, inheriting the throne at age 21, "shall say to several millions of people, older and wiser than himself, 'I forbid this or that act of yours to be law.'" Paine's ridicule fits any modern martinet forbidding us from governing ourselves.

An unquenchable thirst for superiority drives power-addict leaders to control all lawmaking. Whatever form the coercion takes, despots will suffer no laws to be made that do not suit their purposes.

"Watch out for the fellow who talks about putting things in order!" warned Enlightenment encyclopedist Denis Diderot. "Putting things in order always means getting other people under your control."

We may be as effectively enslaved by the lack of laws protecting our liberty, Paine cautioned, as by submitting to laws abridging our freedom.

Leaders with haughty minds will scarcely refuse to ratify any law placing them into as strong a position of power as possible. They will not gladly suffer the passage of any law removing from them authority they abused. Powers granted in a crisis endure. After "9/11," countries widely enacted intrusive security laws. Decades later, most are still in effect.

Is any power jealous of our freedom, Paine asked, the proper power to decide the laws governing our lives?

> Whoever says No to this question is an independent, for independency means no more than whether we shall make our own laws, or whether the king;

What if public opinion in any land demands the repeal of all unjust laws. Our rulers will try stay in power even a day longer by co-opting the popular will. They will revoke their own laws at once. They will try to do by fraud in the long run what they cannot do by fear in the short run. Beware of despots enacting autocracy in the name of democracy.

5. Propaganda Manipulation Will Reign

Authoritarian regimes unduly massage the mass mind. They rely on propaganda. Facts and reason would expose their absurdities and crimes. Kings call themselves our friends, Paine wrote, but they "do not change from enemies to friends by the alteration of a name."

Despots use propaganda to win the loyalty and unity of the populace. What if we foolishly reconcile to sacrificing our free minds for security? Can anyone doubt our rulers will act to ensure we think as we're told? Can anyone doubt we soon will think opinions are facts?

In societies serving kings by any title, reason and looking within for truth are intolerable. Any chance to cultivate honest personal democracy is anathema to despots. Paine knew we are remote objects in the orbit of regal politicians. They consider our good no farther than suits their ends. Their self-interest leads them to suppress our mind, lest contrary thinking interferes with them. Be not fooled by alluring lying leaders only out for themselves. They would rule our minds and lives if we let them.

6. Alpha Male Wars Will Rage

Our world is too thickly planted with despots to stay peaceful long. Bullies need to prove might makes right. They are prone to war. Autocratic rulers are always fighting enemies, foreign and domestic. All disrespect provokes their retaliation and vengeance.

Paine said conquest is always "a temptation to enterprising ruffians." Once a king is firmly enthroned, he said,

> ...that degree of pride and insolence ever attendant on regal authority swells into a rupture with foreign powers in instances where a republican government, by being formed on more natural principles, would negotiate the mistake.

Why do wars break out? A leader's pride, envy, greed, lust, or egoist insecurity. In war, the economic security of all is waylaid. Taxes get diverted from better uses. The Costs of War project at Brown University has tracked U.S. spending for wars since 2001. It's past $8 trillion with 900,000 deaths. What could the USA do with those tax dollars? Rebuild the national transportation and communication infrastructure. Install solar or wind electricity for 8 billion households globally. Fund healthcare for 2 billion low-income children. You get the idea.

The United States spends more on its military than all other nations combined, says Jane's Information Group. Military spending comprises 54 percent of the total U.S. discretionary budget. Just six percent goes for education. Military funding comes from "deficit spending," borrowing repaid by taxes. Interest on military debt enriches lenders, but it drains money from government investments in our communities.

How can we preserve humanity from future wars? Get free of our addiction to alpha authority. Why keep consenting to turf wars over who's top dog? "Where there are no distinctions there can be no superiority," Paine said. "Perfect equality affords no temptation." Equality in any democracy lets freedom flourish. Society gets more creative, and so more prosperous. Prosperity is the best guarantor of peace. Until we let go of needing kings, we will let leaders wage their wars in our name.

7. Climate Change Will Wreak Havoc

Our compulsion to conquer nature fits the traits of alpha male rule and authority addiction. Our habits caused our global ecological crisis. If I see reality clearly, little short of freeing our minds from authoritarian thinking can preserve us from worsening climate disasters.

The earth is at risk (see the next chapter). Fears about the future are reasonable. What's irrational is letting fossil-funded alpha leaders make climate policy decision for us. Our ancient autocratic habits incline us to trust leaders to save us. It's absurd. We can save ourselves! We the people "have manifested such a spirit of good order," Paine wrote, that we have shown constitutional government works. We've amply proven our talents for problem-solving in a democracy. We need no kings.

Until we alter our habits, alpha rule endangers all life on our planet.

〰️

1997: BOGOTA — *Flying into Colombia at night totally disorients me. I'm arriving to talk at the nation's first Internet World conference and trade show. The "network of networks" only recently entered South America.*

I'm in a window seat behind the wing. On the ground far below, I see scattered lights in the darkness of the countryside. Looking up at the hazy night sky, I see scattered stars in the heavens. Earth and sky merge and flip. I feel upside down. The sensation is symbolic.

This is my very first trip outside the United States. I'm finally becoming a global citizen in fact as well as theory.

My orientation returns to normal as the plane reaches its destination. Below are the lights of Santa Fe de Bogotá, a sprawling city of 6.3 million. Landing at El Dorado International Airport, I find my name on a driver's placard. He takes me to a grand hotel in the city center.

The next morning, the conference director greets all the speakers at the Gonzalo Jiménez de Quesada Convention Center. Nestled on the lower levels of the Coffee Bank building, it's part of the International Trade Center, built in 1980. He extols his country's virtues and promise.

I think of my advance research on Colombia, called the most Spanish of South American nations. Pure Spaniards, comprising 20 percent of the population, hold minority rule over mixed mestizos, mulattos and zambos. Thirty percent are below age 15, so the internet is catching fire.

Colombia, led by Simón Bolívar, won independence from Spain in 1821. The nation has swung between liberal and conservative governments. Lots of dictators and assassinations. The current government of Ernesto Samper is accused of secret financing by the drug cartels. The CIA is blackmailing corrupt Samper, I gather, to give the U.S. a free hand in the country.

The conference director says we need not fear the Marxist guerrillas, FARC (Fuerzas Armadas Revolucionarias de Colombia) and ELN (Ejército de Liberación Nacional). Both rebel groups are funded by drug trafficking to the USA, where prohibition keeps the crime cartels in business.

Internet World Colombia poses a threat to the rebels, I figure. If the internet boosts the economy, drug lords will lose clout over public officials and the rural poor. I don't know if the insurgents miss their shot or if security is tight, but no incidents disrupt the conference.

I'm glad my auditorium talk goes well. I present practical yet idealistic thoughts on media literacy in an interactive world. The interpreter in my earpiece keeps pace with me. The audience response leaves me feeling heard. Perhaps I left a few ripples in a few minds.

That night, I'm feted with all the speakers to a feast featuring succulent Colombian beef. Sultry women on staff invite me to go dancing with them. Too exhausted, too tired to tango, I decline, regretfully.

After three days of trade show networking. I'm driven to the airport. The boulevards are packed with cars, trucks and motorbikes. I'm struck by the colonial-era buildings tinged black by soot from millions of internal combustion engines. I realize pollution control is not a priority concern in popular consciousness. What I deem vital is not so here. The worldview in Colombia is not the same as mine. It's disorienting.

In a window seat on my flight home under hazy night skies, once more I cannot tell the lights below from the lights above. Once more, earth and sky merge and flip. Upside down again I am.

Delaying Liberation Delays Evolution

In this decade and century, autocracy would set the course for society, if we let it. Paine opposed going along with any form of tyranny:

> Bring the doctrine of reconciliation to the touchstone of nature, and then tell me, whether you can hereafter love, honor, and faithfully serve the power that hath carried fire and sword into your land? If you cannot do all these, then you are only deceiving yourselves, and by your delay bringing ruin upon posterity.

What if we keep appeasing despots, whom we do not love nor honor? Our relationship with government will be forced, more wretched than ever. Despots will cling to power as long as we let them. Any deal we make with them postpones our liberation, postpones our maturation as a species. The state of the world, meanwhile, will stay unsettled. We'll live in fear, Paine warned, as "government hangs but by a thread, is every day tottering on the brink of commotion and disturbance."

A government that does not encourage people to govern themselves maturely is like a parent forever keeping children weak and reliant. Such a government lacks moral legitimacy by any enlightened standard. In no case has nature made the offspring of any species forever dependent on the parents. For us to stay forever as needy children violates natural law. Until we are ready for adulthood, we will always find excuses to remain as children needing parents or alpha leaders to save us.

To persist in believing we must forever live like children is in itself childish and ridiculous. Humanity is now ready to outgrow autocracy and mature into democracy. We need to do so. Our survival as a species hangs on evolving global minds. Now is the time for us to personally awake and act together. Celebrate individuality within unity. Changing how we make sense of the world changes the world. A change is gonna come.

CHAPTER 12

Clear and Present Dangers

2000: FIJI — *I prepaid for a two-night side trip to Fiji on my way home from speaking at the Internet World Australia conference in Sydney. I did not predict landing in the midst of a military coup.*

At Nadi International Airport on Viti Levu Island, soldiers stand guard as I clear customs and find the driver holding up a card with my name. He says that we are safe from fighting in the capitol city of Suva.

On the drive north to Saweni Beach, at each checkpoint, tense soldiers stand with forefingers straight above the triggers of assault rifles. Once they see my U.S. passport, they smile with relief and wave us through.

That evening on the beach behind the hostel, I buy fresh-caught tilapia from a skiff. I sauté the delectable fish for a potluck dinner with the hostel's only other guests, two students. Do they know why Fiji's prime minister and dozens of leaders have been taken hostage? Not a clue.

The next day I board a tour boat for a snorkeling trip to an outer island where the reef is not yet bleached white. I fall into conversation with a genial Englishman who says he works in the British consulate. He's quite willing to talk about the coup, isn't he. I'm quite willing to listen.

He says to me, "This coup, actually, is all about money, land, race, and religion." Leading the coup is a native Fijian, George Speight, the front man for nationalists who'd prospered under the previous regime. They want back in power, so they favor this coup.

I ask questions to get the story behind the story. The diplomat spins a twisted tale of corruption and betrayal.

Liberty and Security

Look around our world. The cultural force of addiction to male rule has shown no willingness to relent. All kings and wannabe kings are bent on ruling every aspect of our lives. This applies to "kings" of every gender. Bullies rule us when we let them — if we consent, if tacitly.

Consider the nations where leaders govern and the people do not. Any minority ruling the majority is a tyranny. People claiming their rights may face mortal peril. Despots stay in power by refusing to admit people have rights. You might be willing to put up with a draconian spouse, job boss or town leader. If life is comfortable, you may tolerate abuses. What if your home will be bulldozed if you protest? What if you'll be arrested without trial, tortured or killed? Will you speak truth to power?

The Shock Doctrine by Naomi Klein shows how leaders exploit crises to foist laws and policies that people would otherwise reject. After 9/11, I saw western governments shift to a fear-based "endless war" footing, as in Orwell's *Nineteen Eighty-Four*. The "USA Patriot Acts" waived Bill of Rights protections, like "sneak and peek" search warrants. I saw this going global. "Security Certificates" in Canada. "Control Orders" in Britain. "Special Intelligence Operations" in Australia. "Protection of Citizens' Security" in Spain. "Protest Law 107" in Egypt. Threats of violence, real or unreal, justify revoking our rights and liberties.

Naomi Wolf in *The End of America* spots ten steps that any nation historically takes on the road to fascism. Invoke a terrifying internal and external enemy. Build a secretive Gulag-style prison system. Develop a private paramilitary army or militia. Set up national surveillance systems. Infiltrate and harass vocal citizen groups. Arbitrarily detain and release dissidents. Target individuals in influential social positions. Control the press. Equate dissent with treason. Suspend the rule of law.

The USA took too many such steps under President George W. Bush. President Barack Obama built on the Patriot Acts; whistleblowers exposed National Security Agency (NSA) warrantless wiretaps to collect telecom activity of *all* Americans. President Donald Trump tried all ten steps, even a militia. His coup failed. We he retry in 2024?

Similar threats to liberty exist in nearly every democracy on earth. Our leaders vow their security laws are only "temporary" while we fight terrorism or insurrection. Still, can any of us name the date certain when our civil rights and liberties are ever fully restored? Face a bitter truth. Secret police powers, once obtained, however obtained, are never willingly surrendered by the police — or their bosses.

And why have we never been given a chance to vote directly on these security laws? Our leaders may sense that if we were asked, we'd decline. We would reject their autocratic, automated, misconstruing AI tracking. If asked, we'd vote "no." We'd instead vote to live free responsibly.

Western nations claim they must defend us from evil eastern nations, like Russia, Iran or China. Such regimes *do* violate human rights, yet they serve as hobgoblins for scaring us into sacrificing liberty for security. Any enemy is useful for uniting followers in fear behind the leader.

Losing all our human and civil rights is too terrible to contemplate. For example, consider the right of *habeas corpus,* which assures freedom from indefinite detention without charges. The threat is not new.

Alexander Hamilton said, "Arbitrary imprisonments have been, in all ages, the favorite and most formidable instruments of tyranny."

George Washington warned, "It will be found an unjust and unwise jealousy to deprive a man [*sic*] of his natural liberty upon the supposition he may abuse it."

Ben Franklin said, "Those who would give up essential liberty, to purchase a little temporary safety, deserve neither liberty nor safety."

Good government keeps us both safe and free. Safety need not be at the expense of freedom *if* our laws make common global sense.

〰

The diplomat on the boat explains the cunning coup in Fiji.

It began with a surprise 1999 election victory by the Indo-Fijian Labour Party. That party mainly represents immigrants from India. They came as laborers, leased farmlands and prospered. Fijian natives in power failed to realize the Indian voters outnumbered them. So, they did not bother to steal the election, he tells me. This coup a year later is their solution.

The new Indian prime minister began an anti-corruptions campaign. He ousted officials taking bribes from plantation owners, fuel refineries and tourism interests. He ended lax enforcement of tax laws and environmental regulations. For those reliant on graft, this coup is their solution.

Fijian tribes own all land by heritage. As 60-year agricultural leases to Indians expired, tribes began renewing leases at inflated rates. The prime minister began subsidizing Indian leases. He spoke of revoking tribal land ownership. For tribal chiefs and Fijians, this coup is their solution.

The diplomat leans closer to me at the boat rail.

He tells all about the coup leader. George Speight is a timber executive. He was arrested with cronies for looting economic development funds given to Fiji by Australia, New Zealand, and the International Monetary Fund. The coup happened one day before his trial.

I'm told Speight entered the Fijian capitol building with a commandos chosen by a top general, Commodore Frank Bainimarama. They captured the prime minister and 35 government leaders, mostly Indians.

The military took control of government. Instead of calling Speight a hero, the general is calling Speight a criminal and demanding his surrender. The diplomat says Speight was double-crossed.

Now I hear about the Great Council of Chiefs. Its chairman led a 1987 coup that stopped an earlier anti-corruption drive. He's demanding a return to civilian government, but only if under Fijian control.

Fiji's Christian Council is urging restrictions on Hinduism. New laws may push out enough Indians to restore native Fijians as a voting majority. The diplomat predicts Christian laws will cut away Hindu influence in Fiji. The nationalists, back in power, will rule Fiji for generations.

He finishes, looks at me, then out to sea. I ask if it will end in civil war? "Too soon to know," he says. "Enjoy the water and forget about it."

Our boat anchors in the emerald green bay of an atoll. I put on snorkeling gear. All thoughts of politics slip away as I slide into the warm South Pacific and glide under low waves. Sunlight ripples through the clear water. I have not felt this peaceful in years. I feel one with the striped fish darting amid the colorful coral. I feel one with the ocean and the earth. Floating in the eternal now, I forget the woes of the world.

Democracy at Risk

Cancer hides from the immune system to keep growing in the body. It drains strength and the will to live. The societal cancer of addiction to authority also hides from consciousness. It drains political will from the body politic. The illness requires urgent healing.

Do we fathom the nature of democracy enough to see what's at risk? As a refresher, below are fast civics on what makes any nation democratic. I'll follow with reporting on the status of democracy in the world.

The Nature of Democracy

What defines "democracy" for me? I cite The Economist Intelligence Unit (EIU) and the UK and Freedom House in the USA. The Universal Declaration of Human Rights guides my thinking.

Below is my synthesis.

Rule of Law — Democracies enforce the rule of law, not the whims of kings. Leaders obey all laws. Laws protect freedom from violence. An independent judiciary upholds due process, equality under law.

Majority Rule — No minority controls the government. A majority vote in elections decides all leaders and laws. Elected assemblies require majority votes. The voters, ideally, value policies over people.

Civil Liberties — Laws protect civil and human rights. Freedom of assembly and association. Freedom of the press, of speech and expression. Freedom of religion, and from religion. Freedom to love and marry.

Autonomy and Individuality — The right to be self-sufficient. The right to be different, one's unique self, free from reprisal.

Election Process — All citizens may vote in all elections. Voting is free, fair, secure. Transparent election systems ensure reliable ballot counts. Little or no voting fraud. Legal challenges are welcome.

Peaceful Transfer of Power — All parties accept valid voting results. Outgoing leaders assist incoming leaders. Smooth transitions.

Political Pluralism — Diverse people and groups freely engage in policy politics. They compete and cooperate. They obey rules for fair play. Anyone may run for office. Anyone my put petitions before voters.

Political Participation — Citizens engage in the political process. They attend meetings and lobby public officials. They discuss and debate public policies with fellow citizens. They vote their conscience.

Political Culture — Popular opinion favors activism and leadership, disdains docility and apathy. Society expects nonviolence.

Government Functioning — Public officials are conscientious. They work in a timely way to carry out laws faithfully and honestly.

Any government with these traits can be called a democracy.

Caveat. Many people call for "defending democracy." Compare their words, deeds and goals to the traits above. Refute gaslighting.

The Status of Democracy in the World

I'll briefly highlight two respected global reports.

Democracy Index — The annual report from the UK's Economist Intelligence Unit (EIU.com) ranks 167 nations worldwide. Going from democratic to authoritarian, EIU in 2024 ranks North America, Western Europe, Eastern Europe, Central Asia, Latin America, the Caribbean, Asia, Australasia, Middle East, North Africa, and Sub-Saharan Africa.

EIU indexes four types of governments.

• *Full Democracy* — EIU says 24 nations have Full Democracies, serving only 8 percent of humanity. The top ten in descending order are Norway, New Zealand, Iceland, Sweden, Finland, Denmark, Ireland, Switzerland, Netherlands, and Taiwan. Germany is #12. Canada is #13. Australia is #14. United Kingdom is #18. France ties Spain at #23.

• *Flawed Democracy* — EIU says 50 lands have a Flawed Democracies containing 37 percent of humanity. The first 10 in descending order are Chile, Czech Republic, Estonia, Malta, United States, Israel, Portugal, Slovenia, Botswana, and Italy. India ties Poland at #41. South Africa is #47. Philippines is #53. Colombia is #55. Thailand is #63.

• *Hybrid Government* — EIU says 34 nations have Hybrid regimes with democratic and authoritarian traits, home to 15 percent of humanity. The first ten are Bangladesh, Malawi, Peru, Zambia, Liberia, Fiji, Bhutan, Tunisia, Senegal, and Armenia. Hong Kong is #88. Mexico is #90. Ukraine is #91. Kenya is #92. Nepal is #98. Turkey is #102. Bolivia is #106.

• *Authoritarian Regimes* — EIU says 59 nations are Authoritarian, containing 39 percent of humanity. The first ten are Kyrgyz Republic, Algeria, Qatar, Lebanon, Mozambique, Kuwait, Palestine, Ethiopia, Rwanda, and Pakistan. United Arab Emirates is #125. Egypt is #127. Iraq is #128. Cuba is #135. Venezuela is #147. Russia is #144. China is #148. Saudi Arabia #150. Iran is #153. Syria is #163. North Korea is #165. And Afghanistan under the Taliban is the most authoritarian on earth.

My mathmind calculates these 74 Full and Flawed and democracies govern 45 percent of us. The 93 Hybrid and Authoritarian nations govern 55 percent — significantly more than half of us on earth.

EIU concludes, "The increasing incidence of violent conflict has badly dented the global democracy score." The overall decline was driven by reversals in every world region except Western Europe.

Freedom in the World — The annual report by U.S.-based Freedom House (Freedomhouse.org) for 2024 finds "mounting damage of flawed elections and armed conflict" in the 18th consecutive decline.

Freedom House cites "widespread problems" with election violence and distorting manipulation that deteriorate rights and freedoms. Armed authoritarian aggressions, like Russia in Ukraine and the Israel-Palestinian conflict, cut political rights and liberties. Yet there's hope. "Pluralism is under attack but remains a source of strength for all societies."

Freedom House scores 195 nations by the Universal Declaration of Human Rights. They reported 83 nations are "Free" (20 percent of us), 56 nations are "Partly Free" (42 percent), and 56 nations are "Not Free" (38 percent). In short, 80 percent of us live in lands with partial or no democracy. Last year, 21 nations improved; 52 nations declined.

• *Free* — Only Finland scores 100 percent, followed by Sweden (99 percent) and Norway (98 percent). The nations above 90 percent include Canada, Ireland, Denmark, Netherlands, Belgium, Portugal, Switzerland, Japan, Uruguay, Australia, Estonia, Chile, Iceland, Taiwan, Austria, Germany, Micronesia, United Kingdom, Italy, and Spain. Nations down to 80 percent include France, Argentina, Greece, United States, South Korea, and Poland, Nations down to 70 percent include South Africa, Israel, Brazil, and Colombia. (Do these rankings dash preconceptions?)

• *Partly Free* — Nations scoring from 69 percent down to 35 percent include Albania, Ecuador, Bolivia, Peru, Fiji, India, Hungary, Liberia, Paraguay, Nepal, Kosovo, Mexico, Philippines, Indonesia, Armenia, Sri Lanka, Zambia, Kenya, Tunisia, Ukraine, Singapore, Nigeria, Lebanon, Hong Kong, Bangladesh, Kuwait, Morocco, Thailand, Tanzania, and Pakistan.

• *Not Free* — Nations scoring 34 percent down to 0 percent include Uganda, Jordan, Turkey, Haiti, Iraq, Qatar, Oman, Cambodia, Rwanda, Ethiopia, Vietnam, Egypt, United Arab Emirates, Nicaragua, Venezuela, Laos, Russia, Cuba, Iran, China, Libya, Belarus, Saudi Arabia, Afghanistan, and Sudan. The three "worst of the worst" authoritarian nations are South Sudan and Syria with Tibet (under China) at the bottom.

"The struggle for democracy may be approaching a turning point." says Freedom House, "While authoritarians remain extremely dangerous, they are not unbeatable." Democracies are "remarkably resilient."

So, democracy is in peril worldwide, and there are reasons for hope.

The Earth at Risk

We face urgent environmental perils caused by alpha rulers needing dominance. I find the addiction to wealth and power, regardless of costs for others, threatens humanity and all life on earth. For brevity, here's my fast summary of the situation on our home planet.

Climate Change Causes

Human Activity — Human activity is the primary driver of rapid climate change. Scientists agree by overwhelming consensus. Our globe has not undergone such a drastic climate shift since 66 million years ago. A meteor hit evidently wiped out the dinosaurs, began the Cenozoic Era. We now live in the "Anthropocene Era," says Nobel laureate chemist Paul Crutzen. Around 1950, he says, we entered an age when our apex human actions affect all planetary ecosystems. What we do alters all.

Since the late 19th century, fossil-fuel interests have shaped local to global policies. The fossil industry dominates markets, leverages governments. Humanity has long gone along with the system. Now we're seeing the costs of our worldwide oil addiction. Mercy mercy me.

Overpopulation — What human activity causes the most damage? Paul Ehrlich calls it "the population bomb." World population in 1900 was 5 billion, tripling since 1500. We passed 8 billion in 2022. At current birth and death rates, we'll reach 12 billion of us by 2100. So many people eating, defecating and polluting! Is this the world we created?

Caveat. Overpopulation can slow or end through contraception and women owning their bodies. But that defies male rule, doesn't it.

Land Use — Humans directly affect 70 percent of the ice-free land surface on earth, says a UN Intergovernmental Panel on Climate Change 2019 report, *Climate Change and Land.* It tells how gases and particles exchange between the land and air. Agriculture, forestry or related land uses yield 23 percent of the greenhouse gases. Transportation accounts for 20 percent of all the CO_2 emissions, and three-fourths of that is from vehicle road traffic. It's been a hard day on the planet.

Our land use often has adverse climate impacts. Loss of biodiversity, says the UN report, harms human health and livelihoods. It causes "food insecurity." The levels of risk vary across regions, even where a risk is not expected. What will be the effects of climate change by 2100? It hangs on "how population, consumption, production, technological development, and land management patterns evolve." In short, it's up to us.

Climate Change Consequences

Here's my summary of the likely climate changes ahead

Atmosphere — Gases and particles entering the air once took about 40 years to affect the climate, finds atmospheric researchers. The weather in the 2020s reflects what went into the air in the 1980s. Pollution in the 2020s will show up in the climate by the 2060s. Ocean warming shortens atmospheric lagtimes. So does land use. The pace is accelerating.

Climate disasters today will increase tomorrow. Expect hyperstorms and floods. Expect droughts and wildfires. Expect desertification around the equator. Deforestation in 100 years may wipe away the rainforests, the planetary lungs replacing carbon dioxide (CO_2) with oxygen. Climate scientists atop Mt. Mauna Loa annually report record CO_2 levels. These match when warm Pliocene seas were 80 feet higher than now.

Oceans — Global warming is melting polar icecaps and glaciers. The speed is faster than scientists expected. Rising sea levels already flood coastal areas worldwide. Water is heavy. More water in the oceans means more weight on the ocean floors. Warm water is heavier than cold water. I expect tectonic plate adjustments. This may explain increased volcanic eruptions and earthquakes along the Pacific "Ring of Fire."

Out at sea is the Northern Pacific Gyre. This huge dead zone of tiny particles, mainly plastic, is as big as a continent. More dead gyres spread in the South Pacific, North Atlantic, South Atlantic, and Indian Ocean. Gyres ruin fisheries. Gyres alter ocean currents and air currents.

Worse awaits. If oceans keep heating, scientists predict the Atlantic's circulating current may collapse in decades. Ocean currents control global climate. Any ocean current shutdown threatens all life on earth.

Mass Migrations — Overpopulation drives competition for living space and resources. Vandana Shiva predicts food and water wars. When a natural habitat is lost, all creatures great and small migrate for survival. Same for humans who lose their habitats, such as from flooding or a war. Pew Research in 2020 reported 86 million migrants in Europe, 85 million in Asia. There are 11 million "unauthorized" migrants in the USA in 2024, says the Migration Policy Institute. If billions of us flee our homes, bigotry toward immigrants in Europe and the USA is a sad predictor.

Overpopulation may compel our migration into the solar system. What happens when the Earth colonies rebel and declare independence? If we carry our wars to the stars, will the galaxy welcome us?

Mass Extinctions — Global losses of habitat are accelerating. One million animal, insect and plant species may perish in the "sixth mass extinction," says a UN report by scientists from 132 nations. They assert habitat loss is disrupting the foundations of our world order.

We humans risk extinction, too, and from several sources. A warmer climate lets our bodies host more microbes. Pandemics far more virulent than Covid may kill billions and collapse civilizations. If tyrants take over, will extermination camps return? Scarier, if resource wars go nuclear or biological, will the apocalyptic survivors envy the dead? Self-destruction is a clear signal of split perceptions and authority addiction.

The Point of No Return?

Where's the "point of no return" for climate change? Scientists widely agree it's when earth's average temperature rises 1.5-2.0° Celsius or 2-4° Fahrenheit above late 1800s pre-industrial levels. Warmer is "irreversible." NOAA says 2023 was the warmest year on record. "It was 2.43°F (1.35°C) above the pre-industrial average." Are we already too late?

The European Geosciences Union published a 2018 study on the timing. Researchers built a state-space stochastic computer model of the global climate from 2015 though 2100. The model predicted we'll reach the point of no return by 2035. Recent computer models predict sooner. Aiming for "net-zero carbon emissions" by 2050 is absurd.

The 2020s and 2030s may be our last chance to slow or reverse global climate change. Nations have begun shifting from fossil fuels to renewable energy. But go-slow voices hold sway in global climate talks. Those vested in the *status quo* sidetrack urgent efforts to change policies keeping them secure. Why do we humans idly accept such selfish folly?

Each delay in evolving a global sensibility brings us all closer to that point of irreversible ecological change. Unless we act fast, the planet may no longer support life as we've know it. Mutating microbes may survive, and probably the cockroach, but will human beings?

Reasons for Hope

We reap what we sow. Our consent to overpopulate the planet and rely on fossil fuels, in effect, enabled (codependently) today's disruptions in our lives from humanity pushing the earth out of balance.

Green lifestyles are necessary, says Al Gore, like recycling or electric vehicles, but individual changes are not sufficient. He advises organizing for collective peaceful actions on a planetary scale. I agree.

We co-create ourselves and our world through our thoughts, feelings, words and deeds. We created the mess we're in. We can fix it. More than a billion of us already have a global sense of life, a global mindset. We are finally organizing ourselves as a movement to build a free and safe future for ourselves and our children. Our abilities give me hope.

Each year that passes without us slamming on the brakes is another year we speed closer to the cliff. Whenever you're reading this book, what's the average global temperature? What are you doing that helps?

Hitting Bottom

Hoping leaders will save us will not save us. Afraid and confused, we've lost our way. We've ignored our unity in a universe of light. We've ignored how our connectivity gives us power in a democracy.

Please consider all the ways we suffer and may always suffer until we release our old addiction to abusive male authority. Everything right and proper pleads for us to reject authoritarian thinking. As Paine would say, the blood of the slain and the weeping heart of nature cry aloud for us to awaken into awareness of our global oneness.

I could never stop exposing all the perils from authority addiction and male rule. I find no lasting benefit from it. How many must die before we recover from dependance upon alpha dominance? How hard must we hit bottom before we make a decision to turn our lives around?

In voicing outrage and worry, I do not intend to provoke revenge or despair. I'm giving reasons for actions to shift ourselves and our traditions. Procrastination is profitless. Now is the time to be mindful.

〰

And now I'm done delving into the causes of our urgent global crises. If I had my druthers, I'd rather simply promote high ideals and stop there, but our warrior's journey through shadow was necessary. Now we emerge from the long dark night of the soul into the bright light of hope.

Fear is why we condemn. Hope is why we welcome.

CHAPTER 13

Finding Our Courage

1998: MUMBAI, INDIA — *My hotel driver and guide is frustrated with me. We stand at the Gateway to India in what the British called Bombay. The 25-meter arch, built by the colonial government in the Raj, celebrates the 1911 visit to India by King George V and Queen Mary. This monument to imperialism does not interest me. My guide points out vendors near the arch. I decline his offer. I'm ready to go.*

We return to his battered Tata automobile. He proposes taking me to a bazaar and then a brothel. No, I want to visit a Ganesha temple on this feast day. I want to tour the Bombay home of Mahatma Gandhi. I want to watch a sunset over the Arabian Sea. My driver gets no kickbacks if I spend no money on his clients, so he is frustrated with me.

Trying to figure out the odd American, he asks questions in Hindi-accented English. He learns I'd spoken in Delhi that week at India's first Internet World conference and expo. I tell my guide India is on the verge of a business boom built on software design and computer support call centers. India could become a global economic power in the 21st century. The most populous democracy on earth, India can rival their undemocratic neighbor, China. He is skeptical. What I say does not fit his reality.

Car horns always beeping, we crawl through dense traffic to reach Shri Siddhivinayak, an 1801 temple for Ganesha, the elephant-headed remover of obstacles and patron of new beginnings. On average days, my guide says, the temple draws about 25,000 visitors. More than 100,000 worshipers are expected on this feast day. The crowd is overwhelming.

Inside the temple, we go from station to station. I'd brought chocolate candy as my offering. I give it to a priest at the three-door entry to the sanctum housing an ornate Ganesha. The priest gives back a Prasad offering to set before either of two silver statues of mice, believed to carry prayers to Ganesha. Like my guide, I put a hand over one mouse ear and whisper in the other ear. Like St. Francis, I pray to be a channel for peace.

Earlier, before entering the temple, against my guide's advice, I'd given a piece of chocolate to a young girl. As we exit, she meets me at the curb with a noisy gang of children — all with their hands out.

My driver shoots a reproachful look at me, plows through the mob and opens the car door for me. He gets behind the steering wheel, starts the motor. Horn honking, the car creeps through the screaming children beating on the windows. I feel torn apart inside. Was my gift to that child wrong?

Enough is Enough

I've long seen the advent of real democracy and world peace as an evolutionary breakthrough for humanity that sooner or later must occur. The event need not be far off.

Many of us now admit our authority addiction (even if by another name). We reject the folly of war and empire. As crisis follows crisis, we choose to survive crisis fatigue. We stop hiding from fear with society's traditional "drug of choice." The opiate of the masses (media aside) is the blind worship of leaders who prey on our insecurities and anger to rule our hearts and minds. We easily get swept up in the fervor.

How can our leaders dare to declare we are free and then revoke our freedoms on the grounds they do not trust us to behave responsibly? Do our leaders know us? Do they know if we've evolved a global sense of our unity in life, so violence is unthinkable? No, they do not know us, yet they presume to decide for us. Their faith lay in cynicism. They presume we are guilty of original sin, collective guilt or flat stupidity.

Despots feel entitled to violate our rights as fits their fancy. They do not ask our permission first. They betray us when they rule in our name but without our consent. A government that fails to keep us both safe and free has lost moral legitimacy.

Paine asked, to whom does any government belong? Reason told him, tyranny and democracy have different owners. Tyranny belongs to the tyrant alone. Democracy belongs to us all.

A free and democratic government of our own is our natural right, but authority addiction deters us from democracy. If we release the habits of trusting alpha male rule, if instead we practice mindful self rule in our daily lives, then we can govern ourselves sanely with global sense.

We hear proud praise of liberty and democracy, but can you name any government without a *de facto* king? Governments revolve around a central figure, regardless of title, like president or prime minister. If that leader is female or nonbinary, doesn't that person use alpha-male tactics to wield power? Why give in to the old impulse to trust any shining hero anointed as a savior king? That way tyranny lay.

For us to enjoy individual and world enlightenment, let us combine personal growth and social change. If we fail to unite these two activities, we may negate centuries of toil and sacrifice to win our freedom.

Our liberty and survival is at risk. If we do not act with global sense now, our ancestors and descendants may rightly condemn our failure. When do we trust our souls and say enough is enough? When do I?

〰

We weave through south Mumbai traffic and turn down a side street to Mani Bhavan, *the private residence of Mohandas K. Gandhi from 1917 to 1934. The house is now a museum and global heritage resource.*

As my guide watches impatiently, I slowly move through every room. I see Gandhi's belongings, his books, his desk, the pallet where he slept celibate without his wife. I study photographs and dioramas showing major events in his life, like his travail in South Africa, the salt march to the sea, the end of British colonial rule, partitioning India and Pakistan, assassination by a fundamentalist Hindu. Each exhibit carries my mind and heart deeper into the life and heart of this world teacher. His spirit touches me.

Feeling Gandhi's presence so directly forever changes me. I know in the core of my being that I no longer can be the man I was before.

Standing Up for Ourselves

Henry David Thoreau aptly wrote that most of us "lead lives of quiet desperation." We go along to get along, then we hate ourselves for living a lie, or I do. Over time, we get so strained and stained by inner conflicts and shame, hidden and denied, that we can never speak up for ourselves. We stay silent at our cost, or I do.

It's reasonable to fear objecting to injustice. We may face threats to our safety for voicing global sense in any words. As long as we stay afraid of fear itself, our fear tips the scales of justice and peace on earth. What if injustice demands action? If we step past being a victim, dare we poke the bear? If we survive, dare we speak out again?

We may proclaim, there must be justice before there can be peace. If by "justice" we mean restoration, repentance and forgiveness, I agree. Peace emerges from justice as justice emerges from peace. If by "justice" we mean revenge, since vengeance inflicts injustice, hate grows.

"The old law of an eye for an eye leaves everybody blind," said Martin Luther King, Jr., echoing Gandhi or maybe Sholem Aleichem. My refusal to forgive any person traps me in resentment that only harms me, not those I resent. Forgiveness frees me with cleansing love. When I do it, even partially, love flows. Love lends courage to honesty.

For too long, I've been part of what journalist Amy Goodman calls "the silenced majority." Fearing rejection, humiliation or retaliation, I've kept the ideas in this book to myself. Insecurities arose as self-talk to silence my voice. Who am I to think I can create a book that matters? Forget writing tonight. Wash the dishes and go to bed.

"All tyranny needs to gain a foothold is for people of good conscience to remain silent," Edmund Burke or Thomas Jefferson possibly said, but that's unverified. John Stuart Mill did write, "Bad men [*sic*] need nothing more to compass their ends than that good men should look on and do nothing." Given our urgent dangers on earth, I no longer can do nothing. I cannot stay silent and stay true to my soul. Can you? I'm a nobody, yet my life issues are universal, making me everybody, same as you.

Standing Up for Democracy

All despotic regimes invent foes and disdain dissent. Leaders exert their strength to silence ideas they don't control. Voltaire astutely wrote, "It is dangerous to be right when the government is wrong."

Consenting to tyranny is equally risky. If we profess our tyrants are moral, what stops them from arresting and killing us anyway? What stops them from concocting pretexts to declare martial law? I notice examples in the Philippines, Thailand and Peru. The situation is more risky or fatal for people asserting their freedom than for leaders refusing to admit the common people have just cause to feel aggrieved.

To reiterate Paine, despots see themselves as separate from us and above us, above the law. Laws are for them to make, not follow. Their self-interest alone matters to them. They leave us alone only if we do not get in their way. We are but distant pebbles in the field of alpha leaders. They suppress our rights whenever it gives them advantage. They regard our good only if it serves their goals. They limit our liberties and silence our voices in decisions that affect us. Free speech frightens and angers them. Despots see democratic participation as vile interference.

Beware whenever books are banned or burned, when journalists are jailed or killed. Beware when leaders act like Soviet dictator Joseph Stalin, who stated, "Ideas are far more powerful than guns. We don't allow our enemies to have guns. Why should we allow them to have ideas?"

And when we must dissent, only peaceful dissent will do. Violence by anyone harms everyone. Spilling even one drop of blood is too high a price if the karma wounds our spirits. Violence is a surrender to our inner tyrant. "And if it is a despot you would dethrone," advised Kahlil Gibran, "see first that his throne erected within you is destroyed."

Standing Up for The Earth

Climate change is real and accelerating. We are running out of time to avert irrevocable shifts. All of our global efforts so far are insufficient. Why delay adopting policies rooted in global awareness until it's too late to avoid ruin? How can we put realism into practice now?

Climate changes require global actions. We need to shift from debate to cooperation. Everything said in the debate has ended at the same point — delay in effective policies. Replacing fossil fuels with renewables is an accelerating undertaking. Inventing alternate technologies has paid fruit, like hydro, solar, wind, and materials chemistry. But fossil interests warn against shifting too rapidly; they want more time to adjust.

Environmentalists, meanwhile, argue about how to produce policy change faster. One side proposes force or violence, the other friendship. Factually, the first has failed; the second has limited influence.

We're told industrialization creates prosperity. We're asked to ignore the motive for industry is self-interest, not world service. Corporations exploiting the planet to sell energy don't do it for our sake, but for their profit. They help us prosper only to retain us as customers.

Thomas Paine wrote, "Alas! We have been long led away by ancient prejudices and made large sacrifices to superstition."

Since survival of the fittest means adapting to new conditions in the right way, the adaptation of becoming eco-wise makes common sense. Like it or not, our world is going global. More than one billion of us are transmuting "globalization" into a positive cultural force for awakening humanity to our oneness. Thinking globally, we tend to get active locally. We live free ethically. Here at childhood's end, we each in our way are helping humanity mature into adulthood.

Living with global minds, we forget the narrow limits of towns and countries and see our friendships on a larger scale. We claim kinship with all life on the planet, and we triumph in the generosity of spirit.

"It is pleasant to observe," Paine wrote, "by what regular gradations we surmount the force of local prejudice, as we enlarge our acquaintance with the world." He added, "Wherefore, I reprobate the phrase of parent or mother country applied to England only [or any one country], as being false, selfish, narrow and ungenerous."

The whole planet can be a wide open market for free and fair trade. By denying our oneness, we alienate and fight with people in other lands, as wrote Paine, "who would otherwise seek our friendship, and against whom, we have neither anger nor complaint."

Let's release prejudiced or superstitious loyalty to destructive habits. The unbridled power of aristocracy over government and the earth sooner or later must have an end. A good heart can draw no joy from the thought of unjust and corrupt economic and political systems enduring forever. Parents can feel no joy from knowing the government cannot ensure their children inherit a free and sustainable world. Since we are putting future generations into debt anyway, often for armies, let's instead invest in earth recovery. Otherwise, we abuse our heirs meanly and pitifully.

"In order to discover the line of our duty rightly," Paine said, "we should take our children in our hand, and fix our station a few years farther into life; that [future] eminence will present a prospect, which a few present fears and prejudices conceal from our sight."

Disasters will prompt policy changes, so be forewarned. If popular opinion demands ending bad policies and practices, our leaders may do or say anything to placate the unrest. Expect elites to wheedle and whine to retain their wealth and power even one more day.

Refute gaslighting with facts, reason and global realism. Organize, lobby and demonstrate to protect and serve our descendants on the planet. Stay nonviolent. Be fun. Hold the moral high ground. Express inner peace by uniting with life. Unite consciousness and politics for lasting shifts in society. We still can prevent the worst — if we stand up for ourselves, for democracy and for the earth. Our better angels keep us going.

∿

In early evening, I'm driven to the Priyadarshini seaside. I'm stunned silent by Gandhi's home, by feeling his presence so powerfully.

We park at the shore. I see children frolicking in low waves. Once out of the car, I remove my shoes, roll my pants up to my knees, and wade into the warm surf. I close my eyes and breathe in serenity.

Something taps my leg. I look down at trash and filth sloshing against my ankles. I rapidly leave the water and wash my feet at the public spigot. Putting on my shoes, I'm feeling sad such waste is normal here.

I stand alone on the walkway in pungent, humid air and gaze out to sea. The setting sun ignites horizon clouds red and gold.

At last, my voice returns, strong and clear. I walk over to my guide. "I'm ready to go back to the hotel now. Thank you so much for driving me around today." I plan on giving him a big tip.

He sighs and follows me to the car. I reach for the door handle, but he steps around, waves aside my hand and insists on opening the door for me. He grandly gestures for me to enter, his face sardonic.

Clearly, my guide is still frustrated with me.

Coming into the Light

When most people believe a false idea is true, its popularity makes us think the idea must be right. Saying the idea is wrong evokes a loud and perhaps violent outcry from the defenders of tradition.

Billions of us are loyal to a belief that we each exist apart from the rest of life, that we are born evil, that we cannot be trusted with freedom. A growing body of us rejects such crippling beliefs. Instead, we say each one of us is born good, intelligent, capable of enlightenment, capable of self rule in our lives, capable of democracy in the world.

We do what we can to be one with the One. We sense how our global connectivity empowers us to transform the world through our thoughts and feelings and actions. Global sensibilities are reaching a critical mass in popularity. More than a billion people comprise real cultural force. Each new world crises draws more people into global thinking.

We stand at a crossroads. Will we abide more tedious tyrannies, or will we create dynamic democracies? Will we fall under oppression more terrifying than the darkest cyberpunk nightmare, or will we rise to create societies anchored in a global sensibility? Will we annihilate ourselves through nihilistic hate, or will we realize our highest human potential through forgiving love, inner peace and inventive creativity?

According to *Spiral Dynamics* by Don E. Beck and Christopher Cowan, human societies naturally generate values-based cultural memes (vMemes) as societies evolve. For instance, a classic American vMeme is that "Competition is better than cooperation." All vMemes exist at once. Together, they form an ascending spiral that trends toward an integral, spiritually awake and diverse global community.

The vMeme of reliance on kings and other masters has shown no willingness to relent. If anything, despots today work harder than ever to control us. Witness the upsurge of autocracy, the coups and attempted coups to overthrow duly elected governments.

We observe more tyranny in the world these days because humanity is coming into the light, dispelling the shadows hiding dark habits. The "ruling class" realizes global enlightenment is coming. They strive harder than ever to keep us in the dark, to keep their wealth and power as long as possible. They see we're slipping out of their grasp. In desperate efforts to dominate us, we're seeing the tyrants' last stand. As global sense grows, we're seeing the demise of the bully.

Welcome the Dawn

In facing cancer, I opened wide to mindfulness to remain alive. As I keep opening my mind to enlightenment, I notice ways I still trap myself with split perceptions and self-deceptions.

I no longer tell myself a story that changing unhealthy habits is too much work, a big lie to excuse inertia. From my own small traumas, I'm learning what Viktor Frankl and Elie Weisel learned in Nazi death camps. Freedom is the inner choice to rule my own mind.

I accept life on life's terms. I accept "survival of the fittest" depends on adapting to life, not making life adapt to me. The smartest adaptation to globalization is adopting a global sensibility, and acting on it.

"Never doubt for a moment," affirmed Margaret Mead, "that a small group of committed, thoughtful people can make a difference. Indeed, it's the only thing that ever has." More than a billion global thinkers are greater than a small group. Let us cooperate for world enlightenment. We may be the only generations who ever can or ever will.

Maybe you believe the world will end soon, or you will depart soon in some Christian, Hindu or New Age rapture or ascension. Maybe you believe space aliens will descend soon to save us, or erase us as a menace. Maybe you think our world problems are too big to solve, or you feel too small and weak to matter, so why bother trying? What's the use, anyway? Forget the dishes. Just go to bed.

Feeling puny ignores our power. Everything, everything, is connected to everything else in an infinite multidimensional networks of light and time called life. What anyone does affects everyone. What we do with our minds and hands transforms our world daily. We draw courage from knowing the darkest hour comes before dawn. As we gain enlightenment, our natural goodness shines.

The leaders we need on earth look back at us in the mirror every morning. One need not be perfect to be perfect for leadership in the right place or right moment. We can pull a Gandhi and be the change we wish to see in the world. Are we willing to take action as we "let go and let God"? Am I? Immanuel Kant says, "Have the courage to use your own reason. That is the motto of enlightenment."

Humanity is awakening to the universal power flowing through our global wholeness. We need only welcome the dawn. Thomas Jefferson said, "Enlighten the people generally, and tyranny and oppressions of body and mind will vanish like evil spirits at the dawn of day."

We are like sleepers rudely roused from our slumber by cold water dumped on our beds. We dislike being awakened abruptly. Now that our eyes are open to the light of unity, we cannot return to living in a stupor again. We no longer can tolerate bullies in the world or in ourselves.

I'm saying this to myself, mind you. I'm aware childhood scripts of rejection and abuse still hold me back from being too outspoken. I aim to inspire, yet I risk ire if *Global Sense* has a response akin to *Common Sense*. I need to stand up for global ideals and for myself. Am I ready?

Paine wrote, "I love the man [*sic*] that can smile in trouble, that can gather strength from distress and grow brave by reflection."

PART IV

Our Ability to
Change the World

Those who expect to reap the blessings of freedom must... undergo the fatigue of supporting it.

THOMAS PAINE

CHAPTER 14

Personal and Social Transformation

1985: NORTHERN COLORADO — *After my failure with the writers network, to find my lost courage, I choose to jump from an airplane.*

My fear of failing is holding me back from going after my dreams. I've worked through depression, with help, yet I'm still holding back as a writer. The cult book has since evolved into a book on self rule. It defies some norms. I fear rebuke or humiliation. To stop thinking like a victim, I figure, if I can overcome the fear of fear itself in a real life-or-death situation, my imagined fears may lose power over me. That's the plan.

Eight of us from a self-esteem group enroll in a two-day jump course at a private airfield on the prairie near Greeley. The first day, we learn how to open an Army parachute if the ripcord fails, how to steer the shrouds, and how to do a safe parachute landing fall. Tuck and roll. Hours of jumping from a platform onto a pile of mattresses make it instinctive. Tuck and roll. Tuck and roll. I dream of it that night. Tuck and roll.

At the airfield next morning is a Cessna high-wing aircraft, its right door removed and back seats pulled out. The plane caries four jumpers per flight. I'm on the third flight, giving me time to be nervous.

Inside me still lives a scared little boy too afraid of heights to jump off the high diving board at the swimming pool. Now I'm past thirty and about to board a small plane, ascend to 2,000 feet, hook up a static line, step out on a wing strut, let go of the plane, drop like a stone, count to ten, and check chute. If it fails, pull the ripcord handle. Yes, I am nervous.

I stand by the runway with classmates to watch the first flight. The plane levels out and flies over the drop zone. A parachute plops open under the plane, which banks right to circle and fly level over the drop zone again. A second chute opens under the plane. Two more passes. Two more chutes. As the plane returns to the landing strip, we watch the jumpers gracefully float down to the ground, when their chutes collapse flat.

All the jumpers but one tuck and roll, A man playing paratrooper tries to land on his feet. Macho man fractures both ankles. The next flight departs. I borrow duct tape, triple wrap my ankles inside my hiking boots.

I'm more nervous now than ever.

Personal Growth and Social Change

Real and imagined fears are powerful. Freeing us from fear's power, the inner and outer work of transformation inspires courage.

"To put the world right in order," advised Confucius, "we must first put the nation in order; to put the nation in order, we must first put the family in order; to put the family in order, we must first cultivate our personal life; we must first set our hearts right."

To set my heart right, I strive to practice *mindful self rule.* To put the world in order, I strive to practice *personal democracy.* These two aspects of the whole, inner and outer, are necessary and sufficient for us to change ourselves and change our world at the same time.

What do I mean by these two terms?

Mindful self rule is the art of using global sense to guide life choices, so we live true to our souls. Awareness we are living light creating reality each moment, a global sensibility, helps us govern our natural free will. Extremes of selfishness and altruism melt away into unity consciousness. Choices balance the self, all humanity and all life on earth. That's the ideal. I clearly am *not* exemplary, yet a tiny sampling may be useful.

When I eat organic food, that is an act of mindful self rule. When I integrate scientific and holistic healthcare to treat cancer, that is an act of mindful self rule. When I cultivate emotional literacy for knowing and sharing feelings, that is an act of mindful self rule. When I garden, sensing life at my fingertips, that is an act of mindful self rule. When I meditate or pray or pause to watch a sunset. when I rejoice at beauty, that is an act of mindful self rule. And when I forgive another for any real or imagined injury, that very definitely is an act of mindful self rule.

Personal democracy is the art of using global sense to improve our relationships and our world. When a global sensibility guides conscience, we mindfully make daily choices that benefit our homes, schools, jobs, communities, nations, and planet. We think globally and act locally in our private and public lives. Not lip service. Real deal.

When I share a vulnerable conversation with a friend, that is an act of personal democracy. When I sign a petition to stop naval sonar testing that harms breeding seals, porpoises and whales, that is an act of personal democracy. When I do reiki healing, that is an act of personal democracy. When I attend a community meeting on a vital public issue, that is an act of personal democracy. And when I vote my conscience on Election Day, that very definitely is an act of personal democracy.

When global sense guides mindful self rule and personal democracy (said in any jargon), our awareness and actions are in harmony. We live in integrity. Whenever I do it, my true self shows up in authentic presence. I radiate love, joy, peace, gratitude, generosity, compassion, patience, and humor. I notice others' feelings. I think clearly. If I can do it, if too rarely, so can you, or anybody. A global sense of life transforms our lives and our world. As within, so without. As above, so below.

Reason and conscience are central for mindful self rule and personal democracy. Uniting personal growth and social change opens doors for creative solutions. Uniting the two may upset those keeping them apart. Nevertheless, personal growth and social change are one.

≈

I board the airplane and sit in the back. By the time we reach altitude and the first jumper exits, my nervousness has become anxiety. A metallic taste taints my mouth. The second jumper steps out and drops. I'm next, so I scoot on my butt toward the open door. The heavy parachute pack strains my back. My anxiety has become fear, honest fear.

I hook up my ripcord, swing my legs out the door and plant both feet on the strut. I hoist myself out the door. The wind nearly rips off my helmet. I sit back down in the doorway, shout to the jumpmaster that my helmet is loose. He leans over and helps me tighten the chinstrap. By now we've missed the drop zone, so we must circle back into position.

The plane banks right. The open door is at my feet. If I'd lean forward, I'd easily side out. I lean back. We're again above the drop zone. I step out onto the strut. I am no longer afraid. I am terrified!

I close my eyes and release my death grip on the plane. When I let go, my mind goes blank. I do not count ten. I do not check chute. Air screams in my ears. In darkness, I am falling, falling, forever falling.

A sudden jerk yanks me upwards. My eyes snap open. I look up to see strands unsorting as the parachute billows into shape.

I hear silence, serene silence. The gentle descent under a parachute will linger among the most graceful moments in my life. Below is a checkerboard of farm fields, slowly drawing closer. A raven approaches me, its wings a whisper. The totem bird glances my way and flies on.

I drift off target, a giant bullseye painted on the ground. I pull on the shroud handles to steer my glide path, sighting the target between my feet. In my elation, I forget to slow my descent before landing by turning the chute to face into the breeze. I'm coming down with a soft wind at my back. I land hard. Tuck and roll. My ankles are unhurt, yet I compress my spine. Amen for yoga. The physical pain is worth the personal gain.

In the following years, my fear of failure largely dissolves. I'm willing to take greater risks in life. I go back to school, build an international career as a media trade journalist, survive cancer, forgive abuses, write this book. Fear does not stop me like before, yet I still feel fear. I still need courage.

Mindful Self Rule

Having power over myself is better than having power over others. The better I govern my emotions, thoughts, words, deeds, and energy fields, the better I get along with myself and others, the better my life flows. The more I sensibly govern my impulses and free will, the more I trust myself to live safely free in society, the less I need another to manage me.

Insecurity and external validation are habits. Do I do what others expect me to do (to please them), or do I do what I do from knowing what is right and true? Do I react fast on autopilot, or do I observe and respond from mind and heart? Self-knowledge guides self-government.

Awareness of our natural unity, our interconnectivity, propels and restrains our inborn freedom (*internal locus of control*). Alertness to our oneness carries intrinsic responsibility for our impacts on other people and the world (*external locus of control*). Balance is vital.

Elizabeth Cady Stanton said, "Nothing strengthens the judgment and quickens the conscience like individual responsibility." My freedom of choice is guided by conscience, reason, spirituality, emotions, experience, and a willingness to be accountable when I goof. When all of me resonates like a clear bell, my choices work out well.

Our daily choices shape our lives and our world. If we have global consciousness, we tend to make life choices that benefit our body, mind, heart, and soul. For me, living well is a juggling act. Lots of balls in the air. Life unfolds best when my free will is governed by self rule.

To suggest options, to help you imagine the gazillion ways you can rule your own life, below are a few things I do — offered as hints for your own discoveries. Please, do not limit yourself to my examples.

Body Sovereignty

We have a right to rule our bodies. I believe, "You are what you eat." Since my diet affects my health and the planet's health, I eat organic and natural foods. I avoid genetically modified foods and processed foods with preservatives. I take walks and go swimming, as I can.

Since physical health reflects and reinforces emotional, mental and spiritual health, for me to survive cancer, I use allopathic, naturopathic, homeopathic, nutritional, herbal, and energetic remedies. I study effects, side effects and contraindications. I assist my neurochemistry by evoking endorphins, serotonin and dopamine. Dancing enlivens me.

My body belongs to me. Unwanted touching is a boundary violation, unless and until invited. Heartfelt safe sex is a surprise at my age. Violence is always taboo. My life belongs to me. Your life belongs to you.

I research longevity, trusting verified science over profiteering bunk. In surviving lethal illness, I accept the inevitability of death, be it days or decades away. Gratefully, as sung in *Spamalot*, "I ain't dead yet."

Mind Sovereignty

We have the right to rule our own minds. "You are what you think." Paine wrote, "There are two distinct classes of what are called thoughts: those that we produce in ourselves by reflection and the act of thinking and those that bolt into the mind of their own accord."

I claim a duty to govern my thoughts. I seek to monitor self-talk, subtexts, what I say to myself and others about what I believe is true.

I'm leery of my own lazy thinking. "Sluggish reason," lamented Mary Wollstonecraft, "supinely takes opinions on trust, and obstinately supports them to spare itself the labour of thinking."

Confidence can mask ignorance or arrogance. I'm wary of my need to be right. Edmund Burke warned against those who "defend their errors as if they were defending their inheritance."

"It is error only, and not truth, that shrinks from inquiry," Paine said. "It is an affront to treat falsehood with complaisance."

Rhetoric persuades us. Propaganda deceives us. Treating lies as facts is how leaders fool us. I'm skeptical of what I hear and read on the media. My opinions can only echo others when I'm too busy or tired for research and analysis. I ask myself, am I thinking for myself or reciting slogans? "Once you teach people to say what they do not understand," Rousseau said, "it is easy enough to get them to say anything you like."

I explore the realms between subjective mind and objective reality. I trust critical thinking and scientific method. Facts that belie beliefs are gifts. I'm alert to "magical thinking" mindtraps, wishing without reasoning. Thus, I study decision-making and problem-solving methods.

Reason and common sense are necessary yet insufficient. I cultivate mindfulness. Healing split perceptions is easiest when I sense our oneness. I can shift from brain-stem reactions to conscious frontal lobe responses. Since brainwaves and neurochemicals guide my words and hands, when I am fully present, I unify as a whole being. I am more me.

Heart Sovereignty

We have the right to rule our own emotions. "You are what you feel." *Emotional intelligence* helps me know what I feel in my heart and gut. E*motional literacy* helps me read others' feelings, so I respond mindfully. My ongoing lesson is living from my heart more than my head.

When I can quiet the mental chatter to enter the heartspace or belly stillpoint, my head choices are cleaner. My outcomes are better.

I do personal growth work. I do bodywork and lightwork sessions. I explore the neurobiology of emotions. I seek to heal old wounds, release impulse triggers. I act to heal traumas limiting my ability to love.

I read self-help books. I attend classes and workshops. I explore many modes of psychotherapy; I don't use therapists as a journal, which I buy cheaper at art stores. I only consult counselors or facilitators who've done their shadow work, so they won't divert me from delving where they fear to tread. In general, I seek clean catalysts for going deeper faster.

My emotions belong to me. No matter what happens in the world, I alone choose what I feel. Loyalty to habitual emotions is a choice.

I am personally responsible for emotions I transmit into the world like a telecom tower. If I feel irritation or resentment at another, I look for a mirror. I dislike in others what I need to accept and forgive in myself. This opens me to compassion and healing. Hawaiians say *Ho'oponopono:* "I'm sorry. Please forgive me. I forgive you. Thank you. I love you." From doing it, I confirm the practice invites healing, even miracles.

Soul Sovereignty

"You are that you are." We have a right to rule our essential selves on earth, and any hereafter. I welcome feeling unified with life, the Lifesource, releasing fear and ego, so spirit shines. The paradox of surrender.

I agree with Paine that my religion is the world. if pressed, I define my religion as eclectic "natural Judaism." Monotheism, one Source of all life, makes sense to me, as does deism, faith in discerning the natural laws of life. Those seeing life as pure light alive in us all share a *new spirituality* that transcends and unites religions and humanism.

I remind myself separation is an illusion. To help shift from duality to unity, I study world wisdom cultures. My energetic sensitivity evolves in spurts. As a Reiki healer, at best, ego steps aside, my mind quiets, and intuition guides my hands. I may sense edges of auric layers.

I planted my soul to grow in the soil of this lifetime. When my spirit sheds this body, can I try life in a body again? Will I want or need to try? What dreams may come, I am the I AM being me and all that is.

While I still live, I claim the natural right and duty to be conscious in relationships with myself, other people and the world. I cultivate my capacity for spiritual freethinking. When I get present, I love me as I am. As best I can, I practice being present. Chop food; carry laundry.

Body. Mind. Heart. Soul. This fast survey of a few ways I seek sensible self rule barely begins to suggest things you can do on your own.

Please do not judge the validity of such ideas from my frail example. (Notice how authority addiction shapes our view of authors.) As a writer advocating self rule, I've found audience responses reveal their mindsets

Personal Democracy

We express mindful self rule through personal democracy.

Self-knowledge and worldly knowledge together help me balance personal sovereignty and self-restraint. All actions have consequences, so before I speak or act, I want to pause a beat and ask myself, what makes common global sense? I'm getting better at it. The more I mature, the less I reenact the insecure ego pretensions of my youth.

So, I how do I know if what I'm doing in life is good? Kant gifted us the Categorical Imperative. If everyone on earth does the same thing, would it make sense or become absurd? Jefferson advised, "Whenever you do a thing, act as if all the world were watching."

You may care to help repair our world, but feel clueless what to do, so you let others do it for you. You may think, "I'm just one person, and I can't do everything." That's true enough. But you can do *something* — anything. Once we choose to help, what shall we actually do? Among the gazillion options open to you, below are five ways I engage.

Green and Healthy Lifestyles

The internet and bookstores offer plenty on green and healthy living. For my part, I'm a conscious consumer willing to buy organic and green products or services (scale reduces prices). I read labels for sustainability and health, I skip wasteful packaging. I bring shopping bags.

I assess my "ecological footprint" with online quizzes. I reduce, reuse, repair, and recycle. Not yet at zero waste, I don't dump without permission. I drive a used electric car. As a home renter, I use LED light bulbs. If I ever can buy or build, I want solar panels and LEED green construction.

Honest and Fair Relationships

We reflect our closest relationships. My life warns me against giving away my power to others, nor letting others give away their power to me. Codependent authority addiction is a risk in any relationship. "The mere impulse of appetite is slavery," wrote Rousseau, "while obedience to a law we prescribe to ourselves is liberty."

I alone am responsible for my own feelings, not for others' feelings. Others do not make me angry; I *choose* to be angry. Emotional literacy and a global sensibility help me be more present and pleasant.

Loving unconditionally is the heart of personal democracy. When I love myself as I am, loving others is easy, and so is letting others love me. My relationship problems are from putting pain, shame, fear, and safety before love and faith, putting grievance before gratitude. Assumptions and expectations foul relationships. Do I want to be loved or be right?

Emotional intelligence informs emotional literacy. By knowing what I feel, I better sense others' emotions. If I'm afraid, or defining myself as a victim, I may fail to think how my words or deeds land on others. When I see myself co-creating each relationship, I listen better. Others feel heard and valued. I respect them and myself. When I feel safe, I show love more easily. Vulnerability allows intimacy in honest relationships.

I work to abide by what don Miguel Ruiz calls The Four Agreements (my bugaboo is #2.) Given my history, empathy takes effort for me. I ask what life must be like for others. Carl Rogers' book, *On Becoming a Person,* helps me drop judgments on others' stories, view them in the process of becoming their highest and best selves. I can open my heart.

In the spirit of Martin Buber, I seek to see others as "capable of inner development." As we forgive others' faults, he said, we generously create space for them to be genuine with themselves and with us. We empower them to be their true selves. Works for me when I do it, if I do.

Education and Literacy

As did Paine, I believe a good education is our natural human right, not a privilege of birth, rank, wealth, or station. I imagine education being free for everybody, funded by fair taxes paid gladly, a bargain at any price. Upholding democracy in every new generation is priceless.

Let us teach our children well to love themselves as they are, so their growth comes gentler. Intervene early to reinforce grounded self-esteem. Lifelong learning keeps brains active. My parents read bedtime books to me as a child. Reading for fun keeps our minds young.

Teaching has been a sideline for decades. I favor evidence-based teaching for multiple learning styles. Blended learning, I find, ties reason to curiosity. Experiential learning in teams teaches real-world knowledge and interpersonal problem-solving skills. I love class under a tree.

As for curricula, science, technology, engineering, and mathematics (STEM) serve workforce development and innovation — necessary but not sufficient for life. I value "liberal arts and sciences," the humanities, language arts, all arts, geography, history, philosophy, ethics, and *civics.* A cross-cultural education supports freedom in any democracy.

I value our multiple intelligences. I advocate teaching how to think, not what to think, like Edward de Bono's work on lateral thinking. Teach critical thinking, media literacy, and rhetoric. Read Plato's *Gorgias* and *Phaedrus*. Study *Manufacturing Consent* by Edward Herman and Noam Chomsky. Learn linguistics and semiotics to pierce propaganda.

Support local schools and public libraries. Oppose book banning and censorship favoring *any* ideology. Challenge teaching beliefs and bias as indisputable facts. Go to school board meetings and speak global sense to power, or lobby leaders, or run for the board yourself, if called.

Organizational Democracy

Authority addiction governs too many corporations, nonprofits and governments. Democratic management overall works better.

While "industrial democracy" is deemed socialist, the literature on "participatory management" is studied from graduate schools to board rooms. My grad school research led me to Michael Pacanowsky's portal writings on organizations as living cultures. Organizations are not feudal manors with lords and serfs. Organizations are not machines with workers as replaceable parts. I explored how metaphors shape cultures.

People in organizations tend to support decisions they help to make. Democracy evokes ownership for group decisions, so there's less rebellion, less slacking. To replace hierarchical top-down structures, Pacanowsky describes a flat "lattice" for equitable and inclusive organizations.

I use a *problem-solving* model with eight steps: (1) Define a problem factually. (2) Identify problem causes. (3) Brainstorm alternative solutions. (4) Evaluate alternatives fairly. (5) Pick a solution to try. (6) Implement the solution. (7) Evaluate results fairly. (8) Return to Step 5 or 1.

I cultivate *conflict-resolution* skills. I prefer negotiation and mediation over arbitration and litigation. Strategies like avoiding, accommodating, compromising, or competing seldom settle genuine grievances. Collaborative problem-solving, done with empathy, resolves disputes.

Visionary *servant leadership* in organizations supports democracy. Instead of being kings or tyrants jealous of their power, good leaders serve and empower people to find solutions. Good leaders hold the vision and advance the mission of the organization, best if decided democratically. Good leaders model habits that enhance the culture as a whole. I advocate thinking of our organizations as democracy workshops.

Community Engagement

Practicing personal democracy in grassroots campaigns shifts ideals from slogans to realities, so democracy grows in our societies. Managing efforts democratically builds community engagement.

I volunteer for grassroots political and public education campaigns backed by coalitions of conscience. I start with homework on issues and the causes of problems. I identify key players and their business models. I follow the money. I seek the guiding rationale, vision or ideology. If this research satisfies me, if I engage, my efforts are more rewarding.

Where I can, I suggest that leaders and staff and volunteers agree to solve problems and make major decisions democratically together. The buy-in from a fair vote in vital choices creates enduring group cohesion. Practicing democracy sends ripples across our communities.

Letting leaders make decisions for us enables authority addiction. It divides leaders and the staff or volunteers into kings and subjects. This undermines any vision of equality and inclusion inspiring the campaign. Democracy enlightens us faster than letting leaders think for us.

In my youth, I read *Rules for Radicals* by labor organizer Saul Alinsky. He promoted gradual infiltration and manipulation of public opinion. He used the dialectic of confrontation and polarization to force disputes to resolution. I first witnessed his strategies used in the movement to end the Vietnam War, and his methods are still widely used today.

After I left the cult, when I began grappling with authority addiction and alpha male rule in my life, Alinsky's demonizing tactics felt contrary to my values. Given our oneness, I cannot condone "us or them" thinking. I prefer Gandhi's nonviolent *Satyagraha*, transforming foes into allies by opening hearts and minds. Empathy, diplomacy, consideration, and co-operation are the most reliable paths to "win/win" solutions.

I seek to be a spiritual warrior. When I feel most outraged at injustice is when I most need to practice peaceful personal democracy.

〰

My dad retires in 1985 at age 65 after 20 years working for a regional paint manufacturer and retailer, rising to vice president of marketing. When his company is acquired by a national brand, he takes a retirement buyout. The new owners finagle away part of his pension, legal if unethical.

My folks enjoy world travel on budget tours. Dad shoots color photos. Once at home, he selects images for painting exquisite watercolors. He takes classes at Denver's Art Students League. He joins the Colorado Artists Guild and eventually becomes its president. His work hangs in juried art shows. He seems happiest when painting in his home studio.

On Father's Day in 1997, dad and I go canoeing on Evergreen Lake. He's unusually vulnerable with me. I ask him why he never pursued a career as an artist. He replies, "I was not good enough." I feel he's mistaken.

We've evolved a comfortable warmth between us. We play pool at the Denver Press Club, where he's a lifetime member through his local PR work. Dad tells others he's proud of my journalism career, but he never tells me. A press club friend will share this revelation at my father's funeral.

Dad has end-stage diabetes. Neuropathy disables his legs. He migrates from cane to walker to wheelchair. He's at last hospitalized in January 2000 when doctors amputate a foot. A blood clot hits his heart. With death near, my father finds peace with himself and with me.

In the hospice, dad asks for my beliefs about the afterlife. I'm surprised. He's long been an agnostic Reformed Jew who believes we live on only in the memory of others. He's been skeptical and dismissive of my mystical bent. Now on his deathbed, he wonders what's ahead, I reply, "When you let go, move toward the brightest light you see. Look for family and friends."

In late January, after mom says she'll see him tomorrow and goes home, I sit awhile at his bedside. He's too hoarse to speak, so we're simply together. As I stand to leave, in his eyes shines the light of unconditional love. For all of my life, I have longed to see that look of pure love in his eyes. Grief opens my heart. The moment heals us both.

Outside, I sit in my car and sob. Dad dies in his sleep that night.

Inner Work and Outer Work

Practicing mindful self rule in myself helps me practice personal democracy in the world. Both inner work and outer work are necessary. In Taoism, the feminine *yin* energy stimulates the masculine *yang* energy as *yang* stimulates *yin*, forming a dynamic loop. They are interconnected and interdependent. In essence, *yin* and *yang* are one. Either without the other is incomplete. The universal circle of life.

In the same way, mindful self rule stimulates personal democracy as personal democracy stimulates mindful self rule. My heart and mind guide my words and deeds in life as my words and deeds guide my heart and mind. They are interconnected and interdependent. Mindful self rule and personal democracy are one. Either without the other is incomplete. When I do both together, even if poorly, life works better. Practicing personal democracy in our workplaces and community groups, further, helps build and encourage robust democracy in society.

A crucial shift in me was discovering I can feel one with the universe *and* retain my individuality. I can love me as I am, be at peace with myself and the world. I can stop trying to control life for safety. When liberation from my inner tyrant makes sense to me, that's when I feel free.

〰

In this chapter, I've explored self and world improvement. In the next chapter, I discuss gender equality and male lib, a pivotal trend in the global sense movement, and then I propose direct republics.

For framing, in this fourth and last part of the book, I'm arguing that we *are* capable of a global shift into personal and societal enlightenment. If we choose, we are the champions of the future.

Mary Wollstonecraft observed, "The beginning is always today."

CHAPTER 15

Gender Equality and New Men

*2005: **DENVER*** — *I go to bed late on Sunday night, October 9, knowing a massive snowstorm is due in Denver by morning. I should go move my car, I think. The aging hatchback is parked under a big elm in front of my rented duplex. The tree still bears leaves from a warm autumn. In my mind I hear a message to let the car stay put. "All will be well."*

Before climbing into bed, I look out the window to see snow is falling in big fluffy flakes. The prospect of getting dressed again, putting on boots and parka for going out into the cold, does not appeal to me. In my mind I hear a message to let the car stay put. "All will be well."

In the morning I look out the window to see my car is covered by snow and green leaves. Once outside. I tug on the nearest leafy twig poking from the snow atop my car. The twig does not budge. I brush snow away to find the twig attaches to a branch. I look up at the tree to see a white gash where the bottom limb had cracked off the old trunk.

Frantic, I dig away the snow to discover the heavy limb fell lengthwise on my car, crushing the roof, creasing it, folding it like a taco. The windshield is shattered in a zillion pieces all over the car seats. I feel shattered. Shocked. Thank you so very much, Mother Nature!

What am I going to do? I have liability insurance, but I am not covered for Acts of God. I cannot afford a replacement used car. Why didn't I move the car when I thought of it? How could I have heard inside so clearly to let the car stay put? Can I truly trust my inner knowing? I'm supposed to be so spiritual and intuitive? Hah! Who am I kidding here?

My one comfort is that I work from home as a freelance media trade magazine journalist. As long as I have a computer, a telephone and internet access, I can earn a living. So, as weather permits I'll walk, bike or bus until I can buy a usable used car. I will get by under a touch of grey skies.

I phone my partner of four years. She's busy at work and not available. I'm home alone and discombobulated.

The woman I call is a sabra from Israel involved with Jewish Renewal. We'd met at a political rally in Denver's Civic Center Park. A mutual friend introduced us. I asked her, "How's your life so far?" She thought I was rude. I knew she mattered. We soon love each other and spend most nights at her place or mine. She calls me her bashert, *her intended one.*

Thanks to her, I adopt my Hebrew birth name as my public first name. I am Judah. Thank you and farewell, Kenny and Ken. Judah is the real me, more authentic. Judah is the tribe that survived.

Friends start calling me Judah, but not yet my family. This morning, I'm little Kenny calling mommy after a tree limb crushes his car.

Gender Inequities

Since the ancient rise of alpha male rule, with rare exceptions, the status of women and nonbinaries has been low worldwide. However, the global movement for gender equality is ending male rule. The process is slow, with setbacks, but the trend is transforming our world.

Generations of addiction to male dominance created our modern world crises. We've let alpha men compete to sire their dynasties, leaving us a legacy of war and ruin. Rooted in natural primal needs for safety and reproduction, old dysfunctional habits are hard to break.

Our sense-making systems have kept alive the core belief that men belong in charge. As more of us evolve global mindsets, gender equality and body autonomy make sense to more people — inducing cultural and social shifts, which triggers a ferocious backlash. What gives me hope is that a global sensibility spurs efforts to protect Mother Earth from rapine. Environmentalism inspires conscious consumers to call for business and government to wake up and go green. Similarly, the women's movement inspires good men to wake up, grow up and do men's work.

Feminism dislodges males' grasp on power. Men adapt in response, if reluctantly. Men begin liberating themselves from old male habits, like treating women as property. Liberated men escape the ancient mindtrap of dominating others to feel good about themselves.

Just as racial equality laws reduce racism, gender equality laws reduce sexism. If any man makes a free-will choice to obey gender equality laws, if he halts predatory words and deeds, he may open his heart and mind. If unconsciously, he releases old alpha male habits. Takes time.

In Western society, a vital early call for female equality was the 1792 pamphlet by Mary Wollstonecraft, *A Vindication of the Rights of Women*, published in England the year after Paine's *Rights of Man.* "If the abstract rights of man will bear discussion and explanation, those of women, by a parity of reasoning, will not shrink from the same test," she wrote.

Women are not inferior to men, but women degrade themselves...

> by receiving the trivial attentions which men think it manly to pay to the sex... This homage to women's attractions has distorted their understanding to such an extent that almost all the civilized women of the present century are anxious only to inspire love, when they ought to have the nobler aim of getting respect for their abilities and virtues.

Encouraging women to strive for "reforming themselves to reform the world," she wrote, "I do not wish them [women] to have power over men; but over themselves." Holds true for anybody, actually.

Paine is credited, if unverified, with the earliest known colonial call for women's emancipation, a 1775 *Pennsylvania Magazine* missive, "An Occasional Letter on The Female Sex." I hear his voice in the writing:

> If we take a survey of ages and of countries, we shall find the women, almost without exception at all times and in all places, adored and oppressed. Man, who has never neglected an opportunity of exerting his power, in paying homage to their beauty, has always availed himself of their weakness. He has been at once their tyrant and their slave.

Insecure men who view women as prey often fear gender equality. A woman standing up for her rights threatens such a man's virility. He may not retaliate if sexism has legal penalties. Stubborn defiance of civil remedies will persist as long as some men hate and fear women

Dr. Jordan Paul writes, "A mother is the first omnipresent authority figure in a boy's life. His physical and emotional wellbeing is totally dependent on her. How she uses that power and his reaction to it deeply imprint his relationship with all women. As an adult, any fear of women's power will rear its ugly head."

Misogyny. Sexism. Gender inequity. By any label, oldthink males deny what's contrary to their identity as a "real man." They fear feminine emotional vulnerability. They attack gay and transgender people to push away emotional authenticity. They repress, often violently, variances in the gender genome. The addiction to male rule is global.

As a sign of repression, the UN reports, women in developing lands, doing unpaid and paid household tasks, work 20 percent more hours than men. The International Labor Organization reports that women, on average, globally earn 33 percent less than men.

Forced and arranged marriages further deny women equal rights. Marriages in India often are arranged by families, for example, yet women are liberating themselves. In the state of Uttar Pradesh, a bride was told that her future husband was educated. When they met at their wedding, she asked him, "How much is 15 + 6?" He said, "17." She walked out of the ceremony. The police were called. All gift were returned.

Women struggle to control their reproductive systems. The abortion debate, essentially, is a fight between men's desire for birthright sons and women's natural right to rule their bodies, body autonomy. "Right to Life" is code for men treating women as breading stock, a ruse to control their wombs. Moral women believe the lie to their disadvantage. Religions ban contraception and abortion, Paine would argue, to inherit generations of faithful believers without actually earning them.

I see religious whites in the USA pushing hardest to ban abortions. The bans mostly affect poor people of color. Races that white supremacists chant "won't replace us" are being forced to reproduce faster. The U.S. Census forecasts a "white minority" by 2045. Banning abortions means "replacement" happens sooner. Zealotry breeds irrationality.

Paine reasoned that nobody is born with an innate right to rule due to their ancestry. I find modern genetic support for him from bioethicist Alice Dreger at the University of Chicago. She studies people at "the edge of anatomy," like intersex and transgender people, when X or Y chromosomes act in ways that defy binary models of gender identity.

Dreger names America's founders the original "anatomical activists." They rejected the idea of monarchy based on birthright in favor of a new concept, that "all men are created equal." Refuting the idea of an inherited right to govern, they laid a foundation for the equal rights of all people, regardless of their gender or outer forms.

Our oneness gives us all natural equality, so natural law debars bias discrimination based on sex, race, age, ability, religion, creed, origin, or any factor. If all life is sacred, anyone from anywhere has a natural right to love and marry anybody on earth, or not.

Gender is not destiny, say women today. As a hetero male in the 21st century, I add that the idea gender is not destiny also frees us men from delusions we have an inborn right and duty to rule women and the world. We "new men" can drop the burden of male rule with a sigh of relief. We can gladly share the leadership load. We can ensure our safety by serving our communities, not by dominating them. We can change. The way we lived yesterday need not be the way we live tomorrow.

〰

My mom surprises me. Until I can afford a car, I can use hers. A recent traffic ticket convinced her to stop driving, she says, "so it's silly for the car to sit in the parking lot if you can be using it." In trade, I agree to take her to doctor appointments and weekly grocery shopping. That afternoon, I ride the bus to her senior apartment building and pick up her car.

Mom and I enter a new phase of our relationship. After shopping or doctor visits, she takes me to lunch. Weeks pass. Our conversations deepen from surface events in our lives to sharing the substance of our lives.

Mom reveals how she's worried about me ever since I was a sickly child, wheezing from asthma. She admits to feeling hurt by my youthful rebellion and then by me joining the Moonies. She admits feeling hurt that I was the last to see her husband the night he died. She admits feeling sad we have not talked like this before. I apologize for all the pain I caused her, and she forgives me. We feel love flow.

I share how her criticism and sarcasm wounded me. I reveal how I felt unloved and worthless when she did not protect me from dad's abuses. She reveals her father's rages at home, how she never knew until watching Oprah that men should not act that way. She lived in a male world of female roles and misunderstood what she was supposed to do. She admits having a sharp tongue, and says she had no idea of the harm she could create. She did not let me be the tender person I am inside. She's very sorry. She apologizes for all of the pain she caused me, and I forgive her. We feel love flow.

For the first time in our lives, my mother and I become friends. We are equals. We attain peace. I'm grateful my years in the men's movement helps me open to feeling the feelings allowing our healing.

The Women's Movement

Modern women have pursued gender equality in four waves. More will be needed. Given widely available histories of feminism, I'll spotlight only the key writings and leaders inspiring women to do the private and public work of liberating themselves from alpha male rule. If these efforts are unfamiliar to you, what follows can be a springboard.

First Wave — Modern feminism tracks back to the 18th century in the United Kingdom and North America. The feminist movement spread to Europe and worldwide by the early 20th century.

Mostly affluent white women, early feminists advocated voting right (suffrage), yet they also won matrimonial property rights, divorce rights, and education rights. Women marched and did civil disobedience. First Wave UK leaders included Millicent Garrett Fawcett and Emmeline Pankhurst. U.S. leaders included Fanny Wright, Alice Paul, Susan B. Anthony, Elizabeth Cady Stanton, and Sojourner Truth (racism in feminism).

Australia was the first to legalize women voting in 1902. UK women partially won the vote in 1918, fully in 1928. U.S. women won the vote in 1920. Saudi Arabia was latest to legalized women voting in 2015. The only state left where women cannot vote is Vatican City (papal male rule).

Second Wave — The movement renewed midcentury in France, the USA, UK, and Australia before going global. Feminists upheld every woman's right to control her own body, her right to enjoy sexual freedom the same as any man, including her right to an orgasm. Men were told to care about a woman's satisfaction as much as their own.

Second Wave issues featured reproductive rights (contraception and abortion), violence against women (harassment, molestation and rape), pornography, plus inequities in jobs, pay, divorce, child custody, sports, the arts, business, and beyond. Women of color spoke up.

Women and allied men backed the U.S. Equal Rights Amendment. (A legal argument can be made the ERA today lacks only one more state ratifying it for gender equality to be the law of the land.)

Launching the Second Wave was a pivotal book, Le *Deuxième Sexe* (*The Second Sex*) by Simone de Beauvoir, published 1949 in France and 1953 in America. The biological fact a woman bears children does not justify treating her as the "second sex" or the alien "other" within society, she wrote. "Woman is shut up in a kitchen or in a boudoir, and astonishment is expressed that her horizon is limited. Her wings are clipped, and it is found deplorable that she cannot fly."

Major Second Wave books included *The Feminine Mystique* by Betty Friedan (1963), *The Female Eunuch* by Germaine Greer (1970), *Sexual Politics* by Kate Millet (1970), and *Our Bodies, Ourselves* by The Boston Women's Health Book Collective (1970). The top magazines are *Ms.*, led by Gloria Steinem and Letty Cottin Pogrebin along with *Cosmopolitan*, led by Helen Gurley Brown. "The pill" enabled sexual freedom, "free love." Promiscuity lost its allure in the 1980s onset of HIV/AIDS.

A push for equal rights is the most enduring legacy.

Third Wave — Feminism revived in the 1990s, initially from punk rock Riot Grrrl music about sexuality, rape, female power, and patriarchy. The DIY subcultures made sense of gender equality as ending all limiting gender expectations and stereotypes, so every person feels pride.

Growing advocacy for gender equality lent courage to lesbian, gay, bisexual, transgender, queer, and intersex minorities (LGBTQI+). Same-sex marriages became legal in 36 nations by 2024.

An early breakout writer at age 22 was Rebecca Walker, daughter of novelist Alice Walker. Her 1992 *Ms.* essay, "Becoming the Third Wave," upended "post-feminism." Clarissa Pinkola Estés, PhD, in 1996 published *Women Who Run with the Wolves,* celebrating folk myths and stories to awaken the wild woman in any whole woman.

Fourth Wave — The 2016 presidential election of misogynistic Donald Trump helped rekindle the women's movement in the USA and globally. The immense Women's March in DC and elsewhere marked the emergence of a fourth wave. People across the gender spectrum have come together to demand equal rights for all people.

Another cultural trigger was the 2017 exposure of sexual predation by a Hollywood mogul who for decades employed bribes and extortion to silence his beautiful victims. Famous movie stars went public. Other women came forward to report sexual assaults on them, too.

The #MeToo movement against sexual misconduct by men spread from a social media hashtag into board rooms, offices, factories, retailers, nonprofits, and across society. The message: "My body does not belong to you. Unless I consent, keep your hands to yourself."

In 2022, the U.S. Supreme Court revoked the 50-year constitutional right to an abortion, permitting state bans. Legislators banning autonomy now face upset women, new men and nonbinaries who vote.

The ancient model of alpha male rule, patriarchy, is losing power in the world. The changes are gradual (too slow for me). The movement to assure gender equality under law (like equality of race, age, ability) seems unstoppable. I invite us to help speed it along.

※

In November, I take mom to her doctor for a persistent dry cough. She's diagnosed with Stage I lung cancer. I begin taking her twice a week to an oncology clinic for alternating chemotherapy and radiation. The cure seems harder on her than the disease. I admire how bravely she handles it.

In December, I get a call from her seniors apartment complex. Mom had a stroke. She's in the ambulance now. I rush to the hospital in her car. My elder sister meets me there, driving from her foothills.home.

Mom lays semi-comatose in the intensive critical care unit. The right side of her face sags. Her right hand lays limp across her belly. Her sunken eyes frighten me. Seems to me her spirit is barely in her body.

A week later, she's transferred to the stroke unit. Her speech clears a bit. She can move her right hand, but not yet enough to feed herself. She begins physical therapy and speech therapy. The doctor is concerned about her irregular heartbeat, the low fever draining her energy and the high risk of pneumonia. She's too weak to resume cancer treatments.

In January, mom starts saying in slurred speech, "I want to go home." She resists standing up and trying to walk. She resists doing speech therapy. She insists she wants to go home.

My sister and I reason with her. You cannot expect to return home to your apartment, not yet. A rehabilitation facility is the next step. She shakes her head at us, struggling to enunciate, "I want to go HOME!"

Oh. Got it. We transfer her to a hospice.

A week later, she has one final piece of unfinished business. She wants to sign over the car title to me. I demure, but she's adamant. So, I drive to her apartment and bring back her title. She signs it and gives it to me. We hold hands. Our eyes smile love. After a while, I go home in my car.

That night, my mother dies in her sleep.

The hospice calls at 3 a.m. My sabra partner and I get up, get dressed, and go to the hospice. In Jewish tradition, we sit shemira beside my mother's empty shell of a body until the mortuary hearse arrives in the morning.

Mom's funeral is two days later, the sixth yahrzeit or anniversary of dad's death. Our family and her surviving friends gather for the ceremony, My close Denver friends show up to support me, Most of them aren't Jewish. I smile at them trying to read aloud the transliterated Kaddish.

Suddenly, in a surge of gratitude, I grasp the messages last October not to move my car the night of the big blizzard. If I had moved my car, it would not have been crushed. I would not have borrowed mom's car and served as her driver. We would not have healed our relationship as mother and son. My soul knew what was best for me all along.

Yes, all is well, and all will be well.

The New Men's Movement

I feel deep hope for us men freeing ourselves from alpha male habits. Resistance is persistent, yet the trend is real and measurable.

My optimism is informed by 40 years in the men's movement. Since my late twenties, I've attended men's consciousness-raising trainings and support groups. I've joined vulnerable men raging or sobbing in pain, fear, grief, and confusion. I've done deep emotional healing with men. I've engaged with men questioning the meaning of manhood. What helps a man to rule himself instead of trying to rule the world?

At their best, men's support groups or circles are a safe place for us men to drop our pretense masks, speak honestly from our hearts, be our authentic selves without macho posing. We stop living in our heads for awhile. We fully feel all our feelings. We own and transform the shadow aspects of ourselves that we hide, suppress and deny. We grieve, release grievances projected onto others. We are accountable for integrity. As we discover our sacred masculinity, we explore our sacred femininity.

At their worst, men's support groups turn into fraternal lodges for "male bonding" by badmouthing women, bragging, drinking, sports bets, all the usual bull that reinforces old male habits.

The new men's movement embraces equal rights. Gender inequality injures men, too. Men die younger than women from stress, violence and suicide. Men risk financial exploitation and domestic abuse from women (or any mate). Men face "male bashing" and reverse sexism in the media, the workplace and the courts. Generations of male rule invite blowback, but it's overblown. Injustice against anyone harms everyone.

Some men construe "men's rights" as code for their right to keep the testimonial promise to protect and rule a wife as a holy duty. They resent and fear women being equals. News about unfair treatment of any man justifies such men in abusing and bullying women

Gentlemen, let's welcome gender equality. We men have ruled long enough. Combative competition damages us men, those we love, and all life on the earth. Gentle men, we need not be in charge to be powerful. Our greatest inborn gift is keeping it real.

Books — The international men's movement traces to a series of early books, which parallel books in the women's movement. If you are not already familiar, here are foundational works:

• *The Liberated Man* by Warren Farrell (1974) boldly redefines masculinity for emancipating men in relationships with women.

• *The Hazards of Being Male* by Herb Goldberg (1976) breaks ground by showing how "masculine privilege" harms men, such as dying younger and shutting off access to emotions.

• *The New Male* by Herb Goldberg (1979) tells how men can move from self-destruction to self-care, still a valuable guidebook.

• *Why Men Are the Way They Are* by Warren Farrell (1986) lays bare the male-female dynamic, what motivates both genders.

• *Iron John* by Robert Bly (1990) inspires men's personal growth with a "mythopoetic" story to redeem the wild man in any whole man.

• *Fire in the Belly* by Sam Keene (1992) offers a path for men to find within the male ideals of strength, potency and warriorship.

• T*he Way of the Superior Man* by David Deida (1992) is a spiritual guide for men facing the challenges of women, work and sexuality.

More valuable books for new men have been written, and the body of literature is growing. We men are centuries behind women in liberating ourselves. My brothers and I are catching up. To support this assertion, below are some sources for your independent research.

Web Portals— Here are three global websites for new men:

• *Good Men Project* (goodmenproject.com) greets about five million visitors monthly with stories and essays on men's work and issues.

• *MenStuff* (menstuff.org) is an old-style website for the USA and the world. Click the links to pro-feminist, mythopoetic, men's rights, and fatherhood groups. The columns offer diverse opinion.

• *XY* (xyonline.net) is an Australia-based global pro-feminist, anti-violence resource founded in 1998. Search for the latest *Men's Bibliography,* compiled by Michael Flood, listing 40,000 books and articles.

Global Groups — Here are five world organizations for new men:

• *Instituto Promundo* (promundoglobal.org) supports efforts for new masculinities and gender equality in developing nations.

• *MenCare* (men-care.org) promotes fully responsible and healthy fatherhood in 45 countries.

• *MenEngage Alliance* (menengage.org) works with men and boys to advance gender equality in 34 countries.

• *ManKind Project* (mkp.org) provides trainings, support groups and initiations for men seeking emotional authenticity in 22 nations.

• *White Ribbon* (whiteribbon.ca) empowers men and boys to end violence against women, girls and nonbinaries in 60 nations.

National Organizations — A sampling: ABandofBrothers (UK), *Aliansi Laki-laki Baru* (Indonesia), American Men's Studies Association (USA), Biidwewidam Indigenous Masculinities (Canada), Cambodian Men's Network (Cambodia), Caribbean Male Action Network (Trinidad), Equal Community Foundation (India), Essentially Men (New Zealand), Male Champions of Change (Australia), *Masculinidades y Equidad de Género* (Chile), Men Advocating Real Change (USA), Men for Gender Equality (Sweden), Men's Resource Centre (Rwanda), National Organization for Men Against Sexism (USA), *Red de Masculinidad por la Igualdad de Género* (Nicaragua), Reform Resource Centre for Men (Norway), Sonke Men as Partners (South Africa), and numerous others.

For regional and local men's movement activities, search the web for your area using keywords like "men's support groups" or "men's circles" or "men's work." Worthy activity may be happening near you.

I'm only scratching the surface of the men's movement. We new men are liberating ourselves, our families, communities, and our world from destructive "alpha male" habits. New men awaken other men.

〰

2020: DENVER — *Today is Father's Day in the United States of America. Yesterday's solstice means it's the first full day of summer. Adding celestial fun, tonight is a new moon.*

I'm in the fourth month of pandemic isolation in a house I rented after moving home. I'm working on two client books and this book, sitting long hours at my computer. Gardening is my meditation.

I live near the University of Denver. Last night, students partying at a house across the street burst out in howls. The distraction from work annoys me. I judge them immature, heedlessly gathering without masks during the pandemic. More howls. This time their young lust for life enters my heart. Old man, schmold man, I want to feel what they're feeling!

I watch livestream Sunday services from my Denver spiritual science church. The speaker talks about reaching closure with his late father. I think of my father, the lovelight in his eyes at the end. Do I harbor regrets on this Father's Day? Do I regret not giving my dad a namesake grandson? Sometimes. Do I regret missing the joys and sorrows of fatherhood? Today I do. Maybe I'm a better man and grateful dad in another timeline.

After lunch, I join the Sunday vidcall with the New Thought center on Kauai. I hear island friends talk about walks by the ocean. I fly there in my mind from the dry heat wave in Denver. Melissa is not on today's call, but we talk by phone regularly. I'm glad we parted as friends. I'm grateful for calls with Denver friends, too. Helps keep me grounded.

In late afternoon I drive to Emanuel Cemetery and place rocks on the headstones of my father and mother and grandparents, a Jewish tradition. Standing at their graves, I talk to my ancestors in spirit.

Here am I. Still alive. Immunotherapy erased the latest node of cancer. I avoid Covid like the plague it is, and I test often. I'm staying alive because I have a soulwork book to complete. I'm changing from a nebbish into that mensch you always wanted me to be.

I address my father. After a lifetime trying to prove myself to you, I'm giving to myself the love I always needed from you, the love you gave me at the end. I believe you loved yourself by then and found peace. As an elder, you fulfilled your youthful dream to become a fine artist. Now I'm an elder, and I'm still working to fulfill my youthful dream to be a fine writer. Guess I'm a lot like you, after all, Dad.

Mom, I bless you for what you must have gone through raising me. As a man, I'll never know your pain and joy in childbirth. Birthing this book is the closest I may come to a labor of love. Will there be nachas?

Standing at my parents' graves, I bless my lineage.

Gender Equality and Global Change

Our ancient addiction to alpha male rule drives the two most urgent threats to life on earth — climate change and autocracy (tyranny).

Gender roles are changing and equalizing. The old male guard resists mightily, yet more of us men than ever now respect the moral principle of natural equal rights and autonomy for all genders, all people. Regardless of how long the process takes, male dominance is ending.

I'm not alone in this view. Herb Goldberg, PhD, a pioneer of the new men's movement, predicts that by the mid-21st century in most western societies, women will lead in shaping cultural consciousness. In a phone interview, he said women have an edge over most men in their fluid ability to adapt to social changes without rage and violence. Women also support one another in ways competitive men do not.

Perhaps women once ruled society or ruled equally with men. If so, across thousands of years, the pendulum swung to male rule. Now it's swinging into balance. Alpha male rule is ending.

For a lasting shift, in binary terms, we need both male and female liberation, for we are the majority. Women can't be free from gender traps until men are free from gender traps. So, for all us hetero men, stop seeing women only as sex objects. For hetero women, stop seeing men only as success objects. Men, stop trading support for sex. Women, stop trading sex for security. Men, stop trying to be a king to feel safe. Women, stop trying to marry a king to feel safe. Same for nonbinaries. The megatrend of "inclusion" extends to all genders, races, ages, and abilities.

As more men shift from competition to cooperation, from conquest to collaboration, as more women claim their equal power, as nonbinaries claim their equal rights, imagine the benefits rippling around the globe. Gender equality and new men give me hope for our future. The shift into gender equality can transform all aspects of life on earth.

CHAPTER 16

A Rebirth of Democracy

2020: **DENVER** — *On Election Day, November 3, I go for a drive-thru Covid test. I'd already voted days ago by drop box — the safest way to vote in a pandemic. That night, I collapse fatigued on the sofa to watch election returns on TV. I drift away to the dull drone of pundits.*

The Democratic Party platform calls for climate-conscious, pro-union progressive policies. The Republican Party platform has just one policy plank, "to enthusiastically support the President's America-first agenda."

The popular vote goes to Democratic candidate Joe Biden, but that's not final. America's founders did not trust illiterate voters. The popular vote does not rule. The presidency is decided by Electoral College votes, one for each state seat in Congress. Currently, 270 votes are needed to win.

I rise from the sofa and go to bed, tracking election results on my tablet. Six swing states are still counting millions of ballots. Most Democrats voted by mail or drop-off box. Most Republicans voted in-person at polling places because. Trump said (sans proof) mail-in voting is a fraud. He says the only way he'll lose is if the vote is rigged. Meanwhile, his Postmaster General "cut costs" by removing urban mailboxes and sorting machines.

I awaken late morning. Recounts are ongoing. The presidency will not be known for days or weeks. My nation is in limbo awaiting election results, democracy or autocracy? I'm in limbo awaiting Covid test results.

I turn on a newscast. Trump overnight prematurely declared he won the election. He says the ballots still being counted in major cities are illegal and should be ignored. He's rebuffed. Counting continues.

Five swing states are still counting on Saturday as Pennsylvania certifies its 20 Electoral College votes go to Joseph R. Biden, pushing him past 270. Joe Biden, a former senator from Delaware, Obama's vice president, a man who bided his time, will be president. Trump refuses to concede.

On media I watch partying erupt in cities and towns across the USA, Europe and worldwide. I think of the celebrations in Star Wars *after the destruction of the second Death Star, the death of the emperor. Local news covers partying in downtown Denver. Most wear facemasks. Wish I felt well enough to join them. Wish I wasn't afraid of being contagious.*

Genuine Democracy?

I offer a visualization. Imagine that humanity is enlightened enough for genuine democracy. Imagine we're all guided by mindful self rule and personal democracy. Imagine self-government actually works.

Return to reality. We humans selfishly injure others and ourselves, so we need some form of government to keep us safe and free. Therefore, we choose the least evil form of government possible, but it is still evil. Government often is a Hobson's choice, or a Sophie's Choice.

Current forms of government are not handling today's crises well. Climate changes cause upheavals on our overpopulated globe. To survive, humanity is choosing between autocracy or democracy. Disasters and instability help leaders gain followers to win empires. They sell thoughts and feelings tapping authority addiction, all hidden by split perceptions. Why let despots lure us into self-deception, self-destruction?

Thomas Paine in *Common Sense* proposed to American colonists a new form of government. He offered a practical plan for changing from a monarchy to an independent republic. As history records, his plan was followed closely. His plan worked. The plan can be updated.

At some point in this century, maybe the next, we will tire of trusting bullies to keep us safe. When we are ready to shift from alpha male rule to mindful self rule, Paine's plan can be helpful for us to establish more democratic forms of government. Paine's success shows a societal shift from monarchy to democracy *is* possible. Changing the way people make sense of government did occur. Why not do so again?

Is the ideal of genuine democracy too wild to contemplate?

Consider how elements for direct democracy are falling into place. We guide elected leaders with public opinion polling. Legislatures place referendums on ballots for voter ratification. Petitions for ballot initiatives (despite corruptions) bypass legislators entirely and go directly to voters. Transparently run clean election systems ensure the security and privacy of voting. ("Election integrity," sadly, often is a ruse for voter suppression and election theft, so be not fooled by clever wordplay.)

About 87 percent of adults on earth are now functionally literate. Given open access to facts, we *can* educate ourselves and vote intelligently. If we promote universal literacy and critical thinking, real democracy may well be doable. That's a theory worth testing.

The power and courage for democracy already dwells within us all. I trust the wisdom of collective intelligence when we vote our conscience. Ideas like "open politics" and "open source democracy" excite me.

Direct democracy has worked in small communities. New England town meetings, by tradition, give each person a fair say and a private vote. On a larger scale, real democracy is too hard, so we have republics.

In a republic, a "representative democracy," elected leaders are our servants, never our masters. Ideally, if we elected ethical leaders to work for us, can our existing republican governments suffice? That would help, absolutely. It's necessary, urgently, but it's not sufficient. The best republics can only hint at the creativity and prosperity possible in a true democracy. When mindful people live free together, society thrives.

The pragmatist in me warns imagining pure democracy is a foolish fantasy. The idealist in me insists that cynicism about genuine democracy is unfair, and it's a deceit. Genuine democracy has not yet been tried by any nation on earth. Our experiments have never been so bold.

So why have we not tried? The deeper truth, for me, is that humanity has never felt ready nor willing to rein in our wild horses. We've never trusted "we the people" can run a government "by the people" and "of the people." We don't let people directly rule their national governments. Democratic republics remain as far as we dare go. Our old addiction to alpha rulers, I reason, deflects us from trying actual democracy.

I contend humanity is evolving toward responsible self-government. As more of us sense our oneness, we stop abdicating from citizenship. We actively voice our conscious free minds in public affairs.

Who is modeling a global mindset most visibly today? Modern youth — young adults, teens, tweens — Millennials, Gen Z and Gen Alpha, and next gens. Youth are idealistic, like us Boomer, but more realistic about the future. Despite despair, today's youth give me hope.

Why consent to the authoritarian governments around our globe? The rise of democracies since Paine shows we are outgrowing our childish need for kings. Study Hitler, Stalin, Mao, Putin, or Trump. Each flirtation with any cult tyrant proves the perils of despotic thinking.

In the rise of autocracy, we're seeing the desperate despots' last stand. Tyrants are terrified we will see our natural global power and assert it. Despots fight back so hard because they're so threatened. They try harder than ever to ensnare our minds. The culture war on "woke," for instance, represses awakening to our equality and unity on one planet.

Let's heal the traumas behind compulsive survival mechanisms like craving kings. We can learn to live peacefully and abundantly free together. Why delay our ascension into enlightened democracy?

I imagine a day of readiness (or necessity) to build the world anew. For that day, I propose an interim step closer to real democracy. I'm updating Paine's plan by proposing the political model of *direct republics*. I offer this idea (mental construct) as a thought experiment.

I start from Paine's Enlightenment principles. All life is created equal with inalienable natural rights. We all have a right and a duty to live free responsibly and pursue happiness mindfully. We have a right and a duty to evolve global consciousness, each in our own way.

Paine proposed "bringing forward a system of government in which the rights of all men [sic] should be preserved." I've adapted his blueprint in *Common Sense* to present a modern blueprint for evolving democracy. I'm voicing ideas for whenever we're ready, if ever, for conversations about how we govern ourselves, about making sense of freedom.

∿

2021: DENVER — I monitor world news in the first week of the new year. Global climate scientists report 2020 was the warmest year on record. Hong Kong police, pressured by China, arrests 50 pro-democracy organizers. The United Kingdom, influenced by Russian propaganda, finalizes "Brexit" from the European Union. The pandemic endures while variants emerge, surging where suspicion of vaccination is rampant. Superstition kills.

In the USA, Trump tries to overturn the election, and nearly succeeds. He quips to a reporter that he's worked harder in the two months since the election than in all four years of his presidency. For once, given his reported 30,000 lies since becoming president, I believe him.

Trump's antics are reported by daily news media, but I won't learn the full story until a year later when the U.S. House of Representatives *conducts a televised investigation of the efforts by Trump and allies to obstruct the Electoral College vote certification by Congress on January 6, 2021.*

For starters, in the press and in the courts, Trump and loyalists accuse Democrats of massive election fraud. Lawsuits in swing states fail in 60 courtrooms from lack of evidence for changed voting results. Crying election fraud without proof sows public distrust, and that's the goal.

After failing in the courts to prove fraud, Trump and his cohort begin calling swing-state officials, pressuring them to "find" enough votes for him to win, as the Georgia Secretary of State recorded Trump saying.

Meanwhile, Trump allies in swing states recruit slates of fake electors for the Electoral College. They sign "alternative" state electoral certifications of Trump's victory for Congress to consider on January 6. (Some fake electors later will be charged with forgery and election fraud.)

Meanwhile, Trump pressures the vice president to go along. Under the Constitution, which he swore to uphold, the VP has a strictly ceremonial role in the electoral vote certification by Congress. Trump asks him by declare the fake electoral votes are valid, a betrayal of his oath. Trump says in public he hopes the vice president has "the courage to do the right thing."

On Wednesday morning, January 6, Congress meets in a joint session to count the state Electoral College votes and certify the election winner. It's usually a pro-forma ceremony for the peaceful transfer of power.

In the joint session, Trump representatives challenge the electoral vote from swing states with fake electors. A challenge requires debate and a vote in both House and Senate, then a vote by the full Congress. If they deadlock the Electoral College vote count, so no candidate gains 270 votes, under the Constitution, the House will decide the election — one vote per state. A thin GOP House majority would ensure Trump wins. Could work.

Meanwhile, out on the Ellipse, Trump riles up a rally of thousands he'd called here for a "wild" day to "stop the steal" because he'd really "won by a landslide." It's plain by now the VP will not go along, so Trump exhorts the crowd to "be strong" and march on Congress. "If you don't fight like hell, you're not going to have a country anymore!"

Trump wants to join the march, House hearings will report, but his Secret Service driver refuses, despite Trump allegedly grabbing for the steering wheel. He's returned to the White House over his objections.

On TV. I see a mob storm the Capitol, scale its walls like a medieval siege, and break into the building (inviolate since the War of 1812). They wave American flags, Trump flags, Gadsden flags, Confederate flags. They erect a gallows to hang the vice president, who hides but does not leave the building. Members of Congress evacuate or hide seconds before rioters enter the Senate chamber and charge the barricaded House doors. Close combat costs five lives, plus later suicides by traumatized police.

The rally and march (House hearings reveal) are coordinated from a room at the Willard Hotel by Trump's inner circle. They're evidently in touch with ultra-right militia groups, mostly White supremacist, who infiltrate the march and lead the Capitol break-in. They aim to capture and hang the vice president, plus catch and kill legislators telling the "big lie" that Biden won. (Militia leaders later will be convicted of "seditious conspiracy.") Seeing all this unfolding on live TV, I recall the coup in Fiji.

In the White House, I later learn, Trump watches live TV for three hour and ignores pleas to call off the rioters and send the National Guard. I think he delays to give the assault time to succeed at obstructing vote certification, or give him cause to declare martial law. (If he'd tried, I learn, top Pentagon chiefs had all agreed to resign.) Finally, the Acting Secretary of Defense, apparently authorized by the VP, gives the order to send in troops.

At sunset, a police line cordons the Capitol grounds. They wear tactical gear behind plastic shields. With steady steps in drilled unison, they edge back the retreating crowd. Seeing this live on a screen, I recall the civil rights and antiwar protests of my youth along with the Black Lives Matter protests last summer. Police then showed no such restraint.

Congress reconvenes in the battered Capitol later that night. They pick up where they left off. As the Constitution requires, Congress certifies Biden is the President-Elect. All but ten Republicans vote against vote certification, insisting the true president is Trump (who'd just put their lives at risk).

A week later, the House impeaches Trump (a historic second time) for "Incitement of Insurrection." Majority Senate Republicans postpone the trial until after Biden is inaugurated. They call no witnesses and cite Trump being out of office as the pretext to acquit him, a foregone conclusion.

By putting king before country, Trump Republicans deny the republic. They enable autocracy in the name of democracy – the biggest big lie.

A Proposal for Direct Republics

Thomas Paine proposed a defiant idea to American colonists. Instead of rulership by a far monarch, they could form an independent republic. He offered a revolutionary plan for a nation without a king. In his spirit, I offer here an evolutionary plan to democratize our republics.

I propose the new political model of a *direct republic*.

The fear of real democracy leaves republics vulnerable to despots. Paine reasoned that a government should respect people's natural rights. I reason that all people possess an inalienable natural right of consent or dissent over the laws governing them. If this is so, then laws should not be ratified by some king or president. People themselves should ratify the laws ruling them. That's a direct republic. If people are educated enough to vote wisely, the system can work.

Summarized below are the principles for any direct republic. These extend the traits of a "full democracy" for citizen empowerment.

The Rule of Law — Society is ruled by laws, not by regal rulers. John Locke warned, "Wherever law ends, tyranny begins."

In direct republics, voters have the last word over the law of the land. The Law, as enacted, applies in all affairs. The law applies equally to all. No one is above the law or below the law. Laws protect all from violence and fraud. Laws can change, evolving as needs and values evolve.

Lawmaking — Voters use ballots to approve or deny proposed laws. Ballot measures offered for ratification by voters may originate as either legislative *referendums* or as citizen *initiatives.*

In direct republics, leaders cannot decree laws by executive orders, like kings. Leaders do not ratify or veto laws. Voters do that. Leaders may suggest referendums and initiatives, of course, as may any citizen.

Legislative referendums and citizen initiatives reach the ballot only with abundant support. This filters out corrupt and insipid dross.

Initiatives can reach ballots only with sufficient petition signatures. Verify signatures from secure voter-registration records. Enforce "truth in petitioning" laws. Outlaw lying to gain signatures.

Deter deceptive ballot measures. Require clear ballot titles with single subjects. Write laws in plain language that literate voters can read and understand. Let people decide fairly for themselves how to vote.

For each ballot measure, citizens may vote "Yes" or "No" or "Revise." An "R" vote says, "I like the idea, but not as written." This innovation lets citizens vote for improvements before a law is finally approved.

A majority vote (not plurality) keeps new laws few but worthy. For truly pivotal policy shifts, consider a super-majority to ratify.

Fix errors. Uphold the right to redress grievances by putting on the ballot a measure to amend or repeal any law. Also, voters may remove or "recall" elected officials. No leader may interfere with recall voting.

Publicly Funded Elections — Elections belong to the people themselves, so curtail private money in public elections.

End legal bribery with private campaign contributions by lobbyists. Private funding of campaigns is not "free speech." That legal fiction disenfranchises those of scant means. Public funding assures free speech for all citizens, like leaflets in a laundromat, regardless of wealth.

How does public funding work in practical terms? Candidates get equal public funds for their campaigns, as do ballot-measure committees.

Special interests can't fund campaigns to sway the electorate. Ban paying for dirty tricks. Enforce truth in advertising. Enforce equal media time for ballot issues and candidates, like the old U.S. Fairness Doctrine.

Voters decide the election rules. Voters set campaign funding levels. Voters set campaign seasons by weeks or months. Allow early voting. The cutoff is Election Day as polls close. Try proportional voting over winner-takes-all. Consider ranked-choice voting. Make voting easy, fast and safe. The more voters the better. Only despots restrict voting.

Confirm all voters' identity. Ensure voters only vote once per ballot. Protect the anonymity of all votes as private acts of conscience.

Every vote counts, so count every vote. Elections expert Brad Friedman (BradBlog) calls publicly hand-counted anonymous paper ballots the only verifiable form of voting. (Test human vs. machine error rates.)

Universal Voter Eligibility — All adults of age are registered to vote. It's automatic as a natural right. Identity verification may not be used for discrimination or suppression. Opt-out must be available as a right, too. Forcing people to vote is as undemocratic as denying them a vote.

Legislative Branch — Legislatures are deliberative writing bodies. Assemblies of elected representatives draft laws for voters to ratify. Each "bill" faces committee markups. Every bill faces amendments. Bills that pass by a majority vote in the assembly then go on voter ballots.

Any citizen may suggest a law idea for legislators to turn into a bill. Good ideas draw favor. Neutral legislative staff helps research related facts and legal issues. Staff may help clarify and refine bill language.

Every introduced bill gets a floor vote. No legislator may filibuster or veto a bill. If a legislature is bicameral, a bill passing in one chamber must get a floor vote in the other. Defeated bills may be revised. Legislators innately will limit workloads by introducing fewer bills. Any bill the body finally passes is referred to voters as a *referendum* or *proposition*.

Judicial Branch — Form an independent elected judiciary. Publicly funded elections ensure judges are accountable to citizens, not private donors. No appointments by politicians. Jurists serve a medium to long term. No lifetime terms. Judges are not kings in medieval courts. Judges must uphold the highest ethics and be loyal to the law alone.

Judges may be nominated by citizen initiatives or nominated by elected leaders in any branch of government. As a general rule, be wary of judges nominating themselves. Voters may recall judges.

To reach the ballot, judicial nominees must first pass a "bar exam" on legal principles and procedures. They must survive ethical scrutiny, disclose all income and affiliations, vow to recuse in all related cases.

In civil and criminal cases, judges apply the rule of law as enacted by voters. Jurists may set precedents in applying the law, subject to appeal. Judges may not invent laws or polices by their rulings; they are not kings. Judges can rule a law unconstitutional, subject to appeal. Legislators may revise that law, or not, subject to re-ratification by voters. Judges also may propose or change laws with ballot initiatives, as may any citizen.

Courts enforce civil and human rights. Equal justice for all under the law is a right. In criminal or civil cases, if guilt is found, make parties whole. *Restorative justice* is "unitive" rather than punitive.

Law Enforcement — A tested corps of professional peace officers is vital to protect our safe use of free will, to guard our lives and property. Let voters decide the extent of police powers.

Who qualifies as police officers? Screen for emotional intelligence and cultural sensitivity. Seek officers who value human and civil rights. Sift out power addicts. Officer bias and misconduct merit judicial inquiry and media exposure. With transparency, society polices the police.

Prison is reserved for the recalcitrant. Uplifting lives cuts recidivism. Prisons and jails must be humane, restorative, accountable. Government alone runs all jails and prisons. No private prisons. Crime should not be a profit center. Getting rich off inmate labor is like slavery.

The Military — The more we mature, the less we need armies. George Washington wrote, "My first wish is to see this plague of mankind, war, banished from the earth." If the world outlaws conquest, armies are solely for defense and disasters. Amies may not act as police.

Executive Branch — Power in a direct republic resides in the hands of the people, not the leaders we elect, not any hereditary ruling cliques. So, where is the "king" in a direct republic? There is none! Paine warned that nothing brings ruin upon society like kings.

Elected executive branch leaders and professional staff administer the laws ratified by the voters. Leaders do not sign a bill into law, nor veto it. Only voters ratify laws. Leaders create policies to enact laws. Leaders may never decree laws on their own that the courts must enforce.

Emergencies are an exception, but expediency opens doors to despots. Urgent measures must sunset soon, so voters enact a valid law.

I advocate the 12-Step movement's Second Tradition. Elected leaders are but "trusted servants." They do not govern.

The Press — The Fourth Estate is the diligent watchdog of government. A free press is vital for a free society. Fair and balanced reporting of facts must be rigorous, not a sly slogan hiding lies and bias.

Uphold press freedom. No censorship or book banning. Libel and slander laws place the burden of proof on plaintiffs. The presumption of innocence hinders lawsuits from muzzling the press.

I favor nonprofit journalism for press reliability. When a newsroom becomes a profit center, beware of silent self-censorship. Truth-telling is how good journalists sleep with a clear conscience.

Caveats: A free press protects democracy best when media literary is common. Also label all AI-generated content; protect copyright.

Checks and Balances — A balance of powers among government branches is crucial. Let them be co-equals who fairly check one another. The executive branch poses the greatest risk of autocracy, yet true power does not vest in the legislature, the courts, the executive, or the press. In a direct republic, voters hold the ruling power.

To paraphrase Abraham Lincoln, government *of* the people and *for* the people must be equal to government *by* the people. The best check on abuse of power is educated citizens exercising the right to vote.

Corruption Control — Government service is an honored duty and privilege. Officials do their jobs and go home. Term limits hinder graft and autocracy. Professional standards, good pay and benefits draw good people. Do public jobs pay private-sector rates? Let voters decide.

Whenever anyone gets power, human frailties and vices surface. So, forbid gifts, favors and promises. When evidence of corruption warrants, levy indictments. *No immunity for illegal acts while in office.*

An equally foul crime is filing false charges to hobble a public official. Prosecute it as a violent felony, a brutal assault on the body politic.

Separate Religion and State — Never allow any organized religion to dictate government policy. Decide public policy by public votes.

Do not let True Believers control lawmaking, so their beliefs become the law. The faithful might feel a moral duty to enforce their faith on all. Consider how 13 nations today execute atheists. Likewise, beware when secular unbelievers take over and turn militantly autocratic.

Limited Government — Jefferson wrote, "That government is best which governs least." Good government empowers self-government.

How much should government do for us? How do we pay for services like fire and police or roads and sewers? Social democrats fund services with taxes. Conservatives and libertarians favor privatization. Public or private, either way, we pay. Do we get fair value? I imagine educated voters deciding issues like the size-and reach of government.

Now you have an overview of direct republics. I invite you to talk about these ideas, play with them, test them in real life. Start small.

≈≈

2022: DENVER — *As the year begins, I follow environmental news. The 26th world Conference of Parties negotiates another weak climate change deal. From phasing out all coal, they wind up winding down. Weeks later, a mile-wide tornado flattens Kentucky towns to matchsticks.*

As for the future of democracy, I track two major news events.

Massed Russian armed forces in February invade democratic Ukraine. Putin proclaims Ukraine is Russian by right of historic empire (fled by my ancestors). His troops fail to capture Kyiv. They do occupy southeast Ukraine to reinforce Crimea, annexed in 2014. The USA and Europe unite to send munitions and funds for Ukraine's defense and counter-attacks. As war drags on, ever-fewer Russians brave arrest to protest czar Putin. I think of Hitler annexing Austria before invading Poland in 1939 — the start of World War II. Is this the start of World War III?

Back in the USA, the hot "breaking news" is Congress investigating the January 6 "insurrection" a year ago. Testimony by 1,000 witnesses confirms a million documents. Trump evidently knew he'd lost the election but simply refused to accept it. Seems he cannot admit to being a "loser," so the election had to be stolen. I deduce that Mr. Trump tried to trump the Constitution and conspired to overthrow the duly elected government.

In my civics books, that's called a coup. It's authoritarian as hell.

Most Republicans, and a third of all voters, believe Trump's big lie that he won the 2020 election, that it was rigged, despite 60 courts dismissing his fraudulent election claims for lack of actual evidence. Fact vs faith.

Republicans decry Democrats' big lie that Biden won. President Biden, despite historic achievements, bears a faux mantle of illegitimacy, fabricated by weapons of mass deception in the worldview wars.

Polls say 40 percent of Republicans and Independents condone violence against an "illegitimate" government like the Biden administration. I hear talk of civil war and revolution. I hear militia "patriots" liken themselves to the "Sons of Liberty" who proudly hail the "Spirit of 1776."

Today I heard a Trumpie pundit call Thomas Paine a hero and mis-quote him to defend fighting America's "illegal government." I doubt Paine would return the favor. He disdained lies and illogic. Paine would declare dismay the nation he inspired to be free is now craving a king.

I write these words as a journal entry to make sense of the situation.

Thoughts on World Governance

If we let ancient authoritarian habits endure much longer on earth, we will be abusing our descendants. We will be leaving to them the work of liberation we ought to do ourselves. What if, instead, we leave to them a settled form of global governance that's both safe and free?

Trying to create a "world government" is risky. It may be perverted into a dystopian global dictatorship. "Globalization" instead can generate a world rebirth of democracy with equal rights for all under law.

A more valid reason for delay is that no practical blueprint for world governance has been presented. Lacking a clear design, we wisely hesitate to replace old structures with new constructions.

For guidance, I turn to Paine's blueprint in *Common Sense.*

Paine proposed declaring independence and then electing an assembly to write a constitution for the new nation, which may take years, he said. Once a constitution is drafted and approved, the drafting assembly would be dissolved, its members given due praise and honors. That body then would be replaced by the first officially elected congress.

Those drafting the constitution must not immediately serve in the government, Paine warned. Nobody should write into law a power base for themselves. Leaders must do their jobs and go home.

The founders followed his plan. Six months after *Common Sense,* on the Fourth of July, 1776, the Continental Congress signed the Declaration of Independence. Once the difficult war was won in 1781, a constitutional convention convened. That body drafted and revised a U.S. Constitution, adopted in 1787. The first elected Congress sat in 1789.

Copying Paine, we could elect a global constitutional convention of delegates from all nations, representing the whole of humanity. (Could the UN conduct a publicly-funded election?) That elected assembly would admit NO politically appointed delegates. None. Give delegates a good stipend. Ban gifts and bribes. Track lobbying. Open meetings and open records. Clean and transparent. If any delegate departs, the nation elects a replacement. Delegates do their jobs and go home.

This world constitution will affect all life on earth for centuries. Let the drafting assembly take years to deliberate. Write tight and get it right. Democracy takes time. Worth the work.

Once a world constitution is drafted, put the charter to a secure vote in a global referendum. If it fails to pass, revise and vote again, and again and again. If a world constitution is ever ratified by a popular vote, ideally a consensus, dissolve the drafting assembly. Give delegates due praise and honor. Hail the seating of the first elected world congress.

Is it an impossible dream? The League of Nations failed. The United Nations fails from vetoes by villains. I'm planting the seedthought of direct republics. Utopian visions need political will to grow.

2024: DENVER — *On November 19, two weeks after the U.S. election, four days after a super full moon, the day Pluto enters Aquarius for 20 years, I'm sitting on my bed and writing. I'm replacing this narrative, written before Donald Trump won the election. I'm journaling to find realistic hope.*

I'd distilled in this section my evidence and logic for voting against Mr. Trump. I reported on civil juries convicting him for years of business fraud, plus sexual assault and defamations of his victim. I reported indictments by four federal and state grand juries on 88 criminal counts. I focused on the federal charges alleging conspiracy to subvert and obstruct vote certification by Congress on January 6, 2021, to defraud the United States, and to violate voters' civil rights. Under law, he's innocent until proven guilty.

Trump told his base, "I'm being indicted for you." They're coming after me, he said, because I'm defending you. He played victim and rescuer, I felt, to hide guilt as a perpetrator. He called all the charges "political" and "election interference." I called them accountability and democracy at work.

Trump did stand trial on New York State charges of hiding hush-money to silence a porn-star lover before the 2016 election. He deployed Roy Cohn's tactics for tainting jury pools by attacking judges, prosecutors and witnesses in the media (as his diehards made death threats). He predicted a "bloodbath" if he was sent to jail. Despite this, a Manhattan jury last May convicted him on 34 fraud counts, upheld on appeal. After the election, the judge sentenced him to "unconditional discharge." Under law, Trump is a convicted felon, but no punishment. He's free to go be the 47th U.S. president.

Meanwhile, the Justice Department dropped all federal charges against Trump. An internal memo forbids prosecuting any sitting president (thus he skirted first-term charges tied to Russian election meddling). I'm grateful the special prosecutor's report documents evidence on the public record.

Trump delayed all his federal trials by claiming "presidential immunity," appealing to the U.S. Supreme Court. (He'd appointed three of the Federalist Society justices.) The highest court in July ruled (6-3 vote) that the president has "absolute immunity" for all "official acts" as president. In effect, the U.S. President is a virtual king above the law! This unconstitutional distortion of the Constitution, I contend, defies and defiles what Paine and the original founders established — a republic free of monarchy. I'm heartsick.

After the Supreme Court ruling, I'd hoped the Democratic presidential candidate would beat Trump. Biden withdrew (age issues) and endorsed VP Kamala Harris, who fought Trump in a crazy tight race. On November 5, with 270 Electoral College votes needed to win, Trump swept the swing states for 312 votes. He's not disputing the result, as he'd do if he'd lost. Trump won. Deal done. He beat Harris in the popular vote by just 2.4 million votes with a 49.9 percent plurality, not a majority, not a "mandate,"

Democratic pundits are rationalizing Trumps' victory in dizzying ways, from conspiracy theories to finger-pointing. None of it is provable nor fruitful. In my view, Trump won because authority addiction won.

My Moonies sojourn helps me sense the mindset in the "cult of Trump," as Dr. Steven Hassan dubs it. For instance, at a July outdoor Trump campaign rally in Pennsylvania, an assault rifle bullet grazed Trump's right ear. Secret Service agents bustled him offstage; they spotted and killed a rooftop sniper, age 20, a local "loner" likely seeking notoriety (big security lapse). The faithful hailed the near-miss as "divine intervention." We all are sinners; and God is using sinner Trump in these Last Days. Belief creates reality, True believers anywhere conflate facts to fit faith. Split perceptions reign.

2025: DENVER — *On January 21, the day after Trump's inauguration (sun conjunct Pluto), I fear refugees from reason could cancel the republic. Trump promised he won't be a dictator "other than Day One." Yesterday he signed a record 26 executive orders, like ending DEI efforts (white male rule); declaring a national emergency at the Mexican border (nationalism), exiting the World Health Organization and Paris Climate Agreement (anti-science), and (unconstitutionally) revoking "birthright citizenship."*

Trump is enacting "Project 2025," the federalist Heritage Foundation's 887-page plan for a "unitary executive" (autocracy). He's said he seeks "a unified Reich" (a one-party state) with "election integrity" laws (rigged voting). "You won't have to vote anymore," he's declared. "It'll be fixed."

Trump was stymied before by (ethical) officials in his administration. Now only lackeys get jobs. He's firing "rogue bureaucrats who are deliberately undermining democracy" (purging its defenders from government). He vows reprisals. "I am your retribution," he's told fans, warning his foes, "If you go after me, I'm coming after you." His "weaponized" Justice Department will proptect him, prosecute enemies, Democrats and the press, he's proclaimed,, are the "enemy within" and "enemy of the people" (tyrant talk).

He's begun (militarized) "mass deportations" of undocumented (non-white) immigrants (1920s Palmer Raids on steroids). He wants "cheap land" near cities to build "detention camps" for "radical left thugs" or other "vermin" (Hitler's term). The homeless will go to "tent cities." If protests turn unruly, he may "restore order" under the 1807 Insurrection Act (martial law).

Globally, given his "America First" (isolationist) stance, he's imposing (protectionist) tariffs that hike inflation, incite trade wars. He's warned NATO he might tell Russia "to do whatever the hell they want" in Europe. In Israel, he's backing Netanyahu (recently indicted for war crimes).

Most perilous for the planet, Trump is reversing "climate hoax" policies, telling big oil to "Drill, baby, drill!" I hear a dismal American tune.

I draw hope from political realities. Trump faces hurdles that can hinder or halt him from becoming the king he evidently wants to be.

In Congress, dysfunction may check Trump. Republicans won the U.S. House and Senate by a thin edge. They'll often need Democrats to pass bills. Will compromise dilute Trump's plans, or will deadlock stop him cold?

As Trump bypasses Congress with his executive orders, expect lawsuits. Will courts uphold him? I hope conscience overrules obeisance.

I feel stronger hope that Trumpian tyrannies stir pushback and peaceful (playful) mass demonstrations. I trust global sense in action.

If Trump runs again in 2028, if he can be defeated, will he get indicted for "unofficial" crimes? If he's jailed, will his faithful react in rebel rage? Or, will they find a new messiah? Will that end Mr. Toad's wild ride?

Paine said, "Those who abuse liberty when they possess it, would abuse power could they obtain it." A century ago, Hitler went to jail in 1923 for a failed putsch (coup). Elected Nazis ruled Germany by 1933 and Europe by 1940. In 2024 USA, Trump eluded jail for a failed coup and got reelected. He covets the Panama Canal, Greenland and Canada. Given America's "Arsenal of Democracy," will brainy Trump try to take over the world?

That's really up to us, isn't it?

Hints for Wiser Minds

Amidst global political and ecological crises, in lieu of humanity ever maturing into direct democracy for resolving problems, I'm offering the interim political model of *direct republics*. I'm proposing that laws be enacted with the informed consent of educated voters. As Rousseau said, "Every law the people has not ratified in person is null and void." This is a pivotal shift in the way we think about democracy. Such a shift in our thinking about government and citizenship is long overdue.

I merely offer hints for wiser minds to develop. Your ideas may be better. I hope you publish them. Questions arise in me, and I'm the one making the proposal, for which I thank Thomas Paine. He speaks for me in *Common Sense* when he writes:

> Wherefore, security being the true design and end of government, it unanswerably follows, that whatever Form thereof appears most likely to ensure it to us, with the least expense and greatest benefit, is preferable to all others.

I believe our natural oneness equips us for conscious liberty through personal and social responsibility, guided by a global sense of our unity. Ordinary people restrain despots with consumer choices and activism. The power for mindful self rule and personal democracy lives in us all, no matter our words for it. If I'm able to do it, if inconsistently, anybody can. We can create a better future for ourselves and our posterity.

My greatest fear in today's global crises is that we terrified humans may default to our old habit of trusting kings or other masters to save us. My greatest hope in today's global crises is that we terrified humans awake to our oneness and work together in peaceful coalitions of conscience. Inner peace creates world peace. Free minds create a free world.

To update a famous 19th century call to action: Global thinkers on the earth, unite! We have a world to win and nothing to lose but the chains we forged ourselves.

CHAPTER 17

Begin the World Anew

*2020: **DENVER** — By Election Day in November, I'm feeling weak and depleted. I barely walk 20 feet before having to pause and catch my breath. After watching election returns from the sofa, I lie limp in bed, afraid I may die before I wake. The veil is thin. Like when I consciously chose to breathe and live, I choose to trust and sleep. I am not done here yet.*

The Covid lab test finds "No detectable virus." Great news! Confusing news. Is it cancer? Since 2016, I'd scanned clear until 2018. Immunotherapy cleared me again in months. Cancer arose last winter as I moved to Denver. Immunotherapy cleared me by spring. Has it returned so fast?

Fresh scans find "deep vein thrombosis." Blood clots occlude both legs, knees to the pelvic iliac. Too many hours in a bad desk chair? My condition is life-threatening, says the doctor, "but we caught it in time." Blood thinner, compression pants and bedrest reopen my veins. Vigor returns slowly.

On December 21, the winter solstice, I go outside to see the "Christmas Star." Astronomically, Jupiter and Saturn align in the constellation Aquarius. Astrologically, the conjunction heralds the Aquarian Age.

On New Year's Day, my focus is house cleaning. I'm raising windhorse, clearing the old year, opening for the new. I begin dancing to a favorite rock song until I must sit, out of breath. I see what condition my condition is in. My body may be disabled, but not my spirit, and I am done disabling my life. I imagine myself whole and free to be fully me. What's in my way?

The Secret of Miracles

If our bodies are congealed light being us in all our unique forms, and if light is alive, even awake and aware, then anything is possible, even miracles. Physics meet metaphysics in quantum entanglements.

The Path of Least Resistance by Robert Fritz offers practical miracles. Accept current reality squarely as we vividly imagine the reality we desire. Magnifying the creative tension of cognitive dissonance, we migrate one decision at a time from the reality we have to the reality we want. Looking back on the arc of our choices, we call our progress a miracle.

Miracles manifest in the gap between vision and reality. If I let myself imagine a future and let go with thanks in anticipation, if I focus on what I want, not how I get it, if I do what's natural and easy, miracles happen. Visualization with gratitude is "the secret" behind Science of Mind, Unity, Divine Science, Spiritual Science, Law of Attraction, A Course in Miracles, Wicca, shamanism, alchemy, lightwork. Gratitude is my open door policy. In contrast, grievances block flow and draw misfortune.

Shifting how I make sense of reality shifts what I think, which shifts what I feel, shifting my energy, shifting interactions, changing my life, changing our world. Miracles are ripples in reality.

Miracles occur when we claim our power in an interwoven universe. Miracles occur when global consciousness unites with social conscience. Miracles occur when we stop seeking saviors to give us the miracles we refuse to give ourselves. Why deny we are miracle workers?

Miracles teacher Marianne Williamson famously wrote in *A Return to Love*. "It is our light, not our darkness, that most frightens us." In 2020 and 2024, Marianne Williamson ran for U.S. President. She'd expand on Barbara Marx Hubbard's Peace Room to create a Department of Peace. Democratic primary voters earned her a podium on the primetime TV candidates' debates. She plainly spoke realistic moral truth to power — modeling enlightened *spiritual politics*. Gives me hope.

To encourage 21st century enlightenment, I write to revive the ideas of Thomas Paine and the 18th century Enlightenment. I reason that their revolutionary ideals can quicken our evolutionary leap on earth.

Uniting personal growth and social change builds the global sense movement to repair our world. Let us see ourselves as a movement and get better organized. Let us manifest the miracle of shifting male rule and authority addiction into mindful self rule and personal democracy.

Our crises on earth will worsen until we can agree on a "whole of humanity" approach. If we do, our descendants will thank us.

⋙

2021: DENVER — *Blood clots! Another wake-up call. After nearly dying three times from cancer, again I face death unless I take care of myself.*

I ponder, are my veins clogged because my life is clogged?

In summer, an intuitive says I manifested clots in my veins by trying to control outcomes to feel safe. My inner tyrant constricts me. I try to know final results up front. I get impatient, lose empathy, lose serenity, live in the past or future, stop being present, block the joy of now. The universe cannot co-create life with me. The clots tell me to let my lifeforce flow free.

Her words resonate. I shift how I make sense of life

I recall life flowing when I moved back to Denver. I saw synchrony as resettling fell into place within weeks — home, car, income. I cherished living solo that first year of pandemic. Amen for calls with Melissa and grounding vidcalls with men's support groups. My hermit harmony faded as wariness of contagion conflated with doubts and fears about the future of this book. Ah, there! Hiding there are shadow forces clogging my lifeflow.

In autumn, I update the book's facts and revise or add narratives, like this one. The book evolves as I evolve. Writing the book evolves me. I believe it's my soulwork, dharma, kuleana, mission. I stayed alive for this book, and if clots express shadow resistance, what is it I fear here?

The book is essentially done, and yet I defer promoting it. Am I afraid the book will fail? No, failure takes me off the hook. Obscurity is safety. I fear the book's success. I fear discovery of my imperfections (imposter syndrome). More primal, I fear backlash from authority addicts.

I'm in conflict. As a reality check, I revisit Takeo Doi. My ideas do not fit prevailing social norms and cultural values, which often disagree with my inner sense of what is natural and right. I see conflicts between my inner truth, outer face, and need for acceptance. My anatomy of self is congested. Did I clog my veins to put off putting out this book?

I'm like a Pushmi-Pullyu in a Dr. Dolittle story, going in two directions at once. I want the book to shift society, and I want to stay securely invisible. So, did I choose to breathe and live for a dream I now dread coming true? Absurd contradictions constrict my lifeflow. Playing small for safety is folly. Fearing my flame being snuffed denies our oneness. I shift.

I agree to show up and shine. I'll never know what I can do unless I try. I'm afraid, and I'm done hiding this little light of mine under a bushel.

Repairing the World

"We have it in our power to begin the world over again," Thomas Paine wrote at the end of *Common Sense*. "The birthday of a new world is at hand." Never again will we stand at such a pivotal moment in time when civilization goes global, so the need to accept our oneness is clear. As Paine wrote, "Every day convinces us of its necessity."

Judaism advocates *tikkun olam,* repairing the world. Guided by a global sensibility, we can repair the world in which we live and breathe and have our being. We need not wait for government to act.

I agree with Paine that good government is due to the nature of the people, not the nature of the government. If we are naturally good, we do not need kings to lead us. We can govern our governments. We can have a fair say in the laws ruling us. We can wake up and grow up.

Those of us evolving global sense already abound in all the power needed to practice mindful self rule and personal democracy. Intelligence flourishes in every corner of our minds. We solve problems as they arise. We feel empathy and act on it. Every day we expand freedom, justice and peace in the world. Nature planted loving feelings in us for good and wise purposes. Love is the guardian of divinity in our souls.

A billion of us on earth are expelling from our hearts and minds the "barbarous and hellish power," as Paine said, that stirs our inner demons to destroy us. We no longer can reconcile ourselves to tyranny inside our minds or in the world. At least, I cannot reconcile it in myself.

〰

2023: DENVER — On the summer solstice, I get terribly ill for ten days. I'm flattened by fatigue, headache, ear ache, runny nose, and a throat so sore each swallow is a grimace. Food and water taste "off" afterwards. My doctor calls it Covid, a variant. Now I'm a pandemic survivor.

An autumn ultrasound finds clots remain in my upper legs and iliac veins, but blood is flowing. As for cancer, a scan finds a .6 cm node in a lung and a "mass" in the hilar area. I resume immunotherapy.

Again I face my mortality. Will I live long enough to do the work I stay alive to do? Feels like now or never. I let the universe do for me what I cannot do for myself. And when I die, dust in the wind, this brainchild book will carry on. Until then, I am curious about life in the world unseen.

At the harvest moon, I do family constellations work with a facilitator in Boulder. My dad shows up energetically. He did not fulfill his young vision of success as an artist, same as I've not fulfilled my young vision of success as an author. He paid bills with a job same as I pay bills with a job. I honor my father by holding back on my dream, same as he did. I mirror him from loyalty and love. Is this what he wants for his wayward son? Catalytic insights alter engrams. I honor my father best by getting out of my own way.

Time for a Global Shift

The present winter of our discontent is worth a lifetime if used for personal and world enlightenment. I cannot propose any other plan short of mindful self rule and personal democracy, in any words, that promises us a full day of certain peace, civil society, gender equality, earth recovery, and the liberty to thrive in ways that make global sense.

We need to unite and advocate global common sense — the fact we all are one. We cannot afford to stay silent. Every quiet strategy for change has failed. The nonviolence of Gandhi and King was never quiet.

If heartfelt prayers for a better world seem to go unheard, we can remind ourselves, nothing may change until we do, or until I do. Let us accept shared responsibility for co-creating a livable world. No matter what positive thing we may do, why delay doing it? Why procrastinate?

We may never again get another chance like today to generate world enlightenment. We may never again have the heart nor the energy to mount another global campaign to create a free and sustainable world that works for us all, not just the few, or at least most of us.

Likewise, we may never get another chance like today to transform our hearts and liberate our minds. Cosmic forces are aligned for human enlightenment, say metaphysical teachers, and social trends confirm it. Given more than a billion global thinkers on earth, given our power from global connectivity, opportunities for personal growth and social change have never been greater — nor has the need, at least for me. Today's rare window of opportunity may close all too soon.

Dare we ignore conscience telling us to act? Too many worthy causes failed to yield lasting change from the lack of one more willing worker with the patience and pluck to knock on one more door, make one more call, send one more text, shuttle one more grandma to the polls. Grassroots democracy takes work. The work elevates everybody.

If we fail to act now, despotic shadow forces may dominate us this century into the next. How many tyrannical parties have been elected or seized power as people hung back for safety? Paine said, "The strength and power of despotism consists wholly in the fear of resistance."

Fearing retribution, we may accept leaders' lies. We may profess an election was stolen, not lost. We may reconcile being untrue to our souls by letting leaders think for us. As despots pursue power amid climate upheavals, the more we give in to fear, let crises overwhelm us, the safer it feels to let leaders rule our minds. But as Paine advised, it is necessary to our happiness that we be mentally faithful to ourselves.

We cannot afford to defer the inner and outer work of self and world liberation. Let's stop looking outside ourselves for salvation from kings and masters. Let's recover from addiction to alpha rule.

"To talk of friendship with those in whom our reason forbids us to have faith, and our affections wounded through a thousand pores instruct us to detest, is madness and folly," said Paine. "O ye that love [hu]mankind! Ye that dare oppose, not only the tyranny, but the tyrant, stand forth!"

2023: KAUA'I — *I'm on island in December to spend the holidays with Melissa. Our relationship is gentle. We've done our soul work. We're siblings from past lives, old friends, like bookends, sitting on a shore bench. We have each other's back. I never imagined at age 23 that I'd feel these feelings at 73, yet here am I on Kaua'i keeping it real as best I can.*

Melissa asks me to wear a Santa costume when she sings, "Santa Baby" on Christmas Eve at the Center for Spiritual Living Kaua'i. When married, we'd created a funny stage routine with a payoff. I enjoy the irony of a nice Jewish boy hamming it up as Santa Claus. I bellow, "Ho, ho, oy!"

We talk story about friends on Maui who lost homes when Lahaina burned. Fires also scorched Canada, Greece, Turkey, elsewhere. Hurricanes and long rains flooded Africa, India, Japan and China, even Beijing, even Melissa's New York. Climatologists call 2023 the hottest year ever.

We discuss world news. The war in Ukraine grinds on. Heavy losses. Putin's mercenary general mutinies; the man's plane explodes in midair. China strains under Xi Jinping building an Asian empire. India under Modi keeps tipping totalitarian. In Africa, a coup ends democracy in Niger.

Sitting on her lanai, we discuss Israel's autocratic prime minister, "Bibi" Netanyahu. He's been leveraging the Knesset to get control over the judiciary prosecuting him for corruption. Huge public protests offer hope.

Sadly, last October 7, Iran-backed Hamas in the Gaza Strip fired 5,000 rockets at Israel as 1,500 militants attacked, killing 1,200, all ages, taking 240 hostages, all ages. Atrocities. Israel united widely behind Netanyahu. He ordered an assault on Hamas in Gaza, home to two million Palestinians. Gaza is bombed to rubble, in time killing 45,000 Palestinians, half women and children, some used as shields by Hamas. More atrocities. Humanitarian protests urge a cease fire, urge Netanyahu to resign. He attacks Lebanon, Iran and Yemen. War can keep him in power, out of prison.

We watch news reports on students and stockholders urging universities and corporations to divest from holdings in Israel, until official policy changes. The tactic helped end apartheid in South Africa. The difference is that Israel is both the perpetrator and victim of apartheid. Seeing personal democracy countering authority addiction, I feel a glimmer of hope amid sorrow.

I lament to Mellissa that antisemitism is rampant, as is Islamophobia.
Why blame all Jews for Israelis electing an ultra-right messianic government
that acts atrociously? If we pick some bad apples, are all to blame?

We agree the greatest danger is regional war. If major nations join in,
will Abraham's feuding sons ignite Armageddon? Many Christians hope so.
I get a map of north Israel, find the Jezreel, locate Tel Megiddo.

On New Year's Eve, we join the CSL community for inaugurating a new
floor-sized labyrinth. Walking slowly to the center of any labyrinth helps me
step into my center. Tonight, I release what no longer serves me. To refill open
space, I step into a willingness to do the work before me, as best I can. I let
the universe do for me what I cannot do for myself. My heart opens in delight.
As I leave the labyrinth, a friend remarks on my beaming smile.

Making Sense of Freedom

Our 21st century is setting the course for humanity and the planet.
Will we feed our old craving for autocracy or new hunger for democracy?
By healing our inner conflicts, seeing our natural oneness and equality,
we may yet avert climate catastrophes and terrible dictatorships.

To end tyranny in our world, first end it in our minds. If authority
addiction and split perceptions trap us in self-deceptions, we may default
to trusting in kings and escaping from freedom.

When I accept as a fact that light is being me in the act of being all,
(first premise in reasoning), I make sense of life as one. I release crippling
victimhood, own my power. I'm a generator, waiting to respond.

My shadow trap is that I want to control outcomes, so I feel secure.
Fear feeds the grumpy old tyrant within, so confusion and doubt overrule
reason and conscience. In youth, I trusted a cult for "truth," so life made
sense. To feel accepted and loved, I lied to myself. Took years of tears and
pain to regain my freedom of heart and mind.

Making sense of liberty in a new way today, I seek freedom from all
abuse of authority, *and* I seek the freedom to be me as I am. I claim the
natural right to be conscious, to govern my own mind, to choose which
wolf I'm going to feed in my head. Seeing our oneness, I can choose to
live free responsibly, creatively, kindly, and gratefully.

The despots' biggest Big Lie is that democracy is a "failure." The hoax is belied by democratic success stories in communities and businesses, like social entrepreneurs. Participative problem-solving and decision-making yields excellence. Collaborative teamwork is more dynamic and effective than letting a boss think for us. If mindful personal sovereignty displaces despotic mental habits, democracy becomes doable.

Aa we sense our natural global power, leader worship loses its luster. As bullies with feet of clay are exposed, if true believers admit heroes lied, their worldview crumbles. The mindmap crumples.

Since January 6, 2021, I'm forced to admit that half of my fellow Americans see reality very differently than I do. They believe Trump won. They feel Biden stole the election. They believe they have a duty to rebel. Beholding the flipside so starkly is unsettling.

Youthful living in a cult helps me honor how Trump can make sense to good people. In every land, anyone can believe a lie is The Truth. The most intelligent of us can become ardent believers if untrained in critical thinking and emotional literacy. Sharing some secret truth makes us feel special, so we buy conspiracy theories, like a Jewish plot to rule the world. Losing our loneliness in belonging, we believe because we *want* to believe. We are "thinking for ourselves" in groupthink silos, research rabbit holes, swirling mindwarp maelstroms. Our minds are not our own.

Tyranny over our minds is the opposite of mindful self rule.

〰〰

2024: New York — *I'm in New Rochelle for Thomas Paine Day, the yearly celebration of his life on the June 8 anniversary of his death.*

We gather Saturday at the 1925 Paine Memorial Building, built for the Thomas Paine Historical Association, founded 1884 to fight the Comstock Act. We're near the 1839 Paine Monument and relocated Paine cottage. All this sits on what little is left of a confiscated Tory estate that New York State gifted Paine in 1784 as thanks for his war efforts.

Paine rented the farm to tenants until he moved here in 1802 after returning to America from France (following imprisonment by the Reign of Terror). When New Rochelle federalists denied Paine the vote, he moved in 1806 to Greenwich Village, dying there at age 72 in 1809. After Quakers denied Paine a resting place, he was buried on the farm. His empty gravesite is now under widened North Avenue. I'm shown the spot.

My affinity for Paine surfaces here. As journalists, we both wrote about new technologies, civil affairs, human rights, and abuses of power. We both broke with publishers over pay. We both did our personal growth work to get along well with others and stay true to our selves.

I feel at home in this eclectic community of diverse freethinkers who make sense of the world with global minds. I offer books (donated to association) because I'm now willing, as Paine advised, to "undergo the fatigue" of supporting freedom." He proved books can change the world. As we face climate change, our world can pivot from tyranny to liberty. Reason says Paine's ideas can guide us. Conscience says I cannot stay silent.

I am wary of hubris and wary of Paine's ostracism. Come what may, with faith and a throat-lump gulp, I consent to a new role as the old hope peddler. Kindly pardon any upset applecarts.

I must ask myself, am I capable of doing all I want to do in the world? Can I live long enough? Here in New York, I hope to find out.

The spring CT scan in Denver found the lung tumors and hilar lymph mass grew since fall to an inch each. Immunotherapy has stopped working. When I tell Melissa, she says, "You'll be in New York. Why not visit Sloan Kettering, like I did?" I call. They accept me on Medicare.

So, on the Monday after Paine Day, I take the train and subway from New Rochelle to the Upper East Side, 72Q stop. I walk dropfoot on crowded streets to MSK's urology clinic on 68th between 1st and 2nd.

A big medicine waiting room. The nurse takes my vitals, draws blood. The doctor will see me now. Melissa joins us by phone. My doctor knows her doctor. All is friendly. We get down to hard reality.

The cancer is aggressive. If I do nothing, I'll die in six months to a year. To stop cancer growth, he advises replacing immunotherapy with the latest "targeted" drug (targets cancer blood vessels). He refers me to a top oncologist he knows in Denver. Melissa afterwards says, "Spirit at work."

〰

2024: Denver — *I'm home before the June solstice. Hottest summer and year ever, until 2025.... On cool mornings, I plant flowering perennials in the yard, affirming I'll see them bloom next year. Life is alive in me as me.*

My new Denver oncologist says the little daily pill can lend me two or three more years. Research continues. I'm living on borrowed time.

In September, I feel mounting fatigue, shortness of breath, weakness, no appetite (food tastes horrid), and I've lost weight. Walking to the bathroom exhausts me. I'm at the veil again. To live, I must act.

I call my doctor, who agrees on hospitalization. Tests and scans reveal my body is overwhelmed by an overlap of immunotherapy fading out as the new cancer drug kicks in. We suspend the pills for three weeks and restart at half the dose. A scan shows cancer nodes shrank visibly. The treatment seems to be working. I rebound in October, regaining weight and vigor.

I return to doing my day job and volunteer jobs as reverberations echo within from nearing death, again. More ego validation ambitions dissolve. Friend death awaits, and first I need to give this book's ideas a fair chance of outliving me. I see who I am, why I'm still here: I feel called to service.

In November, because Trump won re-election, praising democracy and global sense is now riskier for nobody gnats like me. So it goes. I feel about this book the way Paine said he felt about Common Sense: *"Had the spirit of prophesy decreed the birth of this production, it could not have brought it forth at a more seasonable juncture, or a more necessary time."*

By the December solstice, I've swung from hope to fear to grief to determination. I greet 2025 on warm, healing Kaua'i as Melissa's guest, bless her. I'm working on honesty with myself and being in my heart.

I'm back in frigid Denver. It's Thomas Paine's birthday, January 29, a new moon. I sit on my bed, legs under a blanket. I write to report that President Trump is purging U.S. government before anyone can stop him. Meanwhile, my scan this month shows cancer growth.

Do I still have enough tomorrows to finish the work of my yesterdays? In my mind I hear the message: All is well, and all will be well.

Pain abates. Love abides.

A New Method of Thinking

Freedom and reason are persecuted around the globe, lately with violence in the USA, Ukraine and Mideast. Paine said in *Common Sense*:

> By referring the matter from argument to arms, a new area for politics is struck; a new method of thinking hath arisen. All plans, proposals, &c. prior to the nineteenth of April [1775 Lexington Massacre; or the sixth of January 2021 U.S. insurrection and failed coup; or the twenty-fourth of February 2022 Russian invasion of Ukraine; or the seventh of October 2023 Hamas attack on Israel; or the fifth of November 2024 election of a despotic American president], i.e., to the commencement of hostilities, are like the almanacs of last year; which, though proper then, are superseded and useless now.

World events are changing how we think. Old thinking set in motion the technological forces of globalization now upsetting all our lives. Old thinking unsettled earth's natural balance and set in motion the destructive forces of nature now disrupting all our lives. Old thinking set in motion the ancient forces of despotism now threatening democracy.

Each year will feel more difficult and terrifying until we shift how we make sense of living life together on earth. Changing how we make sense of the world changes ourselves and our world. Global thinking dispels the scary alienation tyrants exploit to seduce us, so we won't get fooled again. As I mend split perceptions to see oneness, authority addiction loses its hold on me. A global sense of life balances free will and self rule.

Living with a global sensibility may at first seem strange or difficult. Like all other cultural leaps humanity has made, awareness of our natural unity and equality one day will become familiar and agreeable. Over time, a global worldview will be so normal, so ordinary, we'll think our societies were always this creative, peaceful and free.

We may pause to get up, stand up, and speak up for global thinking. In oppressive lands, dissent risks our lives and those we love. Still, action is necessary. Too much is at stake to stand idle or complain without fixing. Looking back, we'll be glad we did our part. Paine said, "If there must be [good] trouble, let it be in my day, that my child may have peace."

Why accept despair or expect collapse? Why wait until the wooden ships have sailed? The time for useful action is upon us.

For any who still doubt the readiness of humanity to declare global interdependence, I quote Thomas Paine in *Common Sense* concerning the ripeness and fitness of colonial Americans to declare independence:

> As all men [*sic*] allow the measure, and vary only in their opinion of the time, let us, in order to remove mistakes, take a general survey of things, and endeavor if possible to find out the very time. But I need not go far, the inquiry ceases at once, for the Time Hath Found Us. The general concurrence, the glorious union of all things, proves the fact.

Until global sense makes common sense on earth (in any words), we'll be like one who puts off a necessary task that looks harder with each delay. We know it must be done, and hate to get started. We wish it was over, for we are daily haunted by thoughts of its necessity. "When it becomes necessary to do anything, Paine wrote, "the whole heart and soul should go into the measure, or not attempt it." At least a billion of us on earth are globally awake, walking miracles. By doing our personal growth and social change work together, we can get the job done.

The future is unclear. Hard choices ahead. Accepting responsibility for a livable future is daunting. I see why people want saviors these days. Climate change persists as tyrants insist. More turbulence ahead. More healing ahead. How will life unfold for me, for you, our communities, our nations, our planet? Too soon to know. Up to us.

Why fear tomorrow when we can create today as we will?

About the Author

JUDAH FREED (1950–) is a seasoned journalist, award-winning author, speaker, and consultant based in Colorado. A natural freethinker, he evolved a global sensibility by surviving child abuse, cult faith, ego folly, and lethal cancer.

Entering journalism in 1976, he worked a decade for Denver and Colorado newspapers. He then wrote two decades for the top U.S. and European media trade magazines, pioneering coverage of the internet, interactive TV, and distance learning, speaking on four continents about media literacy and the social effects of interactivity. He next edited Hawaii publications for a decade, returning home to Denver in 2020.

Judah earned a 1988 double BA in communication and journalism through the University Without Walls at Loretto Heights College. He researched rhetoric, organizational culture and public communication through the Individualized MA program of Antioch University,

Judah is a member of the American Society of Journalists and Authors (First Amendment cmte.), PEN America, Authors Guild, Society of Professional Journalists, Coalition of Visionary Resources, Colorado Authors League, and historic Denver Press Club. He serves on the national coalition steering committee for Banned Books Week. He's editor of *The Beacon* for the Thomas Paine Historical Association.

For more information, JudahFreed.com

About Thomas Paine

THOMAS PAINE (1737-1809), an English-born writer and activist, is renown for his 1776 essay, *Common Sense,* a pivotal call for American independence and democracy. Paine's mind was influenced by Locke, Burke, Voltaire, Rousseau, Dideriot, Hume, and other *philosophes* in the Enlightenment.

In his late thirties, Paine's activism, writings and scientific interests in London caught the eye of Benjamin Franklin, who in 1774 encouraged Paine to sail to Philadelphia. There Paine became the editor of *Pennsylvania Magazine.*

With rebellion in the air, Paine wrote *Common Sense,* first published January 10, 1776. Among the 2.5 million colonists, 150,000 copies sold in three months. (Paine donated all of his earnings to the Continental Army.) Inspired by his reasoning, the majority of Americans supported declaring independence and establishing the world's first modern republic.

Without *Common Sense* swaying popular opinion, concur historians, the revolution would have failed.

During the war, Paine wrote the *American Crisis* series to sustain support for the grinding war effort. He began with the line, "These are the times that try men's souls."

After the war, Paine sailed to France for their revolution, voicing humanist ideals in *Rights of Man,* published in 1791 — the #1 bestseller of the 18th century in Europe and America. Aristocrats hated Paine's attack on hereditary power.

Honored at first in France, Paine was arrested in 1793 by the Reign of Terror for the "crime" of being English and ties to the democratic Girondin party. Imprisoned near Paris, he fell ill as John Adams' government denied Paine's U.S. citizenship. When Robespierre fell in 1794, the new American minister to France, James Monroe, secured Paine's release.

While a prisoner of conscience and after, Paine wrote *The Age of Reason*, his critique of organized religion. Published in two parts, 1794 and 1795, the book was praised in Europe, where Paine still lived. In the newborn United States, the book yielded a furious backlash, much to Paine's surprise.

At Jefferson's invitation, Paine sailed to America in 1802. He was so ill that he had to be carried off the ship. Paine found himself an outcast, a casualty of the fight between John Adams and Thomas Jefferson, between the federalists and democrats. Settling in New York, he died disdained in 1809. His remains were later dug up for a monument in England that was never built. All but his jawbone has since been lost.

Freethinkers in the 1800s and 1900s rehabilitated Paine's reputation. Today far more people know his name than have read his work. He is regaining wide attention in advance of the 250th anniversary of *Common Sense* in 2026.

Thomas Paine changed our world for the better. On his great shoulders others stand.

For more information: ThomasPaine.org

Acknowledgments

ANY BOOK involves more people than the author can ever thank. My thanks go to my family, alive and in spirit, who witness my journey. Praise and thanks goes to Melissa Mojo, former wife, lifefriend and initial editor. I would not have survived cancer without you. I honor your patience as Source used me to write. Thanks goes to Colleen Murphy, good friend across the decades despite our differing politics; as a proofreader and commentor, you helped me see the ideas through your eyes.

I thank those 20 years ago who generously gave endorsements for this book's precursor, *Global Sense* — Thom Hartmann, Francis Moore Lappé, Rabbi Michael Lerner, Vandana Shiva, and Dave Wann.

Thanks to friends and allies: Martin Adams, Gary Arlen, Jerry Ashton, Phil Bailey, J Bear Baker, Melody Beattie, Gary Berton, Scott Blakeman, Philip Brautigam, Patricia Calhoun, Peter Clothier, Sharon Coggan PhD, Felicia Cowden, Gabriel Dayan, Donna DeNomme, Jerry Deutsch, Jed Diamond, Matt DiLorenzo, Peggy Ellenberg, Jacquelyne Ellis, Revs. Patrick Feren and Rita Andriello-Feren, Richard Florence, Bruce Goldberg, Greg Seth Harris, Marian and Glenn Head, Gary Hooser, Shel Horowitz, Hampton Islan, Josephine Jones, Bill Kauth, Jonno Kinsella, Henry Kroll, Debbie Krovitz, Peggy Lake, Naviella Lapidot, Bob Layer, Cathy Lewis, John-David and MaryAnn Longwell, Christopher Lowell, Bernard Luskin, Lois Martin, Frederick Marx, Marilyn McGuire, Allen McLain, Rev. Susan Miller, Nancy Mills, Marsha Murphy, Steve Norcross, Jordan Paul, Thad Peterson, Ilene Proctor, Char Ravelo, Sheila and Doug Robinson, Andy Ross, Joel Segal, Linda Sherman, Peggy Spencer, Karen Stuth, Aurelia Taylor, Rick Tidrick, David A. Weinstein, Laurie and Jonathan Weiss, Brenda Van Niekerk, Pamela Varma, Jacqueline Weller, and Kathy Zorko. Thanks to my friends and fans on Substack, Medium, Facebook, Linkedin, Goodreads, Scribd, and other social networks. Thanks to professional friends in ASJA, PEN, AG, SPJ, IBPA, CIPA, COVR, CAL, Denver Press Club, and Banned Books Week Coalition — making our world safer for freedom of expression. I bless the men's movement and ManKind Project for my growth as a feeling conscious man. I bless John Denver, Thomas Crum, Bill Kurtis and all my Windstar friends reaching for higher ground.

I deeply thank the Thomas Paine Historical Association for all their expertise and support and guidance.

I acknowledge all the authors and cultural sources I've cited directly and by allusion. (This book is subtly sown with "cultural literacy" seeds planted where they can bear fruit upon reflection.)

And I thank *you* for actually reading book acknowledgments!

Finally, I thank Thomas Paine in spirit for inspiration and wisdom. You seem present at times, as if leaning over my shoulder and whispering in my ear. I pray my work does justice to your love of liberty.

— jf

Appendices

An army of principles can penetrate
where an army of soldiers cannot.

THOMAS PAINE

Voices of Conscience

PEACEFUL mass demonstrations are a powerful trend in the global sense movement. The long arc of justice bends toward freedom.

For evidence* the trend is real, consider the 21st century, so far...

2004-05: Orange Revolution (Ukraine) — Presidential election fraud triggered peaceful civil disobedience that yielded new elections.

2011: Arab Spring (Mideast) — A peaceful revolution in Tunisia sparked protests, uprisings, and revolutions across the Arab League.

2011: 15-M (Spain) — Inspired by the Arab Spring, *Movimiento* organized peaceful actions by eight million Spaniards in 60 cities.

2011-16: Occupy Wall Street (USA, Global) — Occupation of an NYC park decried abuses of wealth by the top "1 percent." OWC camps and rallies soon appeared in 950 cities across 80 nations.

2013-14: Euromaidan (Ukraine) — A peaceful rally at *Maidan Nezalezhnosti* (Independence Square) in Kyiv backed ties to Europe over Russia. The 2014 Ukrainian revolution led Putin to annex Crimea.

2015: Charlie Hebdo (France) — About 1.6 million people rallied in Paris after Islamist terrorists slew the staff at a satire magazine.

2015-2020s: Black Lives Matter (USA, Global) — White police killings of unarmed Blacks sparked massive protests against racism.

2016: Panama Papers (Global) — As world press exposes leaders hiding billions in offshore tax havens, protests unsettle governments.

2016-17: Candlelight Vigils (South Korea) — Peaceful protests of injustice and corruption engaged 1.5 million Koreans nationwide.

2017: The Women's March (USA, Global) — A day after Trump's inauguration, the largest one-day protest in U.S. history gained traction worldwide for women's rights and all forms of human rights.

(*Listing of political protests only. Eco-protests are equally plentiful. Updated August 2024.

2018: March for Our Lives (USA) — After a mass shooting at a Florida school, students rallied at a DC event and at 2,600 U.S. schools.

2019: October Revolution (Lebanon) —Peaceful tax protests led to the prime minister joining the protestors, ending sectarian rule.

2019–20: Hong Kong — General strikes and mass protests by two million people opposed China asserting control to end democracy.

2020: Belarus — Opposing falsified presidential election results, the largest-ever peaceful protests were stopped by brute force.

2020: Argentina — Unprecedented protests won unprecedented abortion and reproductive rights for women, a continental first.

2020-21: Thailand — Peaceful protests over policy grew into giant demonstrations to reform the monarchy, drawing a harsh backlash.

2022: Russia — Mass rallies in Moscow and other cities protested Putin's invasion of Ukraine and a military draft. Thousands arrested.

2022: Sri Lanka — Massive demonstrations to end corruption led to the president fleeing his lavish mansion and the country.

2022: Iran — When "morality police" killed a detained woman, waves of women-led marches protested the male-rule "republic."

2022: China— Strict Covid lockdowns evoked protests in cities and campuses. Blank white papers held aloft decried censorship.

2023-24: Israel — When indicted prime minister Netanyahu tried to gut the judiciary, unceasing protests and strikes support democracy. Protests then demand his removal for the Gaza humanitarian crisis.

2024: Germany — After the press exposed the far-right AfD party would conduct mass deportations if elected, one million Germans took to the streets of a hundred cities in peaceful defense of democracy.

2024: Argentina — New decrees by the far-right president spurred nationwide strikes and massive pro-democracy demonstrations.

2024; Senegal — When the disliked president decided to delay elections, huge opposition protests began in peace; did not stay so.

2024: Russia — Dissident Alexei Navalny mysteriously died in a Siberian penal colony. Thousands braved arrest to gather for his funeral.

2024: Venezuela — Despotic President Madero claimed reelection despite verified evidence he lost. Mass protests won world support.

Author Notes

Bias Ownership

THOMAS PAINE observed, "There are two distinct classes of what are called thoughts: those that we produce in ourselves by reflection and the act of thinking, and those that bolt into the mind of their own accord." The thoughts in this book come from both sources.

Same as every human, my life affects how I make sense of the world, which filters what I say and how I say it. In my writings and my life, I aim to be global and universal. I seek to voice respect and empathy for diverse cultures and natures. If inadvertently I give offense, I apologize.

Making Global Sense is written for those of us on earth now thinking globally, and for the "global curious." For those in denial of our oneness, I'm glad you're here reading , and any discomfort is natural.

My biases? I make sense of life as a freedom-loving "westerner" from Colorado. I grew up in Denver and have lived in New York, Chicago, Appalachia, Los Angeles, Hawaii, back in Denver, plus some world travel. I'm a white male, heterosexual, spiritually eclectic Jewish American Baby Boomer who's young at heart if not in body. These are biases.

Writers "should" write about what they know. I know the history and cultures of the global West and North better than the East and South. So, that's where I go to find transcendent examples of beliefs and practices around the world. (Pragmatically, I lack a research assistant.)

Wherever you go on earth, you may observe the ancient human habits I write about here. For instance, existential fears and self-doubts, in times of peril, too often push us to sacrifice liberty for security. We habitually give away our power to lofty authority figures. My bias favors outgrowing this habit of autocracy and maturing into democracy.

I advocate uniting spirituality and politics in the nascent "global sense movement." If you absolutely insist either politics or spirituality is disgusting and must be ignored, then my efforts to bridge the two may not land well for you. Sorry. Thanks for considering the idea!

As for spiritual biases, I'm an odd admixture of Judaism, Buddhism, Taoism, quantum physics, New Thought, New Age, deism, craft, and indigenous wisdom. I joined a quasi-Christian cult in youth, so I honor honest rebirth; I have felt joy and peace in foursquare communion. Now I'm neither a "Christian" nor an "observant Jew." Like Paine, my religion is doing good, guided by an ineffable sense of our oneness.

As for my political biases, I'm an odd admixture of philosophies on government. My ideas transcend easy liberal, libertarian, progressive, or conservative labels. Along with 18th century Enlightenment thinkers, I'm influenced by the 19th century Transcendentalists like Emerson on self-reliance and Thoreau on civil disobedience as well as 20th century social justice and nonviolence advocates like Gandhi and Dr. King.

My post-cult studies of mindlock reliance on savior leaders, plus my global sensibility, leads me to agree firmly with Thomas Paine in opposing monarchy and all forms of authoritarian regimes. I favor maturing into real democracy. The more we learn to rule ourselves mindfully, I reason, the less we need government to rule us.

Given my biases, I have shared my mind, heart and soul as truthfully and accurately as I can here. I have done my best to differentiate between facts and opinions, to label beliefs as such, to catch motivated reasoning. Any remaining lapses in the writing are on me.

The ideas stand on their own.

Due Cautions

If this book ever is blessed with a wide readership, even if years after I'm gone, it's fair and right for me to offer cautions about comprehension, book misuse and unintended consequences.

Thank you for having an open mind, thinking for yourself about all the concepts here, arising as they do from my life, not yours. Amen if you resonate, and if you do, I hope you do not stop there.

Test all these theories in your life. Seek insights from conversations about the global issues and big ideas here. Others may understand my words differently than you do, or as I meant. We get into trouble when we let anyone lure us or force us into agreeing with them.

In encouraging a worldwide movement for global awakening, please never violate another person's free will. If others disagree, let them and move on. Both "woke" zealotry and "cancel culture" breach our civil rights. Enlightening the unwilling is like trying to teach a stubborn goat to sing; it wastes your time and annoys the goat.

May you never fall into fanaticism, like I tried in my youth. I decry anyone misconstruing or twisting my words to justify any cult fixated on "global sense." May you never succumb to authority addiction. History shows such thinking leads to absurd atrocities.

For my New Age community, yes, "ascension" is real and necessary. I decry mendaciously using the term as a mere marketing gimmick. Cynically profiting from believers is predatory, like hawking relics of the lost cross in old Jerusalem, or selling conspiracy theories like antisemitism. Enabling and exploiting any addiction is unholy work.

I deny any right to use or construe my words for mind manipulation. If you see it happening, please object. If I'm alive, please alert me.

Finally, I offer conscious commerce cautions for our digital age.

Beware of internet marketplace vendors selling new books as "used." Unless they have a real used copy in their hands, it's a scam. Skip websites selling subscriptions to digital editions of print books that are somehow "unavailable" (card data sold on the dark web). Shun ebook pirates, counterfeiters and AI cloners breaching copyrights. Please don't inadvertently deprive authors and publishers of fair livelihoods.

As an indie author hoping to inspire the world while I float the boat, I agree with J.R.R. Tolkien. His work was published and sold without his permission or benefit. In response, for his authorized edition, he wrote, "Those who approve of courtesy (at least) to living authors will purchase it and no other." He speaks for me.

— jf

Definitions of Global Sense

global sense: — \glō-bəl\ adj. [Latin, *globus*; French, *global*, 1676] \'sen(t)s, noun. [ME/MF, *sens*; Latin, *sēnsus*]: (1) [noun] the conscious, rational, intuitive, visceral perception of all life on earth as interconnected or whole or one <She has ~.>; (2) [adjective] descriptive for recognizing the oneness of all life on the planet <Eating organic food makes ~.>; (3) [noun] a construct, a system of reasoning premised on the principles of oneness and interactivity, that all we think, feel, say, and do naturally causes an effect in the world, by design or default <He sees the ~ of spending his money like a vote.>; (4) [adjective] an awareness that evokes accepting personal and social responsibility with accountability for the consequence of choices. <Attending the peaceful protest made ~ to them.>; (5) [noun] a sense-making process using a whole-context perspective <View the systems failure in a ~.>; <We all suffered in a ~. >; <Doreen Massey writes about a ~ of place.>.

Ideas Glossary

HOW WE make sense of our lives and the world shapes our lives and the world. We use words to help us make sense of reality. If we change our language, any tongue, we shift our sense-making, which changes our life choices, which changes our daily realities on earth.

Making Global Sense uses such shift language. Some key terms:

Alpha Male Rule
The patriarchal system of power inherited by fathers and sons.

Authority Addiction
A compulsive codependent relationship with external power.

Conscious Commerce
Free and fair economics duly bound by a global sensibility.

Direct Republics
Citizens hold the right of consent over the laws governing them.

Global Sense
Consciousness of our sacred oneness, equality and individuality.

Mindful Self Rule
Personal sovereignty and responsibility bound by global sense.

New Men
Conscious, feeling men ruling themselves instead of the world.

Personal Democracy
Mindfully interacting with others in ways that make global sense.

Bibliography

Alinsky, Saul. *Rules for Radicals: A Practical Primer for Realistic Radicals.* New York: Random House, 1971.

Beauvoir, Simone de. *The Second Sex.* New York: Knopf, 1953 (1949).

Beck, Don E. and Chris Cowan. *Spiral Dynamics: Mastering Values, Leadership and Change.* Oxford: Blackwell, 2009.

Boulding, Elise. *The Underside of History.* Boulder: Westview, 1976.

Butterworth, Eric. *Spiritual Economics: The Principles and Process of True Prosperity.* Unity Village, MO: Unity Books, 1993, 2001.

Capra, Fritjof, *The Tao of Physics.* Berkeley: Shambhala, 1975.

Chenoweth, Erica and Maria Stephan. *Why Civil Resistance Works: The Strategic Logic of Nonviolent Conflict.* New York: Columbia, 2011.

Chomsky, Noam and Edward Herman. *Manufacturing Consent: The Political Economy of the Mass Media.* New York: Pantheon. 1988.

Darwin, Charles. *On the Origin of Species by Means of Natural Selection.* London: John Murray, 1859. New York: Sterling, 2008.

Diamond, Jed. *The Warrior's Journey Home: Healing Men, Healing the Planet.* Oakland, CA: New Harbinger, 1994.

Doi, Takeo. *The Anatomy of Self.* New York: Kodansha USA, 2001.

Ehrlich, Paul R. *The Population Bomb.* New York: Ballantine, 1968.

Eisler, Riane. *The Chalice and the Blade:* New York: Harper and Row, 1989.

Eller, Cynthia. *The Myth of Matriarchal Prehistory: Why an Invented Past will not Give Women a Future.* Boston, Beacon Press, 2000.

Emerson, Ralph Waldo. *Self Reliance.* New York: Viking, 1983 (1844).

Farrell, Warren. *The Liberated Man.* New York, Random House, 1974.

Frankl, Viktor. *Man's Search for Meaning.* Boston: Beacon, 2006 (1946).

Friedan, Betty. *The Feminine Mystique.* New York: W.W. Norton, 1963.

Fritz, Robert. *The Path of Least Resistance.* New York: Ballantine, 1989.

Fromm, Erich. *Escape from Freedom.* New York: Farrar, Rinehart, 1941.

Ferguson, Marilyn. *The Aquarian Conspiracy.* New York: Tarcher, 2009.

Gladwell, Malcolm. *The Tipping Point.* Boston: Little, Brown, 2000.

Goldberg, Herb. *The New Male. New York*: Morrow, 1979.

— *The Hazards of Being Male.* New York: Nash Publishing, 1976.

Goodman, Amy and Denis Moynihan. *The Silenced Majority.* Chicago: Haymarket, 2012.

Gore, Albert. *An Inconvenient Truth.* New York: Rodale Press, 2006.

Greer, Germaine. *The Female Eunuch.* New York: McGraw-Hill, 1971.

Hawken, Paul. *Blessed Unrest. New York*: Penguin, 2008.

Hoffer, Eric. *The True Believer.* New York: Harper and Row, 1951.

Holmes, Ernest. *The Science of Mind.* New York: Tarcher, 2010 (1926).

Houston, Jean. *Jump Time.* New York: J.P. Tarcher/Putnam, 2000.

Hubbard, Barbara Marx. *Conscious Evolution: Awakening the Power of Our Social Potential.* Novato, CA: New World Library, 1998, 2015.

Kauth, Bill. *A Circle of Men.* New York: St. Martin's Press, 1992.

Klein, Naomi. *The Shock Doctrine* Metropolitan Books/Holt, 2007.

Lappé, Frances Moore. *EcoMind.* New York: Nation Books, 2011.

Lerner, Michael. *The Left Hand of God.* San Francisco: HarperSF 2006.

Levitsky, Steven & Daniel Ziblatt. *How Democracies Die.* New York: Viking, 2019.

Lewis, Sinclair. *It Can't Happen Here: A Novel* (and radio play). Garden City, NY: Doubleday, Doran and Co., 1935.

Locke, John. *Two Treatises of Government: And A Letter Concerning Toleration.* New Haven, CT: Yale University Press, 2003 (1689).

Maalouf, Elza. *Emerge!: The Rise of Functional Democracy and the Future of the Middle East.* New York: Select Books, 2014.

McKibben, Bill. *Falter.* New York. Henry Holt and Co., 2019.

— *The End of Nature.* New York: Random House, 2006.

Myss, Caroline. *Sacred Contracts. New York*: Harmony, 2001.

Orwell, George. *Nineteen Eight-Four:* New York: Harcourt, Brace 1949.

— *Down and out in Paris and London,* New York, Harper, 1933.

Paine, Thomas. *Common Sense.* Philadelphia: Robert Bell, 1776.

— *Rights of Man.* London: J.S. Jordan, 1791, 1792.

— *The Age of Reason.* London: Joel Barlow, 1794.

Peck, M. Scott. *People of the Lie.* New York: Simon and Schuster, 1983.

Pinkola Estés, Clarissa. *Women Who Run with the Wolves.* New York: Ballantine Books, 1996.

Plato (Socrates). *Gorgias* and *The Phaedrus*. Athens, 5th century BCE.

Pretty, Jules. *The Edge of Extinction: Travels with Enduring People in Vanishing Lands*. Ithaca, NY: Comstock Publishing, 2014.

Rand, Ayn and Nathaniel Branden. *The Virtue of Selfishness: A New Concept of Egoism*. New York: New American Library, 1964.

Ray, Paul H., Sherry Ruth Anderson. *Cultural Creatives: How 50 Million People are Changing the World*. New York: Harmony, 2000.

Rousseau, Jean-Jacques, *The Social Contract*. France, 1762.

Shapiro, Rabbi Rami. *Judaism Without Tribalism*. Rhinebeck, NY: Monkfish Book Publishing, 2022.

Smith, Adam. T*he Theory of Moral Sentiments*. London: A. Millar, 1759. New York: Cambridge University Press, 2002.

— *The Wealth of Nations*. New York: Modern Library, 2000 (1776).

Snyder, Timothy. *On Tyranny*. New York: Crown, 2017.

Steinem, Gloria. *Revolution from Within:* Boston: Little, Brown, 1992.

Thoreau, Henry David. *Resistance to Civil Government*. Self-published in 1849. Republished in 1849 as *On the Duty of Civil Disobedience*.

Toffler, Alvin. *Future Shock*. New York: Random House, 1970.

Tolle, Eckhart. *A New Earth*. New York: Dutton, 2005.

Voltaire. Complete Works. Toronto: University of Toronto Press, 1968.

Von Stief. Frederick, M.D. *Brain In Balance*. CreateSpace, 2012.

Watts, Alan. T*he Book: On the Taboo Against Knowing Who You Are*. New York: Pantheon Books, 1966.

Wilber, Ken. *A Theory of Everything:*. Boston: Shambhala, 2000.

Williamson, Marianne. *A Return To Love*. NY: HarperCollins, 1992.

Wilson, Edward O. *The Diversity of Life*. Cambridge, MA: Belknap Press of Harvard University Press, 1992.

Wolf, Naomi. *The End of America*. Vermont: Chelsea Green, 2007.

Wollstonecraft, Mary. *A Vindication of the Rights Of Woman*. New York: Dover Publications, 1996 (1792).

Zukav, Gary. *The Dancing Wu Li Masters: An Overview of the New Physics*. New York: Morrow, 1979.

For the *complete* bibliography
Visit GlobalSense.com

Index

Autocracy

Commerce

History

These proceedings may at first appear strange and difficult; but, like all other steps which we have already passed over, will in a little time become familiar and agreeable.

THOMAS PAINE

COMMON SENSE;

ADDRESSED TO THE

INHABITANTS

O F

A M E R I C A,

On the following interesting

S U B J E C T S.

I. Of the Origin and Design of Government in general, with concise Remarks on the English Constitution.

II. Of Monarchy and Hereditary Succession.

III. Thoughts on the present State of American Affairs.

IV. Of the present Ability of America, with some miscellaneous Reflections.

A NEW EDITION, with several Additions in the Body of the Work. To which is added an APPENDIX ; together with an Address to the People called QUAKERS.

N. B. The New Addition here given increases the Work upwards of one Third.

Man knows no Master save creating HEAVEN,
Or those whom Choice and common Good ordain.
THOMSON.

PHILADELPHIA PRINTED.

And sold by W. and T. BRADFORD.

Common Sense was first published (anonymously) in Philadelphia on January 10, 1776.
Second edition above was published on February 14, 1776. (Later editions named Thomas Paine.)

The text of *Making Global Sense* is set in Adobe Minion Pro, a serif typeface designed by Robert Slimbach, released in 1990, inspired by late Renaissance typefaces. The headlines are set in Adobe Myriad Pro, a Humanist sans-serif OpenType font designed by Robert Slimbach and Carol Twombly with Christopher Slye and Fred Brady, released in 1992.

The block quotes and versa page quotes are set in Caslon Antique, designed in 1894 by Berne Nadall to emulate the chipped look of old metal Caslon type, created in 1722 by the London typographer William Caslon, based on Dutch baroque typefaces. Popular among printers in the colonies, Caslon was used when printing *Common Sense* and the first printing of The Declaration of Independence.

www.ingramcontent.com/pod-product-compliance
Lightning Source LLC
Chambersburg PA
CBHW031149270326
41931CB00006B/205